Political Myth

NEW SLANT

RELIGION, POLITICS, ONTOLOGY

Edited by Creston Davis, Philip Goodchild,

and Kenneth Surin

Roland Boer

Political Myth

On the Use and Abuse of Biblical Themes

DUKE UNIVERSITY PRESS

Durham and London

2009

© 2009 Duke University Press
All rights reserved
Printed in the United States of
America on acid-free paper ∞
Designed by Amy Ruth Buchanan
Typeset in Iowan Oldstyle
by Achorn International
Library of Congress Cataloging-in-
Publication Data appear on the last
printed page of this book.

Duke University Press gratefully
acknowledges the support of the
Australian Research Council,
which provided funds for the
production of this book.

For Ibrahim Abraham

Contents

Preface

Almost a century ago, in the midst of revolutionary turmoil, with all its vivid hopes and crushing disappointments, Georges Sorel (1961: 127) wrote in his *Reflections on Violence*, "We know that the general strike is indeed what I have said: the *myth* in which Socialism is wholly comprised, *i.e.* a body of images capable of evoking instinctively all the sentiments which correspond to the different manifestations of the war undertaken by Socialism against modern society."

The deep agenda, the political passion of this book is driven by the sense that Sorel's program remains unfinished: flawed, piecemeal, running in various directions, it touches nevertheless on the primary need for political myth, for powerful political myths on the Left.

It seems to me that an intervention like Sorel's is sorely needed at the present moment. For Sorel (1961), the revolutionaries at the turn of the twentieth century needed something to keep their hopes alive, to touch their hearts as well as their minds, and that was the myth of the general strike that would bring capitalism to its knees. For all its continued potency, we may not wish to pin our hopes on the general strike at the beginning of the twenty-first century, but what I like so much about Sorel's project is that political myths should be collective, motivational, and irrefutable. Let me spin this out: cast in terms of the fundamental ideas of the group itself, such a myth was primarily a collective project that thrived on various images and metaphors that made the myth irrefutable, providing the deep motivation for continued political action in the face of repeated failures. In short, political myth is "the framing of a future, in some indeterminate time" (124).

Sorel's inspiration lies behind this book, a book I began on a journey to Groningen in the northern Netherlands. On that first journey I found myself forced to leave Sorel's *Reflections on Violence* at home in Australia rather than take it with me. I just didn't want the hapless passengers who ended up next to me to endure the same fate as that nervous neighbor on an internal Australian flight in 2004. You can imagine the scene: as the plane scrambles and shakes its way upward a black book sits on my lap with an image of shattered glass and the blood-red words splashed across its cover: *Reflections on Violence*. My neighbor-turned–potential informer nervously eyes the book and me, glances away, and then lingers longer over the book. Not wanting to replicate such a scene on an international flight over sensitive airspace, I left Sorel's book safely at home. I hardly need to explicate the global situation, for my leaving the book at home is as much a sign of the times as that somewhat anxious fellow traveler's response back in Australia.

If I began this book on the way to Groningen, I finished it in Nuuk, Greenland, looking out, through snowstorms or the Northern Lights, over the ships and whales in Godthåb fjord. Between Groningen and Nuuk, a number of people have been crucial to my exploration of political myth, making helpful suggestions, frowning at my wayward paths, commenting on earlier pieces of the book, and discussing the whole with me. In particular, let me thank Ken Surin, Fred Jameson, Alberto Moreiras, Alain Badiou, Colin Booy, David Garrioch, Athalya Brenner, Todd Penner, Caroline Vander Stichele, Andrew Milner, and David Roberts. Two people, however, deserve special thanks. Without Ibrahim Abraham's work, this book would not have come to life. And to Christina Petterson I owe thanks for many things, not least for not putting up with crap and for urging me to be as clear as possible.

April 2006
Somewhere north of the
Arctic Circle, between Ilulisat
and Sisimuit, Greenland, on
the ship *Sarfaq Ittuk*

Introduction

Where might a viable theory and practice of political myth be found? Indeed, are such things desirable and possible? In this book I advocate and search for a theory and practice of political myth. Let me be quite clear: I am after myths of liberation and freedom from oppression—and I make no apology for such terms—over against those that oppress and tread down.

The book's main thesis may be captured by two phrases: *facing the beast* and *the cunning of myth*. What I mean by grasping the beast from one's shoulder and staring it in the face is that the Left should call the bluff on political myths of reaction by asking what they might look like should they be realized. These myths of the Right always have an underside, so one task of the Left is to bring that repressed dimension to the surface, to tell the whole myth. So I ask three questions: What if we tell the full story? What if the Right should realize its political myth? What might be our response? This is where mythic cunning comes into play. On this matter I refer to a dialectic: however much the forces of political reaction may seek to impose their stamp on myth, there is always a subversive element that escapes such a stamp. Or rather, such reactionary myths produce subversion in the very act of mythmaking—hence the cunning of myth.

Thus, in the first chapter I attempt to develop a theory of political myth. Here my inspirations are, first and foremost Ernst Bloch, Theodor Adorno, Alain Badiou, Jacques Lacan, and Slavoj Žižek. Adorno, Lacan, and Žižek provide much needed cautions about the baleful workings of myth. By contrast, Bloch and Badiou—one willingly, the other less so—show me not only how to focus on what is positive about political myths, but how to read oppressive and reactionary myths for their moments of subversive delight. Indeed, they indicate how one might read Adorno and Lacan for such glimmers as well.

Always anxious about staying in the realm of theory for theory's sake, I move on from the first chapter to my preferred ground of dealing with texts, namely, the first six books of the Hebrew Bible, the stretch from Genesis through Joshua commonly known as the Hexateuch. Indeed, as I explore the various workings of my theory of political myth, I remain in the realm of texts for the next three chapters. Thus, the second chapter, "Women First?," deals with feminism. In particular, I argue that behind much recent biblical scholarship there is the legacy of so-called primitive communism. Further, since these stories from the Bible remain deeply embedded in more recent political myths, I also argue for the persistence of that legacy in those myths. The chapter has two sections. The first traces the resilient assumption or argument that before the emergence of the "state" of Israel—usually understood as the monarchy—there was a much looser organization of social relations and economic forces in which women had relatively greater freedom. I trace back this "domestic" or "household" mode of production from current biblical scholars such as Carol Meyers, David Jobling, and Gale Yee to Marshall Sahlins, Lewis Henry Morgan, Friedrich Engels, and J. J. Bachofen. What interests me is not only that there is such a legacy to trace, but that each of these scholars must deny it in order to develop their theories of the domestic mode of production. The second part of the chapter involves a reading of some key texts from Genesis through Joshua in light of the legacy of primitive communism. Thus, in a range of stories from Eve to Zelophehad's daughters I follow the way the text explores the possibility of very different roles for women while simultaneously showing why that is not viable—an empty gesture, if you like. Thus women on their own, rebellious women, or women as part of a larger "demimonde" or zone outside the camp are all systematically closed down by a text that seems to obsess just a little too much over these matters. Thus, I argue, there is a theme of rebellion underlying Genesis–Joshua, and this rebellion is the signal of a repressed primitive communism. The catch is that in the detailed and extended treatment of such women, the text airs precisely that which it seeks to close down.

The third chapter turns to Freudian psychoanalysis, from which I draw the central category of fantasy in order to describe political myth. Fantasy is the way of dealing with the constitutive exception—that which is both the necessary support of a particular system (politics, philosophical position, everyday reality) and the major threat to that system. Fantasy handles these exceptions by generating a narrative that simultaneously creates and conceals that threat, known as the fantasmatic kernel, for if the naked threat actually appeared, it would bring the system to a shuddering halt. The specific terms of that relationship between system and constitutive exception in the case of Genesis–Joshua are those of creation and destruction, cosmos and chaos, or, in Lacanian terms, the Symbolic and the Real. In Genesis–Joshua, the threat of the constitutive exception shows up in both natural chaos and human rebellion. I track the logic of system and exception through a series of key texts: the creation story (Genesis 1–3), the Flood narrative (Genesis 6–9), the Tower of Babel (Genesis 11), the rebellion of Korah (Numbers 16), and the various narratives of rebellion and "murmuring."

In the fourth chapter, "The Sacred Economy," Marxism comes to the fore. I begin by observing that the state we find constructed in Genesis–Joshua never existed, nor indeed did it ever have any chance of existing. After tracing the main features of such a mythical state-in-waiting— religion, a political system, family structures, and a judiciary—I argue that such a state may best be called a theocratic tyranny. There is, however, a contradiction: the state-in-waiting and the constant opposition to it that we find in these texts is in fact a contradiction that has a very different basis in social and economic terms. However, in order to get there, I turn to a huge neglected field of ancient Near Eastern studies: the work in the Soviet Union from the 1920s until the 1980s. Seventy years of research, scores of books, and hundreds of articles have mostly been ignored in Western biblical scholarship due to the closing of minds during the cold war. Making use of some of this Russian research (more needs to be translated), which balances a healthy concern for heuristic models and archaeological and textual data, I develop the outlines of what may be called the "sacred economy." Its main features are the village commune, the temple-city complex, the despotic state, labor and class, mediations between village commune and state, and what I call theo-economics, which may be described as the theological metaphorization of economic allocation. The system, in other words, is based on allocation at the hands of the divinity, allocation of land, agricultural technology, and women, along with their modes of allocation, including the patron-client relationship, clans, the judiciary, and the war machine. Here lies the contradiction I have been seeking, for what we find is a tension between an economics of allocation and one of extraction, which operated on the basis of tribute and very limited trade.

The focus of the tension lay in the conflict between the village commune and the temple-city complex. The clash of the two economic systems generates the contradiction of the political myth of a state in perpetual waiting and widespread opposition to it.

The final three chapters move from this analysis of the political master myth of Genesis–Joshua to current politics, especially foreign policy.[1] Thus, in chapter 5, "Foreign Policy and the Fantasy of Israel in Australia," I track the way the deeper logic of the biblical political myth shows up in the fantasy of Israel. Here I analyze some speeches by the key players in the long reign of the liberal-conservative government of Australia (1996–2007), especially those of Prime Minister John Howard, Treasurer Peter Costello, and Minister for Foreign Affairs Alexander Downer. I find that in their hands the fantasy of Israel was in fact a Christian fantasy of Australia. By systematically excluding Islam and then Judaism, what we had was a Christian political myth that lay at the heart of domestic policy as well.

In "Christianity, Capitalism, and the Fantasy of Israel in the United States," the sixth chapter, I follow a similar approach to the one on Australia. This time I focus on speeches by the most unpopular president in U.S. history, George W. Bush (2000–2008), secretaries of state Colin Powell and Condoleezza Rice, Speaker of the House of Representatives Nancy Pelosi (Democrat), and one-time Democratic presidential hopeful, Hillary Clinton. In the United States we find a much more explicit Christian fantasy with three main elements: a process of stepping into the Bible and becoming the great protector of Israel, with whom the United States shares a similar story of origins; a culture of geopiety that shows up in the explicit production of myths by Leon Uris's *Exodus*, Holy Land theme parks and exhibits, and the *Left Behind* series of novels; and the reconstruction of the fantasy of Israel as a myth that embodies the values of freedom, democracy, the free market, and the rule of law. Finally, if the Christian fantasy that parades as a fantasy of Israel is far more explicit in the United States, it also shows its contradictions more sharply. These concern the pesky problems of facts and the battle over history (such as Stalin's status as the "grandfather of Israel"), the unavoidable violence of peace, and the anomaly of George W. Bush's apparent support of Islam as a religion that worships the same God as Christians. Bush, however, unwittingly pointed to the tension that will lead to my final chapter: he presented the fulfillment and realization of what has really become the Christian capitalist myth. Following the deeper pattern of the political myth I explored in my discussion of Genesis–Joshua, it turns out that those who propound such a myth could not endure its realization, for that would bring it crashing down. The widespread disparagement of and despair over Bush in the last years of his presidency—a despair that covered the full range of mainstream U.S. politics, all the way from the center Right (euphemistically called "liberals") to the far Right—lay in the fact that he showed a glimpse of that realized myth.

It is all too easy to criticize the dominant and troubled political myths of nation-states such as Australia and the United States, so in the final chapter I turn to reclaim Georges Sorel's program. In other words, I put myself on the line with some mythmaking. I begin by looking at the final stage in the development of political myth that has run so far from the Hebrew master myth of the State-in-waiting to the Christian capitalist fantasy. This final stage is nothing other than the myth of capitalism as propounded by one of its foremost mythmakers, Milton Friedman. While Friedrich von Hayek provided the ideology, captured in infamous statements such as "There is no society" by Margaret Thatcher, Friedman's monetarist programs lay behind the economic reforms of Reagan, Thatcher, and others. Although he is often represented as an opponent of Keynesian economics, his real target is socialism. This appears primarily as big government, which turns out to be responsible for everything from the Great Depression to affirmative action, let alone communism. Apart from being an opponent of big government, Friedman aggressively asserted the ideological link between capitalism and freedom, the unassailable mantra of U.S. foreign policy, as well as holding up the market as the ticket to a capitalist utopia freed from all its hindrances. And Friedman does so by evoking mythical motifs straight out of the Bible, such as Paradise and the Promised Land of plenty. The next section in chapter 7 tells the underside of this political myth of capitalist plenty. It does so by focusing on the crucial contradiction of this myth, namely, the contradiction between unlimited capitalism and a limited planet. If my interlocutors here are the Greens, I make use of Fredric Jameson's argument that globalization is the first glimpse of a full commodification, Žižek's point that capitalism can exist only through a series of limits and restrictions, and David Harvey's argument that the current construction of nature relies upon capitalism to be "nature" in the first place. We end up with the tension between, on the one hand, a myth of unfettered production and consumption and, on the other hand, its self-produced limits, especially that of nature. Yet the myth of capitalist plenty pictures a world that has overcome those limits. Here lie the seeds of a new myth for the Left, one that requires the risky move of calling the bluff of this myth. In other words, I take the same premise as the myth of plenty and ask what a political myth of capitalism would look like if we removed all its constraints. We end up with a rather more bleak picture of the end of cheap oil and large-scale environmental breakdown. I close by suggesting two responses to this full myth of unfettered capitalism: one is to seek the end of capitalism through this deep contradiction between unlimited capitalism and a limited planet; the other draws on the cunning of myth to bring forth its subversive underside. In other words, what if we call on the so-called hindrances to the myth of unlimited capitalism—the greenies, hippies, ferals, feminists, indigenous activists, anticapitalist protestors, religious Lefties and critics, trade unionists, socialists, and anarchists—to realize their political myth?

The context for this book is the secular and religious Left. It comes at a time when the Left is at the beginning of a renaissance, precisely when the old warriors had begun to bemoan its past glory days of the sixties and seventies in the mistaken belief that they are gone for good. The stirrings come from all directions: "Socialism for the twenty-first century" in South America; the radicalized youth from the anticapitalist protests in Seattle, Melbourne, Genoa, Copenhagen, and elsewhere; the links with green politics; the return of anarchism as a political option for secondary school students; what I lovingly call the Loopy Left (the mix of radical politics and New Age spiritualities); and indeed elements of the more traditional religious Left. All you need to do is take part in a protest to see how diverse this resurgence of the Left really is. Organizations such as the International Institute for Research and Education, which is part of the Fourth International, are struggling to keep up with the need for information and advice to those asking questions.

One result of this process is that old questions are being reopened. I am particularly interested in the way religion, and especially the question of myth, has returned as a topic of serious debate among the Left. To be sure, there are plenty of those in the old secular Left who harbor deep suspicions about religion, suspicions that are perfectly justified in light of the connivance between reaction, state power, and religion in the past and the present. But it is also true that religions such as Christianity—especially through the Bible—have been the inspiration for revolutionary movements. A few examples will suffice: Thomas Müntzer and the peasants in sixteenth-century Germany drew their inspiration from the Bible, as did Gerrard Winstanley and the Diggers in seventeenth-century England, as did the fight against slavery and then, with Martin Luther King, the battle against segregation in North America, as did the anticolonial struggles the world over, as did the antiapartheid struggle in South Africa, as did the

"Jubilee" campaign for the cancellation of Third World debt, and as does liberation theology.

I have discussed these matters in more detail elsewhere (Boer 2007c), especially the breakdown of the program of secularism and the program for a "new secularism" that works for a politics of alliance between the old secular Left and the religious Left. So I will not repeat it here, except to point out that this book takes place within that context. In particular, it is a challenge to those on the Left who have condemned myth as a distinctly vicious form of social legitimization. Let me give a few examples. For Roland Barthes (1993) myth is a second-order semiological system built on a primary system of meaning that deforms meaning and is regressive and depoliticized. But it is largely bourgeois myth of which he speaks, and the answer lies in politicized speech that keeps in touch with reality. But here we also find Walter Benjamin's effort to break out of the myth of capitalism and Adorno's resolute suspicion of myth, particularly in the shadow of the Nazi myths of blood and soil. Even Ernst Cassirer (1947) joins these ranks in the aftermath of Nazism, although he comes out of a liberal position, upholding the United States as a bastion of "freedom." Cassirer is disturbed by the outbreak of myth precisely when reason seemed to have triumphed, and he puts it down to a need for deeper emotional certainties in the face of uncertainty and catastrophe, especially in Germany during the interwar years.

I should say a few things about what this book is not. It is not, to begin with, a study of the religious or secular Left per se. They may be the context for this study, their questions and problems may lie behind many of my thoughts, but they are not the subject of the book. Further, since I am engaged in developing a distinct theory and practice of political myth, the book is not a comprehensive survey of theories of political myth, nor indeed of myth as such. There are enough of such volumes available, of which Lincoln's (2000) masterful historical study, Flood's (2002) useful book, and Csapo's (2005) conversational introduction are good examples. However much I am enticed, it is also not an exercise in "mnemohistory," as Jan Assmann calls it, that is, the ruptures and continuities in the history of a motif. Assmann's (1997, see especially 15–17; 2006) great example is "Moses the Egyptian" and the cultural memory of Egypt more broadly. If it were such a mnemohistory, this book would trace the appropriations and mutations of a motif such as Exodus in the French Revolution, the American settlements and revolution, the First Fleet to Australia, the origins of modern democracy, nationalism, and the nation-state (see, variously, Aberbach 2005; Said 1988; D. B. Rose 1996; Docker 2001; Boer 2008;

Deleuze and Guattari 1987). Further, it is not a study of comparative religion or anthropology, however much these disciplines have claimed the study of myth as their own. Rather, my focus is on some of the most powerful and persistent political myths, namely, those found in the Bible, specifically the Old Testament or Hebrew Bible. What fascinates me is not merely the (ab)use of such myths, but their deeper dynamic and the way that dynamic turns up again and again in later uses of those myths.

Finally, this book is not an argument that Genesis–Joshua is a political myth.[2] Some biblical scholars hold on to older assumptions regarding the exceptional nature of the Hebrew Bible: it stands out from and surpasses its ancient Near Eastern context since it begins the process of negating myth through history, however fledgling that history might be. They are perfectly happy to describe *Enuma Elish*, the Babylonian creation story that moves from creation of the world to the creation of the state, as a political myth, but they are far more reluctant to describe the Hebrew Bible as such.[3] Thus, even Damrosch's (1987) predominantly literary agenda pursues such a line more or less vigorously (see also Brueggemann 1982; Westermann 1984; Steinberg 1993). They should know better, and in what follows I assume the position of people such as Athalya Brenner (1994a: 11), for whom this text is an "inauguration myth" or a "liberation-cum-inauguration myth," and Niels Peter Lemche (1998a: 86–132), for whom it is, along with the story of the Exile to Babylon, a "foundation myth" (see also Thompson 1999). Even the cranky conservative William Dever (2001: 98, n1) can write, "No scholar, revisionist or otherwise, thinks these materials anything other than 'myth.'" What do interest me are the workings and perpetual power of this political myth, particularly in terms of feminism, psychoanalysis, and Marxism.

Finally, a brief note on terminology: I use the terms *myth* and *political myth* interchangeably, against arguments by those such as Flood (2002), who distinguish between an older sacred myth and more recent political myth. Nothing is more political than sacred myth, it seems to me, so the distinction is of little use. Indeed, I operate on the assumption that all myth, no matter how sacred or secular, is political. At times I also interchange the terms *fantasy* and *myth*, as in "the master myth of the Hebrew Bible" and "the fantasy of Israel in Australia and the United States." What needs to be borne in mind through these discussions is that since fantasy is a crucial component of myth, it may stand as a metonym for the wider category of myth.

CHAPTER ONE

Toward a Theory of Political Myth

The best definition of myth is the shortest: an important story. Beyond that we move into the endless variations that one would expect.[1] Rather than some catchall definition, my agenda requires something quite different, for I am after a theory of myth that brings out its political dimension in a usable form. In order to do so, I begin with two problems. First, what is the place of myth for the Left, especially in light of the profound suspicion that myth conjures up, suspicion specifically of "mystification" and religion? Second, is myth posterior to the political event, trying to make sense of it and preserve it, or does myth also have a virtual power in producing the event itself?

THE POWERFUL FICTION OF A COMPLETED TRUTH

I want to deal with these problems via Alain Badiou, Ernst Bloch, Theodor Adorno, and Sigmund Freud. Badiou first. In focusing on the stark purity of the event, Badiou positions himself outside the realms of representation, fabulation, and myth. His theory of the event, especially his resort to mathematics as ontology, functions as one of the clearest, most systematic expressions of this need to banish any last trace of suspicion, religion, and mystification from within political thought. Or at least it initially seems to do so. For those not familiar with Badiou's thinking, let me outline what is quickly becoming the canonical reception of that thought (Badiou 2006). Whether in the realm of politics, art, love, or science, an event bursts into, punches a hole into the status quo, which Badiou variously names the

Order of Being, the situation, the "there is." The terms cluster heavily around the event, which Badiou also describes in terms of a supplement to or excess of a situation, or (and here his mathematical bent comes to the fore) a subtraction from the "there is." His favored examples are falling in love, political insurrection, scientific discovery, and the great moment of a work of art. But the pure event can never be apprehended directly; it can be named only after the fact, identified as an event only after it has actually happened. Thus "I love you," May '68, Galileo, and Mallarmé are inadequate statements of an event that has already happened, linguistic traces of something that happened and then disappeared just as abruptly. Yet an event leaves behind what Badiou calls procedures of truth, certain patterns by which truth is constituted in all its contingent particularity (hence what he at times calls the "Truth-Event"). These patterns involve the naming of the event, the constitution of the subject as a result of the event, and fidelity to the event that will draw others in. If an event generates a thorough rearrangement of the coordinates of the way things are, we can know that an event has happened only through its effects, like an earthquake perhaps. Things will never be the same as the result of the event and the truth procedures it sets in motion.

You will perhaps have noticed that philosophy has not made an appearance thus far. It is not one of the conditions of the event (art, love, politics, and science), nor does it generate truth, nor indeed is it the bearer of truth. In fact, the very description or summary that I have culled from Badiou constitutes the task of philosophy, which is to discern the procedures of truth that an event sets in motion. Philosophy's task is very much after the fact, a second-order reflection. Or, as Louise Burchill (2000: ix), the translator of Badiou's *Deleuze: The Clamor of Being*, puts it:

> As a totally chance, incalculable, disconnected supplement that surges forth in a situation and instantly disappears, the event is only recorded in its very disappearance in the form of the linguistic trace that it leaves behind. It is on the basis of these traces that are instigated the *procedures of truth* that it is philosophy's task to seize and organize. In other words, philosophy is not a production of "Truth" but an operation on the basis of the local truths, or procedures of truth, that, relative to a situation, always originate in an event.

For Badiou, then, philosophy is a second-order activity, explicating the consequences of the event. But I want to draw out a second point. As the champion of a reconstituted Platonism, Badiou argues that the philosophical task is mathematical at its core. Or, as he puts it, if philosophy is concerned with ontology, and if mathematics is ontology (and not just a species of ontology), then one cannot shirk the necessity of mathematics in any philosophical endeavor. But why mathematics? One reason, I suggest, is that this is the most thoroughgoing way to banish anything that even vaguely smells of mystification, religion, or myth from philosophy, let alone any political philosophy of the Left.

Badiou (2004: 93; see also 2006: 112–20) makes this explicit in an extraordinary discussion of Spinoza: "God has to be understood as mathematicity itself." Mathematics, if you like, consummates the death of God. Or, in mathematical terms, the banishment of the One and the dominance of multiplicity as the reality of our existence ensure that religion will simply not be part of the equation. Any discussion of the infinite, therefore, takes place in a thoroughly secular manner, that is, by means of the matheme (the smallest intelligible mathematical unit, like the phoneme in language).

So we have reached the point where one of the greatest political philosophers writing today, and a former Maoist committed to political possibilities for the Left—is not his theory of the event precisely such a thing?—systematically excludes any possibility of religion, let alone myth, from political thought.

Well, not quite.

By contrast, it seems to me that Badiou himself provides us with the beginnings of a theory of political myth, or the fable, as he puts it. If I may put my position as starkly as possible: the idea of a necessary fable, one that is unverifiable, unpredictable, or, in Badiou's terms, undecidable and indiscernible, emerges from the very midst of his discussions of Truth.[2]

At this point Badiou is the worthy successor of Sorel. Alongside Sorel's argument that political myth is irrational and motivational, we also find that he pushes for the unverifiable nature of such myths. His primary distinction is the troubled one between rational and irrational, calm planning and emotive power. All of the rational programs for change he found wanting, failing to provide the deep and irrefutable motivation for continued political action in the face of repeated failures. But riding along with reason and motivation is the far more interesting idea that political myth is unverifiable: it will not be deflated by this or that failure. As an example, Sorel (1961: 125) cites the failed apocalyptic hopes of the first Christians—based on the myth of the immanent return of Christ—as the necessary and yet wholly fictional motivation for their achievements.

Back to Badiou: since I remain for all my sins a biblical scholar, let me come at this question from the side of Badiou's biblical reflections. This is the real test, for Badiou (2003c) attempts to read the letters of Paul, especially the epistle to the Romans, in a thoroughly secular manner, as a source of political insight. What interests me about this book, *Saint Paul: The Foundation of Universalism*, apart from what I take to be a fascinating but unwitting Calvinist flavor, is the way Paul's Truth-Event—that which radically disrupts the everyday, run-of-the-mill "Order of Being"—is inextricably tied up with a pure fable. And that fable is the resurrection of Christ. Indeed, Paul's central proclamation is that Christ has been raised, a claim about which the New Testament obsesses. Paul identifies the Truth-Event of Christ's resurrection only after the fact, only in his outright militancy, in occasional pieces written on the run (the epistles). But the event in question, the resurrection, is pure fable; it has no verifiable or historical truth (Badiou is, after all, a resolute atheist). He professes not to be interested in it, though I must confess that I am. But what draws my attention in Badiou's book on Paul is a comment barely made: that the resurrection is not merely a fable, but a *necessary* fable.

I want to push Badiou here and suggest that the very strength of Paul's central claim—that Jesus is resurrected—is that it is pure fable, that it is not tied to any element of the "earthly" life of Jesus, or, more generally, any historical conditions or causes. It is not falsifiable or verifiable in terms of the order of fact, according to any of the canons of scientific or historical inquiry.

I will shortly argue that Badiou's Paul book reveals the truth of his position as a whole. But first, let us see how Badiou might respond to my suggestion that fable necessarily lies at the heart of his theory of the event. Such a response might go as follows. Fable is in fact fiction, as one would expect in the realm of religion. Thus, when we are dealing with religion, the event has the structure of fiction. Even though it is named as an event, even though it produces all of the procedures of truth, even though we find people who act in fidelity to the event, the event itself must be fiction. And so we would expect fable and myth to play a central role in formulating and determining the "truth" of the event. By contrast, in other cases, such as May '68 or the Chinese Revolution, the event has the structure of fact, so there is no room for fable.[3]

Note carefully what happens in Badiou's response (and I do not set him up as a caricature in order to criticize him). Fable slides into fiction, which in turn slides into religion. Once we are in the realm of fable-fiction-religion, we can then quarantine religion as a special instance of the Truth-Event that does not affect the other types. We might read this as an effort to avoid being threatened by hermeneutics or the pious discourse of the phenomenologists, or indeed to forestall the danger of substantializing the category of Truth as a sacred Name, as Presence and a return to the One (see Badiou 1999: 127–32; 2002: 84–85).[4] But what lies beneath Badiou's response is a profound wariness of the idea of fable: the problem is not so much that fable means fiction as that it is tainted with religion. For this reason fable must have a limited and peripheral space.

I have rushed on too quickly, however, assuming that myth and fable are interchangeable, neglecting to ask what should in fact be the prior question: What is a fable? In terms of genre, the definition is straightforward: a fable is a story that takes place in the world of animals, plants, or inanimate objects with a point to make about human society (see Yassif 1999: 23–26). As a genre, fable does of course differ from myth. However, I am intrigued by the fact that the adjectives of fable, *fabled* and *fabulous*, break out of the strict confines of fable itself. "Fabled" designates the legendary and mythical, while "fabulous" touches on such meanings and then moves on to suggest the tremendous and extraordinary. Badiou's usage falls in with the fabled and fabulous rather than fable itself, and I will assume an interchange between fable and myth that brings them close to one another. To put it as plainly as possible, my discussion of fable in Badiou is in fact a consideration of myth itself. Thus, in the same way that fable inevitably appears in the midst of Badiou's discussions of Truth, so also does myth turn up, often uninvited, in the thick of politics.

Let me return to Badiou's response. Does he avoid fable as much as he would like? Is he able to keep fable under lock and key, under quarantine, so that it will not taint the philosophical task of dealing with the event?

It seems not. For fable, event and Truth constantly mingle and rub up against one another in Badiou's thought. The first instance comes, tellingly, from mathematics, Badiou's favored mode of thought. I cannot help but notice that in a variety of texts he broaches what can only be described as a fabulous wonder at the beauty of mathematics *precisely when he asserts the ontological priority of mathematics*. Out of a number of such moments, those of Mallarmé and Fernando Pessoa (in the persona of Álvaro De Campo) stand out. As for Mallarmé, Badiou (2004: 20; see also 2006: 191–98) writes, "The injunction to mathematical beauty intersects with the injunction to poetic truth." But a brief poem from Pessoa is even more to the point: "Newton's binomial is as beautiful as the Venus de Milo. The truth is few people notice it" (20). It is not merely the oft-made observation that underlying Plato's rigorous philosophy lie the Orphic Mysteries, the music of the spheres, and so forth, nor even that Plato struggles desperately with the quarrel between philosophy and art, resorting to images, metaphors, and myths at the limit of thought (Badiou 2005: 19–20), but that at the heart of the stark and courageous discipline of mathematics we happen upon a Platonic wonder at the beauty of mathematics (Badiou 1999: 11–13). It reminds me of the mathematician, whose name escapes me, who was overcome with the beauty of the simplest of formulas. Is it perhaps a wonder at the fabulous—and here I take the word in all its nuances—nature of mathematics?

The second instance of fable's unavoidable presence follows from this first example. Let me put a question to Badiou: Is mathematics the only way to identify the procedures of truth that follow the event?

> I have always conceived truth as a random course or as a kind of escapade, posterior to the event and free of any external law, such that the resources of narration are required *simultaneously* with those of mathematization for its comprehension. There is a constant circulation from fiction to argument, from image to formula, from poem to matheme—as indeed the work of Borges strikingly illustrates. (Badiou 2000: 58)

The play of oppositions is crucial here: narration and mathematization, fiction and argument, image and formula, poem and matheme. And, I would add, myth and Truth, as Plato's myth of Er the Pamphylian at the end of the *Republic* with all its "traps and bifurcations" (Badiou 2000: 58) shows only too well. Except that they are not so much oppositions as a series of points in a continual circulation, or perhaps an Adornoesque dialectic (that will come soon enough). So it seems that narration, fiction, image, poem, and myth, all of these are as necessary for dealing with the Truth of an event as are argument, formula, and matheme.

I would love to tarry much longer in the militant detail of Badiou's philosophy, but that is another task (see Boer in press). But I do want to stress that I seek the theoretical necessity of fable, or what I will call more generally myth, in the midst of politics, especially the political events that interest Badiou so much. Thus far it seems that Badiou's own thought provides some of the philosophical backing for such a position, however much I have read Badiou against himself. But then there is always the precedent of Badiou's reading of Deleuze, if not Deleuze's own practice of sneaking up behind other philosophers and seeing what unexpected thought he gives birth to.[5]

If we go back to my initial questions—the suspicion of myth, fable, and religion on the Left, and the question of whether myth is posterior to the political event or productive of it—then I have really concerned myself only with the former. And on that score I found that for all Badiou's efforts to quarantine myth and fable from his philosophy of the event, they are integral to that thought. But they remain posterior, after the fact, trying to account for what has happened. Is there, however, a productive or virtual power of myth, one that may in fact generate an event by whatever means? Or, to put it in Sorel's terms, is there a motivational as well as a reflective power in myth?

For a fuller answer to that question I will need to resort to Adorno, Bloch, and Lacan. But before I do, a few hints from Badiou himself, hints as to the workings of fable. On a few occasions Badiou speaks of the event in terms that simultaneously describe, to my mind, the workings of fable or myth. The first comes straight out of his fascination with set theory: the event, he argues, is an excess to any situation, unaccountable in terms of the situation in question. Here is Badiou (2004: 76–77): "Thirty years ago, Cohen demonstrated that this excess is *unassignable*. In other words, no measure could be prescribed for this excess, since it is something like an errant excess of the set with respect to itself." Note the various terms he uses to speak of the event as excess: it is "unassignable," it is an "errant excess" to which no shape can be given, for which nothing can be "prescribed." Need I say that myth also is unassignable, an unprescribable, errant excess? Or rather, that these terms will be the first ones in my search for a theory of political myth.

Another instance where Badiou's theory of the event is bursting with implications for myth comes again from mathematics: this is the process of subtraction, a drawing under rather than drawing from out of (extraction). But what interests me is that at its core, subtraction involves the threefold schema of the undecidable, the indiscernible, and the generic.[6] Again, let us see how his comments on these modalities of the event also speak of myth.

First the undecidable. The undecidable statement is one that subtracts from the norm of either veridical or erroneous statements. We are no longer in a situation of deciding one way or the other. In other words, it simply does not compute to say that fable or myth may be verified or falsified. Myth is simply not of this realm. Second the indiscernible. In this case it is no longer possible to provide any reasonable criteria to distinguish between two terms, to identify any mark of difference. For instance, in a fable it is not possible to say that an elephant is bigger than a mouse, nor indeed that a mouse is bigger than an elephant (through a ruse or whatever). Third the generic. The generic (subset) is where subtraction operates by means of excess; that is, no singular concept is able to contain the generic. In other words, the generic is a pure multiple that evades language, or any fixing by means of a singular concept. A rather simple working hypothesis for myth is that it speaks in a way that cannot be fixed; hence the suspicion in which myth is held by both theologians and antitheologians. Myth works cunningly.

My rudimentary collection of terms is increasing, for now I can add the undecidable, indiscernible, and generic to my earlier ones of unassignable, unprescribable, and errant. But there is a significant weighting in favor of negatives here that borders on an apophatic definition of political myth. In Badiou's terms, however, this is at should be, for this is precisely what happens whenever "language loses its grip" (Badiou 2004: 109; see also 2006: 69). In this respect myth is like poetry, which marks the moment when language begins to slip: "Poetry makes truth out of the multiple, conceived as a presence that has come to the limits of language" (Badiou 2005: 22). Further, if for Badiou (2004: 235) the poem is language's delicacy unto itself, then I want to suggest that myth is the *labyrinth of language*.

And yet, this is not quite the virtual power of myth that I seek for politics. What I have done is read Badiou against himself, finding that even this resolutely antifabulous and antimythic thinker in the end comes out in favor of myth. Or rather, his thought points to the inseparability of politics and myth, but only, like philosophy, posterior to the event. However, thus far in my search for the virtual power of myth Badiou has given me some key ideas for the definition of myth itself—as the point where language loses its grip, as cunning and labyrinthine—but no real sense that myth may be empowering.

Except for the idea of "forcing," or more completely, the forcing of a truth. Again, the idea comes out of mathematics, specifically Paul Cohen,[7] but what interests me is Badiou's suggestion that the form of speech proper to Truth is the future perfect. Thus, it is not so much that the event happened at some moment in the past and that philosophy attempts to discern (and myth tries to narrate) its truth procedures. Rather, the "almost nothing" of the event inaugurates a process that at this moment remains incomplete but will at some moment in the future be realized, and on that basis is it possible to state a truth. In Badiou's (2004: 127) words, "Forcing is the point at which a truth, although incomplete, authorizes anticipations of knowledge concerning not what is but *what will have been if truth attains completion.*" Thus the very possibility of saying anything about a truth relies on the fact that at some moment that truth *will have been* realized, *will have been* true.

Forcing, applied now to myth as well as Truth, will become crucial for the notion of political myth I seek to develop here. I will in due course embellish it, with the help of Walter Benjamin a little later in this chapter and then the category of eschatology from the Hebrew Bible. But for now, let me draw on that same Bible in order to see how forcing might apply to myth. The text is the Exodus from Egypt (Exodus 1–15), a useful counterpoise to Badiou's interest in Paul's fable of the resurrection of Christ. It is, however, much more overtly political than the resurrection and has been one of the motivating myths of any number of political movements, both revolutionary and reactionary—including Thomas Müntzer's peasants, Winstanley and the Diggers, the Boers in South Africa, Zionism, the Pilgrim Fathers in North America, African American slaves, anticolonial struggles, and, more recently, liberation theology.

However, what interests me about the Exodus is that its power relies on the fact that it is a myth, not a cosmogonic or theogonic myth, but a political myth. The most that we might say is that "Israel"—whatever that term means—was an indigenous group, that it was drawn from the Canaanites rather than some external body that broke into Canaan from the desert, either by invasion or in a long process of infiltration. Indeed, it is doubtful that anything known distinctly as "Israel" existed before the Persian province of Yehud in the fifth and fourth centuries BCE, that is, well after any supposed Exodus, or conquest, or David or Solomon, or divided monarchy of Israel and Judah (see my discussion in chapter 4). Let me make my point clear: it seems as though there was no Moses, no enslavement in Egypt, no entity known as "Israel," no Exodus out of Egypt, and no conquest of the Promised Land. Myth is, of course, more than just fiction, although it is dependent on fiction. Yet the Exodus has been and remains a powerful, motivating political myth. In terms of my argument, the political truth of the Exodus relies on the fact that it is a myth, and necessarily so. But what truth does the Exodus then speak? Certainly not one based on an event that took place. We cannot say, as Badiou (2004: 112) says at times of the event, "This took place, which I can neither calculate nor demonstrate." Rather, we need to say, on a political register, At some future point, this political myth *will have been.* The political truth of Exodus, as Bloch was so keen to point out, remains to be realized. In other words, forcing is perhaps one of the best ways to describe the virtual power of a myth such as Exodus. It is, if you like, the "powerful fiction of a *completed truth*" (Badiou 2003b: 65).

ESCHATOLOGY, MESSIANISM, AND APOCALYPTIC

This last phrase, "the powerful fiction of a completed truth," cannot in the end be contained within the ascetic beauty of Cohen's mathematical formulations. Badiou, it seems to me, has said much more than he perhaps realizes. Let me analyze what I have drawn from him in two ways, first by means of the category of eschatology and then through Walter Benjamin. Is not the category of the future perfect, of a political myth that will have been true, eschatological? Indeed, as my earlier invocation of Sorel indicates, one of my arguments is that it is time once again to affirm the eschatological dimension of Marxism. Long an element of criticism—is not Marxism at heart another religion?—eschatology is central to Marxism's continuing appeal and the source of much of its political strength.

I wrote "eschatology" quite deliberately, for there has been a tendency in some circles to speak of messianism or the messianic, particularly without the messiah. Walter Benjamin is for many the (implicit) inspiration for this, and following him we find Georgio Agamben, Judith Butler, and even Jacques Derrida. So let me distinguish briefly between eschatology, messianism, and apocalyptic from a biblical perspective. Far too often, as with these critics, the three terms are confused with each other, understood as alternatives for the same phenomenon, namely, the end, usually by destruction, of this age and the inauguration of a new one. By contrast, they are distinct categories, each with their own features. Further, they are both literary categories and interpretive frameworks or worldviews: as genres of biblical literature, eschatology, apocalyptic, and messianism also provide modes of interpretation.

Some rapid definitions are in order. Eschatology is the broadest category and probably the earliest. Its concern is with the transition from the present, somewhat undesirable age to another that is qualitatively better by means of an external agent, who usually turns out to be God. This external source of change will become crucial for my search for a viable political myth for the Left, for which "God" may be understood to stand as a place marker. The word "eschatology" (from the Greek *eschatos*) is a little misleading, since it focuses on the end; eschatology in the Hebrew Bible is concerned more with process than result. As a literary genre, eschatology emerges fully with the prophetic literature (e.g., Isaiah 35: 5–7), where we find the theme of an end to social, economic, and bodily ills in favor of a new age of freedom and plenty. As an interpretive framework, we find eschatology in the political master myth of Genesis through Joshua that I discuss in the following chapters.

Messianism, too often regarded as a defining feature of eschatology, is actually a subset of eschatology. In this case a particular individual, divinely appointed and directed, effects the transition from old to new (e.g., Isaiah 11:1–4). The messiah, or "the anointed one," is in the earlier material mostly a royal figure based on King David. Later, especially in the intertestamental period and especially at Qumran in the Dead Sea Scrolls, there is a royal, priestly, and even a prophetic messiah. Of course the Christians will claim Jesus as messiah as well, but by this stage messianic eschatology has a long mythic tradition (see Thompson 2005). For all the interest in messianism, especially among the secular Left since Benjamin, I find it problematic due to its reliance on a redeemer figure. I won't go into the reasons that I have explored elsewhere, particularly the Christological logic of messianism since Christianity (Boer 2007a), but messianism bedevils any political movement that tends to put its faith in a particular person, that holds such a person up as model and exemplar—in short, it is the problem of the personality cult. However, one could object that the interest in the messianic since Benjamin is of a peculiar sort, namely, that it is messianism without a messiah—a mythical way of dealing with the possibility of economic and political change, if you will, without redeemer figures. But then the better name for this would be eschatology.

Finally, apocalyptic refers to both a means of interpretation and a body of revealed knowledge (*apocaluptein* in Greek), acquired by divine message or on a journey to the heavens. Apocalyptic may either interpret past texts for the sake of understanding the present, as with many of the Qumran documents, or it may involve a coded way of speaking about the end, usually through calendars and numerology, as with Daniel in the Hebrew Bible. The two modes are not mutually exclusive, as the book of the Apocalypse in the New Testament shows. In apocalyptic we find a stark dualism between good and evil, God and his spirits versus the devil and his spiritual army, metaphoric and often hyperbolic language. Apocalyptic literature after the Bible, and perhaps within it, is usually a sign and an expression of intense political and social oppression. Without any hope in this world, we rely on deliverance from outside it. And that is the major problem with apocalyptic, for it cannot do without a radical dependence on divine intervention, specifically in the form of a savior or redeemer figure—the last thing we want in any new political myth and a constant failing of the Left in its personality cult. While apocalyptic is intriguing as a genre of literature and at times of political action, I am as skeptical about its benefits as I am about messianism, if only because of the reactionary crackpots who engage in apocalyptic speculation today. All the same, apocalyptic is not completely without virtue, for it cranks up the expectation of the end, rendering it imminent rather than off in a somewhat distant future. Yet, while such a fervor for the end means you can't get comfortable in the present age, apocalyptic is also notorious for failed predictions and futile political action that expects God to arrive with his chariots and horsemen.

My preference falls squarely on eschatology. On one level we can understand eschatology as the base category, the primary genre of which messianism and apocalyptic are both derivatives and subgenres. But I would rather push the distinction in another direction and stress the absence in eschatology of redeemer figures and the fevered, closed-in speculation characteristic of messianism and apocalyptic, respectively. An eschatology concerned with *process* rather than result, with the process of passing from hardship to peace, and one that does so by a means that is *external* to human agency is the one that interests me for the definition of political myth. Indeed, the elements that I draw from Benjamin and Bloch are eschatological in this sense.

FUTURE PERFECT: MYTHIC WORLDS

Now I turn to Walter Benjamin in the second phase of analyzing Badiou's idea of forcing in terms of political myth. Benjamin also enables me to move to the next major phase of my argument, the all too neglected work of Ernst Bloch. For Benjamin, the insight I seek is inadvertent, a consequence of what I have argued elsewhere (Boer 2007a) is the failure of his project to develop an alternative way to deal with a major problem among the Left: how to envisage the possibility and nature of the breakout of capitalism. Let me provide a few comments on that project before spelling out how his failure provides an insight into the function of myth.

Benjamin seeks the breakout of capitalism by drawing on the final or anagogic level of the old allegorical mode of biblical interpretation, with its vast schema that runs from creation to the end of the world, the eschaton. To begin with, in the extraordinarily influential last chapter of *The Origin of German Tragic Drama* (Benjamin 1998) he offers a deep reworking of the fourfold medieval allegorical schema—literal, allegorical, moral, and ana-gogic—to argue that in the Baroque mourning plays we find the marks of a fundamentally Christian mode of exegesis that is possible only with the Fall. For in a fallen world only ruins and traces remain of the prelapsarian world; allegory then becomes the means of a failed deciphering of salvation in those ruins. If in his book on the mourning play (*Trauerspiel*) Benjamin sets his sights on simultaneously describing and developing a theory of allegory, in *The Arcades Project* (Benjamin 1999) he would come to use the method itself in all its fragmentary and broken form—hence the curious status of the work as a vast collection of quotations and commentary.

The shift from the former to the latter work leaves its mark by a transi-tion: the concern with creation and the Fall in the Trauerspiel book moves decisively to the other end of the scale, the eschaton, in *The Arcades Project*. Here this "inveterate adversary of myth" (Wohlfarth 1997: 67) focuses his energy on various ways of thinking through the breakout of the mythic hell of capitalism itself, represented in its most advanced and decayed form in nineteenth-century Paris. He does so by means of the dialectical image, the caesura of the explosion out of history, of waking from a dream. Yet the mark of his failure in this project lies in the very language he uses. For he resorts, as has been well noted in feminist criticism of Benjamin, to sexual language, particularly in terms of women and maternal functions.[8] But the very same language saturates the biblical myths of creation and eschaton. Even when he doesn't explicitly invoke the Bible in his writing, the mark of the Bible's presence in his texts is where they overflow with the language of sexuality, the gendered text, women as mythical other and the in-cessant repetition of birthing metaphors. In other words, at the point where he seeks a way to think through the breach in the myth of capitalism he reverts to biblical myths, especially those of Genesis and the eschaton, a reversion marked by the language of the maternal function.

However, in this failure, in this reversion to myth in the effort to rupture myth itself, Benjamin unwittingly provides a way of rethinking the category of myth. It is not so much that we must seek to escape myth; rather, in his very use of myth it seems to me that Benjamin begins to imagine the pos-sibility of the future not by taking terms from our present and projecting them into the future, but by working in reverse. The terms and concepts of a better future, whether socialist or something as yet unimagined, and however degraded and partial they might be in our present perception and use of them, provide the way to think about that future itself. In other words, the very eschatology of the biblical myths themselves—the ones that Benjamin uses and others that he does not—suggests that myth is one crucial way we might reach across the divide between our capitalist present and a very different future to draw terms from that future itself, however imperfect those ideas, images, and terms might be. The problem is that if the future is as radically distinct—however gradual or sudden a transition it might be—as Marxists like to think, then the very ways of thinking and arguing will also be qualitatively different. Here lies the reason for the unwitting insight of Benjamin's focus on myth: the inescapably mythic nature of the material with which he works—the narratives of creation, eschaton, and even the messianic—suggest that the language of myth, with all its promises and dangers, provides one way of imagining a very different future.

In many respects I have extracted this insight from Benjamin, forcing, if you like, a certain truth from his work. But then I do have Deleuze and Badiou himself as models for such an approach. Let me connect my point from Benjamin more closely with Badiou's notion of forcing. Let us be clear: Badiou's focus is on an event that has happened but whose truth is not so much a present reality as one that *will have been* if such a truth attains completion. By means of my reading of Benjamin I want to shift the basis of that truth from the past to one in the future—a shift that is implicit in Badiou's suggestion that we may make (tentative) truth-statements now on the basis of the truth that will attain completion at some future point.

There are two implications of such a transfer. First, it brings me a little nearer to an understanding of myth as a virtual power, one that is productive of political events rather than merely a reflective act, posterior to the event. For if the truth of the event remains to be, indeed will have been at some future point, then the anticipation of that truth becomes not so much a completion of an event that has already happened as an element in *producing the event that will give rise to that truth*. If the truth will have been, then so also will the event have been.

Second, in my brief discussion of Benjamin I bordered on suggesting that this future actually exists in some sense, that it is the point from which myth draws its images and terms. If so—and apart from the dialectical point of making such a move—then that is to my mind part of the magic of the future perfect *and of myth itself*. This point gives a distinct twist to the commonplace point that myth creates a world or worlds: myth constructs or postulates world(s) whose truth will have been upon its completion. Or, to use Badiou's extraordinary phrase, such a world created by myth is the powerful fiction of a completed truth.

And so we can add to my makeshift theory of political myth. Not only is myth the labyrinth of language, the marker of the point at which language loses its grip, but myth is also eschatological: it *forces the event itself* by creating worlds in which the political event will have been.

THE DISCERNMENT AND CUNNING OF MYTH

At this point I would like to introduce the stern prophetic figure of Ernst Bloch, all too readily forgotten in contemporary debates. While Badiou and Benjamin, and indeed any number of others on the Left, are suspicious of myth, seeing it as something to be passed by at a distance with disapproving looks, Bloch is the great proponent of the value of myth for the Left. Rather than close down myth and its baleful influence, Bloch cautions against such a sustained dismissal, for myth can be revolutionary as well as reactionary. Although he understands full well the reasons for being "wary of the mythical sphere in its entirety" (Bloch 1998: 296; 1985, vol. 9: 339) after the Nazi myths of blood and soil, he argues that the "myths" the Left is all too keen to dispose of are precisely the myths that contain stories of murmuring, subversion, and rebellion. What happens with the ban of myth, argues Bloch (1972: 34; 1985, vol. 14: 64), is "that the primitive, uncultured specters are thrown out, but the directives and announcements from on high remain to haunt as they always did." Adorno would make a similar point: the eviction of myth from the reasoned politics of Marxism faced the danger of replicating the patterns of oppression from the very myths that they sought to discard.

In Bloch's championing of myth, he goes a step beyond one of Lévi-Strauss's theories of myth. This is none other than the famous idea that myth is a "cultural trouble-shooter," as Csapo (2005: 226) puts it. Lévi-Strauss's problem was that myth seems to run roughshod over the laws of logic and experience, following what he called a "pensée sauvage" (1966) or "thought gone wild" in which all possibilities are open, and yet myths with the same patterns appear throughout the world (see Lévi-Strauss 1968: 206–31). His solution is not some recourse to a deep mythic consciousness or collection of archetypes, but the point that myth shares the common feature of a solution to a cultural contradiction. He would take this conclusion well beyond the study of myth—into art, the spatial arrangement of settlements, and so on—but the point was that the effort to solve the contradiction was not so much a solution as a displacement. In other words, a social contradiction would show up as a formal contradiction in art and myth, as his example of facial art among the Brazilian Caduveo tribe shows so well. In its formal tension between two axes in face painting, one along the natural lines of the face and another at an oblique angle, with no other means of dealing with social tensions within the tribe, the Caduveo used facial decoration to ameliorate and repress such tensions (Lévi-Strauss 1973: 229–56; 1968: 245–68).

Lévi-Strauss's theory is useful because it provides one path to the social and political situation of myth, but it remains a reactive theory—myth is a response to a social contradiction—similar to Badiou's theory of truth. Bloch, however, goes well beyond Lévi-Strauss. Not one to embrace myth without some reserve, his greatest contribution is what we might call the *discernment of myth*. His second contribution, often regarded as his trademark, is the anticipatory, utopian function of myth. Indeed, what Bloch does is provide myriad details and content to the theoretical framework for the virtual power of myth that I have constructed with the help of Badiou and Benjamin. Bloch's vast collection, spilling out beyond his massive *The Principle of Hope* (1995) into any number of other books, supplies almost more materials than I need to fit onto the carefully planed and joined frame I have constructed thus far.

Bloch's discernment of myth is in fact a dialectical reading of myth that does not throw myth out wholesale nor take myth uncritically as a positive dimension of human culture. It provides, in other words, a sustained exercise of a more sophisticated Marxist ideology critique. Bloch's deliberations on biblical myth draw my gaze, particularly in that extraordinary but neglected work, *Atheism in Christianity* (1972). For Bloch, myth is neither pure false consciousness that needs to be unmasked nor a positive force without qualification. No matter how repressive, all myths, like ideology, have an emancipatory-utopian dimension about them that cannot be separated so easily from deception and illusion. In the very process of manipulation and domination, one finds a utopian residue that has not been entirely incinerated in the white heat of reaction, an element that opens up other possibilities at the very point of failure (see Kellner 1997; Jameson 1981). Bloch is particularly interested in biblical myth, for the subversive elements in the myths that interest him are enabled by the repressive ideologies that show through again and again. If the Bible is not always folly to the rich it is at least the Christian Church's bad conscience.[9]

Bloch's most lucid discussion of the role of myth comes in his debate with the outstanding New Testament scholar Rudolph Bultmann (1952–55, 1958, 1966), who proposed a program of demythologization of the Bible and theology. For Bultmann, the Bible inescapably contains the forms of thought, language, and belief of the time in which its various parts were composed. Indeed, the dominant mode of expression was myth; for the gospel, the *kerygma*, to be meaningful in the contemporary situation of the early twentieth century, this mythological structure must be excised from the Church's message. Not merely the accretions to the central message were in Bultmann's sights: he urged that the basic components of Christianity derived from the New Testament, such as a three-tiered cosmos with heaven above and hell below, the miracles of Jesus, especially the empty tomb and the resurrection, the coming of the Holy Spirit and the return of Christ on the clouds at the end of history, should all be discarded as unworkable and unbelievable myths. This is only a basic list, but once the demythologizing task was complete, Bultmann called for a remythologization in terms of contemporary patterns of thought, specifically the existentialism that had swept through European philosophy.

In place of a program such as Bultmann's, Bloch feels that it is the purpose of such materials that counts rather than the prescientific ideas they contain. Do they speak of transformation and liberation? Do they have cunning heroes who win through a ruse? But this requires some distinction within the broad category of myth, too often a blanket term without specificity, lumped together by Marxists and others in Engels's phrase "the imbecility of the primeval forest" (quoted in Bloch 1998: 297; 1985, vol. 9: 339)—distinctions between the despotism and domination of myth proper and those that, like later fairy tales, subvert such domination (see also Zipes 1979, 1983). The story of Prometheus in Greek mythology or the serpent in Paradise in the Bible give voice to this fairy tale element in myth. Bloch would much prefer to keep both the conformist and nonconformist elements of myth rather than no myth at all, since the banishment of myth discards the "joyful message," the "deepest utopian theme" (Bloch 1998: 300; 1985, vol. 9: 343) of mythology along with all that is oppressive.

If the first step of his argument is to seek out the purpose of myth in order to make a political distinction, his second step involves distinguishing further between different types of myth. In part, this is because Bloch does not want a wholesale recovery of myth, for this would render him an anti-Enlightenment thinker beyond the wide circle of Marxism. And so the results of fear, ignorance, and superstition may go, but those that give expression to the quality and wonder of nature should not. Fairy tale, legend, saga, and myth all become separate entities. Here he invokes Greek art, science (Kepler), and the Romantics. He is, of course, trying to run myth through dialectics, "destroying and saving the myth in a single dialectical process" (Bloch 1972: 37; 1985, vol. 14: 67).

Toward a Theory of Political Myth · 25

At his best, Bloch's discernment of myth is an extraordinary approach, for it enables us at least to make a start in identifying those elements within a myth that are oppressive, misogynist, racist, that serve a ruling elite, and those that are subversive, liberating, and properly democratic (i.e., socialist). What we need, he suggests, is a "particularly sober and discerning mind" that does not take myth at face value, without shades of difference (Bloch 1972: 37; 1985, vol. 14: 67). And yet he does not always live up to the rigors of his dialectical approach, falling prey too often to the spurious notion that "earlier is better." Thus, the stories of rebellion, he suggests, belong to the earliest and supposedly pristine layers of myth. Indeed, the earliest mythology comes out of the world of primitive communism, a world before the division of labor and the formation of classes; only later do they become the imaginative normalizations of social contradictions, that is, ideologies (Bloch 1988: 35, 114–15). The biblical scholarship of his time, to which he was heavily indebted, is partly to blame, and its desperate search for origins remains a defining feature today.

Rather than these assumptions, what we need from Bloch is what I have called the discernment of myth, an exercise that takes place precisely because of myth's *cunning*. Thus, the exercise of discerning the subversive content and purpose of myth is also a recognition that the enabling conditions for subversive myths are precisely those myths that are not so, that through and because of the myths of dominance and despotism those of cunning and nonconformism can be there too.

We can now extend our theory of political myth a little further, for Bloch is the great exegete of the *cunning of myth*.[10] He provides an answer to this question: If myth is the point at which the firm foothold of communicative language begins to slip into the labyrinth of language, when we enter the eschatological process characterized by the future perfect—what will have been—then what are the political possibilities of such worlds? The answer is twofold: these myths and their political possibilities are ambiguous and contradictory, for reaction and subversion operate in a dialectical tension. And so the potential for subversion arises in a sly and cunning manner.

ADORNO'S WARINESS

What Bloch has done is shift the emphasis decisively to *political* myth. Politics was of course implicit in my readings of Badiou and Benjamin, where one condition of the event is indeed politics (Badiou) and part of the agenda is to seek a way out of capitalism (Benjamin). Yet in both cases politics itself was partially concealed, waiting in the wings until Bloch was able to bring it forth. But something else has also been there, behind the curtain, standing side by side with politics: dialectics. If my take on myth and truth in Badiou touches on an older, dialectical Badiou of *Theorie du Sujet* (and one who reemerges in *Logiques du Monde*), and if Benjamin's insight in the midst of his failure carries on the dialectical logic of his work, then Bloch's dialectic is at the forefront of his recasting of myth.

Yet for all the dialectical interplay of oppression and subversion within myth, Bloch sides quite decisively with the possibilities of myth for political revolution, for its contribution to a socialist agenda. This is the reason for my interest in his work, but I cannot avoid a certain wariness about his program. It is not just that he slides from the discipline of his dialectic to seek some pristine and authentic subversive voice beneath the layers of reaction that have been placed over such mythical substrata. Rather, my wariness comes from two angles: one is Adorno's unremittingly negative characterization of myth in the famed dialectic of myth and enlightenment, and the other is the psychoanalytic objection that any program for reading the political possibilities of myth faces the Real, the psychoanalytic version of the constitutive exception. Both objections are closely related, it seems to me, for both operate with a dialectic that is reminiscent of Bloch's.

The curious thing about Adorno is that the dialectic of enlightenment produces the firm conclusion that myth is oppressive, all but closing down any possibility for reading myth positively. But it is worth listening to Adorno's reasons, for they form the backdrop to my discussion in chapter 2, "Women First?" Perhaps his most well-known argument comes from the discussion with Max Horkheimer that became the first two sections of *Dialectic of Enlightenment* (Horkheimer and Adorno 1999). Here Odysseus becomes the prototypical bourgeois, the prime instance of the way enlightenment—which Adorno and Horkheimer trace back to the Greeks— inevitably brings myth back in the very process of banishing it as so much superstition. Or, to put it in the terms of the classic Adornoesque dialectic, if we push enlightenment far enough, to where it hardly wishes to go, then we will flush out the myth that is inseparable from the program of enlightenment itself.

The point of all of this is that, apart from a moment when, in the correspondence with Benjamin (1999: 127–28; 1994: 168–69), he explores what myth that has been thoroughly demythologized might look like, Adorno finds myth unremittingly baleful. It is synonymous with deception, false clarity, fixation, domination, exploitation (not least of women), and the repression necessary for individual subjectivity to emerge. Myth must be uncovered and countered in whatever way possible; thus, to argue that myth is already enlightenment and that enlightenment generates ever more virulent forms of myth is a critique of enlightenment itself and not a retrieval of myth. Given the context in which Adorno did much of his work—the Nazi appropriation of myth in terms of the Blond Beast and of blood and soil—we can well understand the ideological suspicion that a Marxist of Jewish background would direct at myth. In this respect Adorno shares the deeper wariness of Badiou and Benjamin.

Let me give two examples of this argument. The first comes in the reading of the episode of the Sirens in Homer's *Odyssey* (Horkheimer and Adorno 1999: 33–37; Homer 1999). Here Odysseus blocks the ears of his rowers with wax so they will not be tempted and seduced by the sirens' song, but Odysseus himself orders them to tie him, as tightly as they can, to the ship's mast so that he can hear the song but do nothing about it. Of course, Odysseus begs and cries out to his men to release him when he hears the song, but they calmly keep rowing, oblivious to their master's cries. For Adorno and Horkheimer this is a prime instance of the dialectic of myth and enlightenment: here we find the simultaneous separation and subjection to one another of those who labor and those who do not (Odysseus bound to the mast and the men to the oars); the rationalization and ordering of labor, which is now done under compulsion and without pleasure, becoming part of the machine while being unable to communicate; the parting of the ways of the enjoyment of art and manual labor (whereas Odysseus can hear and contemplate the beauty of the song, the rowers do not hear it at all); the separation of intellect and sensuous experience in order to unify the former and subjugate the latter. In short, it is Hegel's master-slave dialectic avant la lettre: the proletarians who can no longer hear about their situation in contrast to the immobile master trapped in the immaturity of domination. Odysseus is, in short, the prototypical burgher.

But it is the last point that overlaps with the remarkably sympathetic reading of Polyphemous the Cyclops (Horkheimer and Adorno 1999: 64–69). Apart from the tension of subjectivity—the play on Odysseus and Udeis, "Nobody"—that enables Odysseus's escape, Adorno and Horkheimer point out that the source of the remarkable power of the Cyclops is that they are older than the gods. That is, they come from before the law and social organization, so whereas they seem to lack the laws of civilization—they eat human beings and fend for themselves—they show compassion to their animals and one another, a compassion lacking in Odysseus. For law and organization are in fact the objectifications of domination, and what we find in myth is the exploration and establishment of law and organization of society, as well as the patterns of the subjugation of women.

At this point Adorno shares the second of Lévi-Strauss's ideas of myth, particularly as we find it in *The Raw and the Cooked* (1994). In an extraordinary tour de force Lévi-Strauss relates 187 myths from South American indigenous tribes to one fundamental structure: the passage from barbarism to society through the motif of food. The preparation of food, a process of moving from what is raw to what is cooked, marks the moment of social formation and ordering, in short, culture. In contrast to the passage from raw to cooked, the other passage is from fresh to rotten, the mark of the lack of culture, of society and organization. The difference from Adorno is that Lévi-Strauss's narrative is somewhat more benign, a necessary process rather than the imposition of an oppressive regime.

I would not wish to dismiss Adorno's points lightly, for as we will see with the narrative from Genesis to Joshua, we do in fact find the suppression of rebellion, the delivery of the law, the emergence of a state, the conquest of a land, and the organization of society and of the relations between the sexes. Thus the narrative shift that takes Odysseus from Circe, who tries in vain to get him to stay, to Penelope marks the transition from matriarchy to marriage: woman becomes both courtesan and wife (Horkheimer and Adorno 1999: 69–75). Here we find an assumed but never developed schema in which the first term marks something lost in myth: matriarchy to marriage, savagery to barbarism (Lewis Henry Morgan [1877] peeks over the page at this point), animal to human individuation and subjectivity, magic to myth. The catch is that Adorno and Horkheimer refuse to explore what magic, matriarchy, human animality, and savagery might actually entail.

But now my reason for drawing Adorno into Bloch's dialectic of myth comes to the fore. Adorno explicates more fully than Bloch the oppressive functions of myth: rationalization, social organization, codifications of class, establishment of the law, and so on. However, as Bloch shows, this is not all that myth does. For myth does not merely lock these into place; it explores the tensions and contradictions that make these problems in the first place. To be sure, myth often closes down the contradictions in the end, but not before it has given considerable space to them, and they are *precisely those contradictions that would render a social and economic order unviable*. Myth enables the airing of such contradictions precisely because they cannot be entertained within certain social organizations.

However, just as I read Badiou and Benjamin against themselves (in fact, such an immanent method I derive from Adorno), I want to read Adorno in the same fashion. For it seems to me that in the midst of his trenchant criticism of myth he yields some valuable insights. What interests me here is not so much the dialectic of myth and enlightenment as the other great pairing of myth, this time with history.[11] The reason for my interest is that the virtual power of myth lies not merely in its motive force, but directly in its relation to history. In other words, how might myth effect historical change?

One of the best exhibits of the dialectic of myth and history comes in Adorno's first philosophical and deeply theological work, *Kierkegaard: Construction of the Aesthetic* (1989). Concisely put, his argument is that in the same way that Kierkegaard's mythless Christianity relies on myth, so also is Kierkegaard's effort to escape myth through a radical inwardness based on myth. The catch here, however, is that the very notion of inwardness is itself mythological, that is, part of the deepest ideological structure of liberalism. And this myth—the myth of the free individual—is inescapably tied to the historical situation of the bourgeoisie in early capitalism. So we get to the point where the myth of radical inwardness cannot but speak of its historical situation *and* that situation generates the myth.

Even though Kierkegaard worked ever so hard to break the mythical spell that hung over Christianity, ridding it as far as possible from the mythical world in which it first arose (three-tiered universe, heaven and hell, and so on), and even though Adorno astutely locates the other myths that creep in (Nordic, chthonic, gnostic, Orphic), what Kierkegaard has in fact done is construct an extraordinarily persuasive myth in their place. And that myth circles around the autonomy of the isolated individual that emerges from radical inwardness. To put it crudely, even if Kierkegaard may have *demythologized* Christian thought, he has *remythologized* it in terms of an existentialism of which he was the founder. Myth and history come crashing back together at this point: the myth of radical inwardness gives way at every moment to its political economic situation, *and* that situation generates such a myth in response, a myth that becomes its deepest ideological expression.

But let me move beyond Adorno and pick up another example, this time from Freud's last text, *Moses and Monotheism* (2001, vol. 23). A short sentence from Jacques-Alain Miller (2004: 28) opens up a problem at the heart of Freud's little book: "Freud wanted him to be real." Wanted whom to be real? Freud wants a historical Moses, so he could then become the father, who in Freud's account is God. Or rather, Freud wants a *real* Moses and a *Real* father-God—the play on the Lacanian Real/real is crucial in Miller's sentence. The father-God is the Real, the unnameable, untouchable, and unrepresentable absent cause of Freud's text (for Miller) and of the Hebrew Bible (for Freud). But Freud also wanted a real, historical Moses, a figure whom he could discern behind the smoke of legend and myth. And so he sets out to find this Moses, who in fact turns out to be a double, two Moses figures that merge into one. Moses himself is the Egyptian, bringing the spiritualized and ethical religion of Aten with him, whereas the unnamed Midianite priest who is blended with this Moses comes from the wilderness, bringing an angry storm god, Yahweh, a "coarse, narrow-minded, local god, violent and bloodthirsty" (Freud 2001, vol. 23: 50). Once the two groups represented by these two figures have united in the wilderness, the people react to the strict monotheistic reforms of the Egyptian Moses, they rebel and kill him, like the primal horde killing the father, and in their guilt they elevate and blend him into the god and thereby conceal the original murder. Less the criticism of monotheism than it seems, here lies the secret of monotheism for Freud, since it enabled the crucial step via the spiritualized notion of one God to abstract thought to which we are all indebted. Now Freud relies on some dubious biblical scholarship to put together his reconstruction of Moses, but what strikes me about this story—praised and castigated since he first wrote it—is that in the very process of seeking the historical Moses and dispensing with myth, Freud constructs his own new myth, one that is extraordinarily powerful. It is, if you like, one of the great instances of Adorno's dialectic of myth and history.

Let us see what Adorno adds to my growing theory of political myth. There are two points I wish to draw from him: the potent force of reaction in myths and the dialectic of myth and history. If myth signals the slippage into a labyrinth of language, into eschatological worlds whose political possibilities may be characterized in terms of a dialectic that is both potently reactionary and cunningly subversive, then myth also has history as its dialectical obverse. To put it slightly differently: not only does history generate myth, but the linguistic labyrinth of myth also generates history, now understood as the cunning of the future perfect. Myth, therefore, may also have a virtual power for subversive change within history. Or to gloss Adorno: as if real history were not stored in the core of each possible myth;

as if every myth that seriously resists reification did not bring the petrified things in flux and precisely thus make us aware of our history.[12]

THE PSYCHOANALYTIC DEMURRER

Alongside Adorno, Freudian psychoanalysis brings a second moment of hesitation.[13] If chapter 2 of this book is a response to Adorno's wariness, chapter 3 faces this psychoanalytic demurrer. Although the content of the psychoanalytic objection to the theory of political myth I am seeking to develop here is somewhat different from Adorno and Horkheimer's, the result is very similar: myth provides us with no path out of our current situation. In fact, myth is part of the problem.

Let me pick up two elements from psychoanalysis, particularly from Freud, Lacan, and Žižek. To begin with, I am going to make significant use of the psychoanalytic notion of fantasy as a key component of myth. Let me cut to the chase, for I will have the opportunity to explore fantasy at more leisure later on: fantasy is *the* way we deal with the psychoanalytic version of the constitutive exception. What does this mean? For psychoanalysis there is a necessary gap between our everyday reality and a deeper, unknown fantasmatic kernel or background of that "reality." This is the constitutive exception, the extraneous item that keeps the system running. Fantasy is the way we deal with, in narrative fashion, what cannot by definition be part of the system and yet is absolutely necessary for that system to operate. Further, the exception is not some benign item that we would like to have but can't (strawberry cake, illicit sex, a high-performance bicycle): it is a traumatic kernel, a horror that would destroy us if we came face to face with it. So fantasy becomes the primary mode of shielding ourselves from that trauma, of enabling our daily personal, social, and political lives to continue without crashing down around us. Now I have refused to name the kernel, for it is ostensibly unnamable and unidentifiable—indeed, there are echoes of Badiou's event here—but even more, *fantasy itself constructs the kernel for which it then acts as a protective mechanism.*

This theory of fantasy that runs through Freud, Lacan, and Žižek relies on what may be called Freud's (2001, vol. 4: 135) depth model: just as in the fantasy life of dreams, myth operates in a relationship in which a latent content lies beneath a manifest content. The trick for analysis and interpretation is to find a way to outsmart the censor in order to get to the latent content.[14] Let me give two examples, one borrowed and the other not.[15] In order to carry on our everyday lives, communicating with people, sharing a meal, having sex with someone, working with others, we do so without thinking consciously about the fact that they sweat, urinate, defecate, menstruate, that their skin has its own zoo of flora and fauna, that their internal organs are perpetually pulsating, gurgling, and pumping. If we did live with such a vivid and constant awareness we would begin to suffer from paranoia, or psychosis more generally, for the world would become nightmarish and treacherous, conspiracies abounding in every action and word.[16] To use another example, this time from *The Lord of the Rings:* The unbearable truth of Gollum/Smeagol is not that he himself has a split personality, a conflict between the more tender Smeagol and the callous, scheming Gollum. Rather, Gollum is the horrible Real of Frodo, the ring-bearer and diminutive hero, that "something in Frodo more than Frodo himself"—he is slimy, smelly, filthy, eternally present—and it is that part that enables the ring-bearer to complete his task: without Gollum he would not be able to destroy the ring. Rather than some silly allegory of little Hobbit Britain fighting free of the evil of totalitarianism, at a psychoanalytic level one could argue that Tolkien's whole fantasy, the vast narrative of *The Lord of the Rings* itself, is concerned with Frodo's disgusting truth.

The objection begins to take shape: if fantasy is the way we deal with the traumatic, fantasmatic kernel, then it perpetuates that kernel. In order to ensure our survival, we must construct fantasies, but this will hardly change the situation in question. This leads to the second, related objection: any political movement will fall foul of the surplus that will eventually undermine it—witness the perpetual failure of revolutions that betray their initial agenda. In fact, any movement for political change becomes a more sophisticated way of ensuring that the system remains in place. But since I seek a way to answer what is a significant question, let me pose this objection in terms of Judith Butler's opposition to it in a crucial debate with Žižek and Laclau (Butler, Laclau, and Žižek 2000). For Butler, Lacanian psychoanalysis in the end closes down any possibility for what is new, for a viable politics beyond capitalism. She focuses on the questions of hegemony and subject, but I will restrict myself to the first. She keeps coming back to the argument that psychoanalysis forbids any step out of the system, that the way Žižek's and indeed Lacan's dialectic works is to generate an impasse at the very point where such a break opens up. Given that hegemony is not a description of the status quo but rather an inquiry into the means of political change, the key issue is that of opposition to domination. But according to the Hegelian and Lacanian logic that Žižek employs, what happens is "that that very point of opposition is the instrument through which domination works, and that we have unwittingly enforced the powers of domination through our participation in its opposition" (28).

Butler puts a series of questions to Žižek, all of them turning on the impossibility of political action from within a Lacan read in terms of Hegel: "But where does one go from here?" she asks. "Does the exposition of an aporia, even a constitutive aporia at the level of the linguistic performative, work in the service of a counter-hegemonic project?" (Butler, Laclau, and Žižek 2000: 28). Or quite directly, where is the possibility of something new, especially in a social and political direction? In fact, what Žižek does, suggests Butler, is pursue the other dimension of hegemony, namely, the myriad ways in which consent operates, particularly what constrains and limits us. "But what remains less clear to me is how one moves beyond such a dialectical reversal or impasse to something new. How would the new be produced from an analysis of the social field that remains restricted to inversions, aporias and reversals that work regardless of time and place? Do these reversals produce something other than their own structurally identical repetitions?" (29).

Now, my sympathies lie with Butler's objection, no matter how hard Žižek tries to answer it. In fact, as I have argued elsewhere, he will need to drop psychoanalysis, however briefly, in order to become a political writer. For all the talk of traversing the fantasy, of the psychoanalytic cure, Butler points to the limits of psychoanalysis. At the same time, however, the two related objections should not be dismissed too readily. Like Adorno and Horkheimer's objection—that myth is enlightenment, that it involves the first moment of social ordering, law, rationalization, and domination (rather close to Lacan's Symbolic)—both the theory of fantasy and the point that any political movement ends up supporting the status quo are all too readily visible within myth. With sickening regularity, myth becomes the way a political economic system is shored up and justified, the way dissent and tensions are managed, the means by which revolution is curtailed and warnings issued about the consequences of such radical change, or even blatant propaganda for reaction. Indeed, for these reasons chapters 5 and 6 in this book explore the ways political myth operates in reactionary political agendas in a number of contemporary instances, specifically in Australia and the United States.

So now my theory gains another thread. Political myth involves the construction of labyrinthine eschatological worlds characterized by a dialectic of reaction and subversion. While reaction potently produces the opposition which it perpetually closes down, while reaction constructs fantasies that carefully conceal a horror that it has constructed, myth has a cunning knack of twisting out of such a stranglehold to offer the possibility that myth is also the powerful fiction of a completed truth. In this sense it may be said to have a virtual power in history.

CHAPTER TWO

Women First?
On the Legacy of "Primitive Communism"

H ere we pass, to gloss Marx, from the plateau of theory to the intricate tensions of texts. In this chapter and the next two I analyze the nature of this political myth via feminism, psychoanalysis, and Marxism, respectively. This chapter tracks a particular moment of denial, first in biblical scholarship and then in the text itself. Thus in the first half I offer a metacommentary on those who argue that early "Israel" may in fact have offered a slightly better deal for women than the oppressive patriarchies of monarchy and empire that have been traced out in detail in biblical scholarship. Lying behind this argument is something all the critics in question deny: primitive communism. What is appealing about the work of these critics is that unwittingly they unearth a function of the text itself, namely, the need to block something that is crucial to the text—what I call a denied moment of primitive communism. Where such a denial shows up most sharply is on the question of women, specifically their presence and absence. If in the critical literature the denied background for a better deal for women is primitive communism, Genesis–Joshua perpetually moves to block the possibility that another world is possible, and the control of women is central to that agenda. This chapter engages directly with Adorno's and Horkheimer's objection to myth, namely, that myth is the first moment of ordering, fixation, and social control.

Less the specter with which I was tempted to begin, primitive communism is alive and well in biblical studies. But it has an all too curious form: not so much the classical Marxist category of the society before want, before the real division of labor between mind and body, but rather the society in which women were at least slightly better off than we might have expected in the overbearing patriarchies of the Hebrew Bible. If the confidence of Gottwald's and Meyer's claims for an egalitarian society that we can glimpse behind the obdurate walls of the biblical text, or perhaps that we can uncover amid the mounds of patriarchal debris, has waned, there remains the suggestion, the hint perhaps, that there lies buried somewhere—in a *tel*, a text, or the psyche—the possibility of a less oppressive system for women.[1]

Primitive communism leaves a curious trail we can follow all the way from Gale Yee back, via Marshall Sahlins to J. J. Bachofen. I begin with the biblical critics before moving on to consider the anthropologists and sundry Marxists, always working in reverse.[2] Although recent biblical studies is a little more skeptical concerning the possibilities for women in whatever society or societies there were "behind" the biblical texts, in certain circles, especially those influenced by social scientific approaches, there remains an assumed background of what has become known as the domestic or household mode of production. For instance, in his argument for a patron-client or "clientalistic" mode of production in the Israel of David, Solomon, and Co., Ronald Simkins assumes a transition from a domestic mode of production to his proposed clientalistic mode, a transition that led to a profound tension between the two as they had to live side by side. Simkins makes use of the standard Marxist category of mode of production, especially the argument that new modes of production do not simply replace earlier ones, but subsume and transform earlier modes.

The major focus of Simkins's (1999) essay is an effort to characterize monarchic Israel in terms of the relationships between patron and client, rather than, say, the Asiatic mode of production (he takes on board the criticisms of the Asiatic mode of production by the disillusioned Althusserians, Hindess and Hirst [1975]). However, what intrigues me is the way such a mode of production follows from what he regards as a well-established category: the domestic, household, or communitarian mode of production. Although they are subordinate throughout the monarchic period, Simkins (1999: 132) suggests that the "components of this mode have been extensively documented for early Israel." However, of all the sources he cites, Marshall Sahlins (1972) is the only anthropologist, and yet he is crucial for the notion of a domestic or household mode of production. Let me quote Simkins (1999: 132–33) on this mode of production (transliterating the Hebrew), since with minor variations and at greater or lesser length, we find a similar description of what has become known as the domestic mode of production in Gottwald, Meyers, Yee, and others:

> The primary productive unit in early Israel was the family unit known as the *bet-av*, consisting of several nuclear families covering as many as four generations, and linked in an extended unit, the *mishpachah*. . . . The *bet-av* was a self-sustaining unit, which owned the means of production—primarily, the land, which was shared in common by the members of the kinship unit. Kinship relations served as the social relations of production and distribution, regulating access to the means of production and determining the distribution of the products of labor. However, within the domestic mode of production, the kinship system functioned simultaneously as the superstructure. The kinship system formed the condition for its own reproduction by regulating marriages. It provided the social framework for political and religious activity, and it functioned as an ideology expressing the relationship between kinsmen and between men and women.

Although Simkins is not taken with any arguments for either an egalitarian social arena (Gottwald 1999 and Meyers 1988), or minimally a slightly better situation for women under such a domestic mode of production (Jobling), Gale Yee is. Against Simkins's argument that there is an ideology of egalitarianism that failed to deal with rising inequalities (that then led to the client-patron mode of production), Yee argues that we can indeed find traces of a domestic mode of production where women and men were somewhat more equal.

By and large Yee agrees with Simkins concerning the nature of the domestic mode of production, or, as she prefers, the familial mode of production, with a few exceptions. First, she finds it more mutually supportive than Simkins would entertain. Second, when weighed in the balance, although she hesitates to speak of an egalitarian situation, for Yee women seem to have been better off under the familial mode of production. Third, she accepts Norman Gottwald's argument for an initial "tributary" mode of production out of which early Israel emerged only to slip back into it under the monarchy (Yee 2003: 60–63). For Yee, Israel no doubt lived under the familial mode of production. Her interest, however, is the effect of this on women. Thus, under the familial mode of production, the "family household was the basic socioeconomic unit" (61).[3] This was undermined by Solomon's division of Israel into twelve administrative districts and the redirection of loyalties to Jerusalem. A key feature of such transitions, in which older forms of solidarity are only slowly overcome, is the control of the sexual behavior of women, particularly the death penalty for adultery. Texts such as Genesis 2–3—a product of royal ideology—seek to strengthen the conjugal bond of the nuclear family and weaken the ties of kinship and subjection to the paterfamilias by shifting them to the king (here she agrees with Simkins). Nuclear families are far less likely to be sources of rebellion against centralized authority. Apart from taking up Gottwald's argument concerning the self-sufficient and mutually supporting and protecting nature of tribal Israel, the picture that emerges between the lines for the familial mode of production is fierce loyalty to the father's house and tribe, resistance to the point of rebellion to efforts to break down such social organization, and the overarching role of the paterfamilias.

We are in fact drawing closer to Marshall Sahlins's depiction of what he first termed the domestic mode of production, particularly the concern with the well-being of the tribal unit over anything else. Sahlins, however, does not appear directly in Yee's discussion. I need to follow the trail back a little to David Jobling (1991), where Sahlins does appear. Two elements of Jobling's work are of interest: the suggestion that women had a better deal under the domestic mode of production and the unwitting connection with primitive communism.

On the first point, Jobling argues that what others call the tension between nuclear and extended families may be understood as tension between virilocal and patrilocal families. The terminology comes from Mieke Bal (1988): focalized from a woman's perspective, either the wife goes to the husband's house (virilocal) or the husband goes to the wife's father's house (patrilocal). To take this a step further, the domestic mode of production is the realm of patrilocal family structures, with the father of the women ruling over a larger tribal group that includes their various husbands and children. By contrast, the mode of production under which kingship operated—for Jobling, the Asiatic mode of production—prefers a virilocal system with *direct control* over women in marriage by their husbands. And this is the key: since the man cedes direct control under a patrilocal, tribal system to the paterfamilias, women find themselves with greater freedom.

I will return to this discussion later, especially in relation to Morgan, but it seems to me that the extended-nuclear, or even virilocal-patrilocal, opposition misses the wood for the trees: the key lies with the basic unit of the gens, which in turn operates with a number of family forms. And the one that comes through quite clearly in these texts is what Morgan calls the syndyasmian family: pairs that live together in larger units in either virilocal or patrilocal patterns.

But let me move on to my second point: that such an argument for a fairer social order ultimately relies upon the notion of primitive communism. This is mediated via an unlikely channel: Karl Wittfogel's (1963) highly problematic *Oriental Despotism*.[4] Let me quote Jobling (1991: 242): "Based mainly on a study of early Chinese society, Wittfogel correlates the shift from primitive commune to the Asiatic mode with shifts (1) from mother- to father-right (a 'patriarchal system of kinship'), (2) from extensive (female-dominated) to intensive (male-dominated) agriculture, and (3) from communal to individual ownership." Seven years later, in the 1 Samuel commentary, from which I quoted a little earlier, Jobling (1998: 146) moves from listing Wittfogel's findings to a more general comment concerning the transition from the household or domestic mode of production to the Asiatic or tributary mode: "The transition from a more egalitarian to a tributary mode is typically accompanied by shifts from female-based to male-based patterns of kinship and social organization, from a low-level agriculture dominated by women to an intensive agriculture organized by men, and from the extended family to the nuclear family."

There are a few transitions between the two quotations, although they do line up quite well. Rather than Wittfogel's communal-individual property transition, Jobling prefers the shift from extended to nuclear family. But the one that catches my eye is the replacement of primitive communism in the first quotation by a "more egalitarian" (i.e., the domestic) mode of production in the second. This is rather astonishing, since *the features of the primitive commune and the domestic mode of production are virtually identical*. Between the two quotations, the one has replaced the other. For all his protestations otherwise—the dismissal of Engels's and Bachofen's evolutionism (Jobling 1991: 241),[5] the criticism of the relics of the primitive commune as it appears in Gottwald's "communitarian" mode of production—Jobling provides the link to primitive communism that lies at the base of the variously named domestic, household, or familial mode of production.

Jobling has now opened the gate for Morgan and Bachofen, but what is this domestic mode of production/primitive communism in his hands?

It is a more egalitarian system, with female-based patterns of kinship, low-level agriculture in which women play a large role, communal property ownership, and the patrilocal family. In many respects Carol Meyers agrees: in her pioneering work of feminist archaeology (Meyers 1988) she argues that we can discern the role of women in the highland society of early Israel, and that their participation in that society was much greater than at first appears.

Although she sidelines Gottwald's explicit Marxism, Meyers builds her argument on Gottwald's meticulously laid foundations. Thus, she accepts his proposal that the Iron Age settlements in the Judean highlands were the result of disaffected peasants rebelling against and escaping exploitation after the depredations of epidemics and warfare of the Late Bronze Age. In Gottwald's argument social revolution underlies the establishment of a new society based on a "communitarian" mode of production. Rebelling against the "tributary" mode, and making use of new iron implements, lime plaster lining of cisterns, and terracing, this new society, early "Israel," consciously developed an ideological, economic, political, and social structure that was distinctly revolutionary (Gottwald 1999; see also Boer 2002). The key point in Meyers's (1988: 52) appropriation of Gottwald for my purposes is that this motley collection vowed "en masse to establish an alternative and egalitarian society, answerable only to their god Yahweh and not to any human master."

And what is the nature of this alternative society? Throwing off the last clods of earth and shreds of misogynist parchment, a "pristine Eve" (Meyers 1988: 77) emerges to show us the "traces of that pristine balance of gender relationships that have been nearly erased" (189). And the context is the *bet-av*, the primary unit of economic and social production. As far as Meyers (1997: 19) is concerned, "The term is perhaps better rendered 'family household' which more successfully reflects the integral relationship between kinship-linked persons and the material basis for their survival." Indeed, the fact that *bet em*, "mother's house," is used in a few places (Genesis 24:28; Ruth 1:8; Song of Songs 3:4; 8:2) suggests, Myers argues, that the "social reality of daily life" has not completely disappeared beneath the weight of an androcentric text (34). In this domestic context, the activities of women were much more highly valued, if not central: the immense task of transforming raw materials into edible food, weaving, pottery, managing the household, the informal power of family law, oversight of household religious practice, the bearing, socialization, and education (hence the close association of woman with wisdom) of many children for the success of the new society. In short, since the household was the primary production unit, as anthropological and archaeological research seems to indicate, and since economic and political arrangements beyond the household were weak, women may in fact have had a dominant role while this situation endured.[6] Is this not a way of speaking about matriarchy without using the term?[7]

But whence the familial or household mode of production? It comes from Marshall Sahlins, and it is Meyers (1988: 142) who made the discovery. Yet it is a curious reference, for Meyers refers just once to Sahlins's book *Tribesmen* (1968), and not the text in which he discusses the term at length, *Stone Age Economics* (1972). (Sahlins, it must be noted, introduces the term with no reference to Marxist debates.) From this slender beginning, the household or domestic mode of production has become orthodoxy in its own right. But now we have two lines that reach even farther back: if Jobling has given us the link to Morgan et al., then Meyers has brought Sahlins into play. I will turn to both in what follows.

Let me sum up. I have traced back the argument that in premonarchic Israel we have a domestic mode of production. Despite the individual variations there is a deeper agreement on the major features of this mode of production: it provided a better deal for women, who were crucial to everything from food production to religious observance. Based around the *bet-av*, variously described as the extended family or patrilocal family (or, to borrow a term from Morgan, the syndyasmian family), the features of such a mode of production were the all-pervasive influence of kinship, agriculture, communal ownership of land, and mutual aid.

FROM THE DOMESTIC MODE OF PRODUCTION
TO THE PRIMITIVE COMMUNE

All the same, it seems to me that we have in these debates in biblical studies a conflation of two related ideas: the domestic mode of production (Sahlins) and the primitive commune (Engels and Morgan, with Bachofen trailing along). But since the biblical critics I have been tracking mention these four writers all too briefly, let me spell out what the debts are.

First, Sahlins and the domestic mode of production, which has three key features:

1. A small labor force differentiated essentially by sex: The inner relations of the household, between man and woman, parent and child, are the primary relations of production in this society. This division

is cultural and not merely physical or natural (Sahlins 1972: 55). "The family contains within itself the division of labor dominant in the society as a whole. . . . It is the dominant form, transcending all other specialization in this sense: that the normal activities of any adult man, taken in conjunction with the normal activities of an adult woman, practically exhaust the customary works of society" (78–79).

2. Simple technology: As an antisurplus system—that is, livelihood is the primary objective and nothing more—only those tools necessary for such a system are needed. Pressure for increased production will therefore be resisted.

3. Finite production objectives, which are all systematically interrelated (see Sahlins 1972: 87): Given that the primary objective is livelihood, and contentment with such livelihood, when livelihood is attained work simply comes to a halt. More people in a given situation do not mean greater productivity; people just work less to attain the same level of livelihood. With a thoroughly different assumption of what constitutes wealth, we have the "original affluent society" (1).

There is one other element, namely, the inherent contradiction of such a mode of production. Sahlins formulates it as the centrifugal relations between the producing units. Economic concerns and objectives pertain only to the domestic unit. Once livelihood is attained for the domestic or household group of whatever shape, work ceases, for there is no concept of producing more for other struggling domestic groups. And yet—here lies the contradiction—unless the domestic economy is forced beyond its own closed circle the entire society will not survive.

Not quite the domestic mode of production we seem to find in the work of Meyers, Simkins, and Yee, let alone Gottwald's communitarian mode of production. To be sure, they all agree with Sahlins's first point, that the domestic unit with its sexual division of labor is the primary unit of production—Meyers's bet-av, accepted by all who cite her. Only Jobling acknowledges the point concerning what he calls extensive or low-level agriculture, and this he takes from Wittfogel. Meyers is simply way off with her assertion of backbreaking labor. (Is this not a common assumption concerning such societies?)[8] Yee and Simkins, to their credit, do point to contradictions; one describes egalitarianism as an ideology that overlies social inequality, and the other mentions the fierce loyalty to the paterfamilias as a primary feature. The domestic mode of production certainly does not provide the basis, at least in Sahlins's formulation, of the cooperative society that Meyers, Gottwald, and Jobling have suggested. The source of this idea of mutual aid, to gloss the great anarchist Kropotkin, must come from elsewhere.

Whence, then, the source for a better deal for women, and indeed the original affluent society? None other than Engels's (1985) classic *The Origin of the Family*. Here we find not merely primitive communism, but an argument for the earliest matrilineal and matriarchal form of the family. And here the denials come right to the fore: while our biblical critics may recognize their debt to Sahlins, they repress his and their debts to Engels, Morgan, and Bachofen. More specifically, *it is the connection to the theory of primitive communism that is denied in such a repression.*

In his flawed but brilliant book, Engels was of course following Marx's notes on Lewis Henry Morgan's *Ancient Society*. They were both drawn to it for the simple reasons that Morgan makes a connection between patriarchy and private property and that he postulates a prior matriarchy. With a wealth of detail drawn from the Iroquois (Morgan's specialty) to the Australian Aborigines, he argued that only with the development of private property could patriarchy—understood quite specifically as the inheritance of goods and the location of power in the male line—emerge. There are two steps to this argument.

First, Morgan (1877: 393–543) distinguished five forms of the family. The "consanguine" family is one in which wives and husbands are held in common, each known as "brothers" and "sisters," the children belonging to the whole group. By contrast, when several sisters share husbands who are not necessarily related, or vice versa, we have the "panaluan" family, or group marriage. Pairing of male and female takes place in the "syndyasmian" family, although not exclusively. The pair would live in groups of similar pairs, sharing space and work, and would stay together as long as it suited either member. Morgan finds the next stage, patriarchal or polygamous families, an anomaly or offshoot. Finally, at the end of the evolutionary run comes "monogamian" (monogamous) marriage, the exclusive cohabitation of single pairs.

Second, for Morgan the change to male descent takes place only with the patriarchal and monogamian familial forms. Relying on the data supplied by Bachofen, he assumes rather than argues for the change. But what he needs, like a crime, is the motive. And that is the gradual acquisition of property: flocks, herds, land, and houses. With property increasingly in the hands of men, the problem became the inheritance, for only with a male line would the property pass on to the father's and not the mother's children: "With property accumulating in masses and assuming permanent forms, and with an increased proportion of it held by individual ownership, descent in the female line was certain of overthrow, and the substitution of the male line equally assured" (Morgan 1877: 355).

So for Engels the moment of primitive communism came before this change, during the time of the consanguine, panaluan, and syndyasmian families. In other words, when the group had husbands and wives in common, or when frequently changing pairs lived in large groups, and when inheritance passed through the female line, we had primitive communism. For our purposes, then, Engels's reading of Morgan provides an argument for a prior social form much better for women and a subsequent move into male dominance. At this basic level, the argument is remarkably similar to those of Meyers, Jobling, and Yee, albeit with somewhat different terms.

Thus far we have the beginnings of a link between the domestic mode of production in biblical studies and primitive communism, but let me focus on Morgan more directly in order to strengthen the connection. For all his appealing quirkiness, [9] I am intrigued by Morgan's notion of the syndyasmian, or pairing, family—one mode of Engels's primitive communism—which comes much closer to the descriptions of Meyers, Jobling, Yee, Simkins, and Gottwald, as well as Sahlins's domestic mode of production. Here is Morgan (1877: 462):

> Several of them were usually found in one house, forming a communal household, in which the principle of communism in living was practised. The fact of the conjunction of several such families in a common household is of itself an admission that the family was too feeble an organization to face alone the hardships of life. Nevertheless it was founded upon marriage between single pairs, and possessed some of the characteristics of the monogamian family. The woman was now something more than the principal wife of her husband; she was his companion, the preparer of his food, and the mother of children whom he now began with some assurance to regard as his own. The birth of children, for whom they jointly cared, tended to cement the union and render it permanent.

For Morgan, then, the syndyasmian family was clearly better for women than the patriarchal family, let alone the consanguine and panaluan forms. It was a stronger unit because a number lived together in a common household, and I am going to assume that the crucial phrase "communism in living" is for Morgan a positive one. In other words, this is far closer to the bet-av or domestic mode of production of our biblical scholars than that of Sahlins. If we recall the three items from Sahlins's description of the domestic mode of production—small labor force based on the household, simple technology, and limited production—only the first is taken up by the biblical scholars in question. There is nothing about cooperation or a better situation for women; for that we must turn to Morgan and Engels. This connection is repressed, however, but that is precisely what interests me.

But the situation becomes a good deal more intriguing. Morgan himself discusses the Hebrew Bible at length, especially the bet-av. It is worth pointing out that he needs to do this to counter the strong effect of the Hebrew Bible on early anthropology of the family. This was particularly the case with the theory that the first form of the family was patriarchal and polygamous. Against this position he argues in detail that the primary form is in fact the *gens*, or clan, based on descent through the female line. It is characteristic of the first three types of family, the consanguine, panaluan, and syndyasmian forms. Narratives such as the purchase of Rebekah as a wife for Isaac, the assertion of Abraham that Sarah was born *not* of his own mother but of his father, making it a legitimate marriage (Genesis 20:12), and of Nahor's marriage of his niece and Amran's of his aunt make sense according to Morgan if we understand descent according to the female line, that is, according to a gentile system.

The key, however, is that for Morgan the primary mark of the gens is the bet-av, a point that reverberates through my preceding discussion. It is the *"paternal house, house of the father,* and *family house"* and "must have numbered several hundred persons. . . . If the Hebrews possessed the gens, it was this group of persons" (Morgan 1877: 380). From this building block we get the phratry (*mishpachah*) as a collection of two or more gentes, and then the tribe (*matteh*). Morgan admits that the material as we have it overwhelmingly speaks of descent in the male line within the gens; that the overt legislation establishes such inheritance, particularly in the case of Zelophehad's daughters (Numbers 36:4–11; 27:8–11; see Morgan 1877: 555–58); and that the earlier structures of the gens have moved on from female descent (the presence of private property in the narratives of Genesis, as Morgan notes [477–78], reinforces his point). All of this is evidence of the shift from the earlier familial forms, from descent according to the female line to descent according to the male line, with the advent of private property; only with the patriarchal and monogamian families do we have male descent and private property. Morgan's status as absent cause of the domestic mode of production becomes ever stronger.

And this is where Bachofen comes into play, for at some level he lies behind Morgan. The main point, based on "vast research," according to Morgan (1877: 359),[10] is that we can discern in the myths of Greece and Rome evidence of a prior stage of matriliny, if not matriarchy. And it is a position that continues to haunt us.[11] For Bachofen, "mother-right" operated in the second stage of human development. This was what he calls the lunar phase, the realm of Demeter, grain, and the passive left side. In this phase women revolted against the earlier, tellurian order of Aphrodite, an era of nomadism and sexual and social anarchy. Without state or agriculture, men held children, women, and property in common. In the second phase, by contrast, private property arose, but it was held by the mother and passed on to the daughter. Women also instituted the lifelong marriage bond; the priority of the mother-daughter relationship and inheritance, especially of the youngest daughter; an awareness of the roles of mother and father in relation to children; agriculture; settled communities; and female deities of home, field, and the moon. Men, however, had the last word and overthrew this order of mother-right, bringing in in three gradual stages the final solar period (of Apollo), which was one of paternal descent, the dominance of the spiritual over the material-maternal, the father-son relationship, division of labor, and male ownership of property.

The connections with Morgan are obvious, especially the shift in the second and third phases from female to male descent and the crucial role of private property in that shift (see Bachofen 1967: 76–79, 92–93, 96–97, 109–10, 114–15, 134–39, 142–44, 148–49, 190–96). But with Bachofen we find the first instance of the idea that we can uncover, whether through the exegesis of myths or archaeology, an earlier stage that was even slightly, if not substantially, better for women.

Let me close this section by returning to Morgan. There is an extraordinary text in which Morgan reads Bachofen's schema through the lens of the gens. But it is also extraordinary for the way it anticipates all of the major features of the proposed form of early Israel that I have traced above: communal household based on mothers of the same gens and their children; extended (syndyasmian) families; common lands; joint tenement houses; a far greater role for women; and communism in living:

> The condition of ancient society, thus brought under review, requires for its full explanation the existence of the gens in its archaic form as the source of the phenomena. This would bring the mother and her children into the same gens, and in the composition of the *communal*

household, on the basis of the gens, would give the *gens of the mothers the ascendancy in the household*. The family, which had probably attained the *syndyasmian form*, was still environed with the remains of that conjugal system which belonged to a still earlier condition. Such a family, consisting of a married pair with their children, would naturally have sought shelter with *kindred families in a communal household*, in which the several mothers and their children would be of the same gens, and the reputed fathers of these children would be of other gentes. *Common lands* and *joint tillage* would lead to *joint-tenement houses* and *communism in living;* so that gyneocracy seems to require for its creation, descent in the female line. Women thus entrenched in large households, supplied from common stores, in which their own gens so largely predominated in numbers, would provide the phenomena of mother-right and gyneocracy, which Bachofen has detected and traced with the aid of fragments of history and of tradition. (Morgan 1877: 359–60, emphasis added)

Is this not Meyers's and Yee's household mode of production, Jobling's conjunction of Meyers's, Sahlins's, and Bal's patrilocal family, and Gottwald's communitarian mode of production? It seems to me that such a passage requires little modification to give us the picture of early Israel's household or domestic mode of production. But what sticks out is the phrase "communism in living," for it becomes "primitive communism" in the hands of Marx and Engels. Let me simply say two things in concluding this section. First, Morgan's description of this primitive commune is uncannily close to descriptions of the domestic or household or communitarian mode of production in biblical studies. Second, while primitive communism underlies these arguments, it is denied in the very process of making them.

But does not the whiff of primitive communism spell the end of any serious scholarship? Is communism not dead? Have not the hopelessly utopian sixties well and truly passed? For primitive communism has all these associations and many more: warm and fuzzy vodka- or dope-filled evenings on some utopian, socialist, or hippie commune that existed only in someone's imagination.

No death knell is sounding here, as may have become clear by now. Rather, the work of these scholars brings out a contradiction crucial to my argument: primitive communism is simultaneously crucial and denied. Or, to put it in terms borrowed from Louis Althusser, primitive communism is the absent cause of this work. Let me spin this out a little before turning to the biblical texts. To begin with, primitive communism lies behind the idea of a domestic, household, or familial mode of production, especially in the sense that such a mode of production was in some way socially more just. After all, this is the argument I have been trying to establish thus far. But it is only the first step. For what many of these scholars do, especially Meyers and Jobling but also Gottwald himself, is offer a moment of denial: primitive communism is denied or dismissed on the path to building a picture of early Israel that is very reminiscent of . . . primitive communism. And we know the reasons: it is evolutionary in the bad old nineteenth-century sense of the word; it is utopian, mythical, and smacks a little too much of paradise.

But the denial is crucial, and that for two reasons. First and rather bluntly, this denial of primitive communism is a necessary step in their arguments; they need to get rid of that albatross before they can proceed, lest their work be tainted by such associations. But, to be a little more sophisticated about this, *primitive communism must be denied since it is a structuring principle in their work*. I cannot emphasize this point enough. This is what I mean by the absent cause of primitive communism. Or, to use Lacanian terminology (and it is often difficult to separate Althusser and Lacan), primitive communism is the Real of this biblical scholarship. In other words, the structuring feature of this biblical scholarship can be central only by being denied, only by being outside the reconstruction for which it is necessary.

UNORIGINAL TALES

The same logic, I suggest, operates in the stretch of text from Genesis through Joshua. Let me be more specific: there is a danger these texts seem to fear, a danger that lies just below the horizon. That danger manifests itself concretely in the text as perpetual rebellion. But rebellion for what? For an alternative world that *must* be blocked in order for the social world of the text to hold together at all. In the remainder of this chapter and in the next I trace the features of that rebellion, only to turn in chapter 4 to explore what is rebelled against.

The following argument is also a direct engagement with Adorno's wariness concerning myth. To a large extent he was right about myth: it does mark the moment of organization, control, and oppression; gender and class and race and species are carefully boxed and delimited in light of an overriding ideological and social order. But, I argue, this is by no means the whole story, and I want to pass through the gate Adorno did not wish to open in order to discover the resistance to that mythic organization that is contained in the heart of myth. So Bloch's cunning of myth will accompany me through the gate.

But which texts am I talking about? Those that focus on women, one of the main concerns of the studies I considered in the first half of this chapter. The texts are Eve and the serpent (Genesis 2–3), the narrative moments of Sarah and Hagar (Genesis 16, 18, 21), Rebekah (Genesis 24–25), Leah and Rachel (Genesis 29–30), Dinah (Genesis 34), Tamar (Genesis 38), Potiphar's wife (Genesis 39), Moses's mother and sister and Pharaoh's daughter (Exodus 2), Miriam in Exodus 16 and Numbers 12, the regulations concerning women in the law codes (e.g., Leviticus 12; Numbers 5; Deuteronomy 21), Zelophehad's daughters (Numbers 27, 36), and Rahab (Joshua 2). I am by no means the first to point out that there are quite a few texts that systematically attempt to control and order women. Or rather, what we have in this complex web of the Hexateuch is a primary instance of the creation of a specific image of "woman." It is the old Foucauldian point: rather than attempt to control and limit flesh-and-blood women, the Hexateuch constructs the category of "woman" through these stories and laws in a way that remains powerfully operative in the subsequent (ab)uses of these texts.[12]

Biblical studies is not immune from the overwhelming tendency of literary criticism to read a text closely, painstakingly. Or rather, we should take an inverse view of the relationship: the long tradition of detailed commentary on biblical texts weighs heavily on the interpretive practices of today's literary critics. So one would expect a detailed reading of one, perhaps two of these texts, a close reading that makes us feel at home in the familiar terrain of literary criticism, or perhaps of biblical commentary and exegesis. Instead, I read synoptically, moving over the vast panorama of these texts rather than spending too much time in the cozy and parochial confines of one text or another. For I am after the synoptic insight, the items that show up only when a number of texts sit together and rub up against each other. I am of course not the first to track over these texts, and some of the points made below derive from this earlier work. But I do have a distinct twist on the text: it seems to me that each of the texts I have listed provides us with a narrative as to *why something could not and should not be*. They are, if you like, *unoriginal* tales, stories of *nonorigin*. They tell the stories of why certain social, political, and economic formations, specifically regarding women, cannot and should not take place. The various stories concerning women in the Hexateuch show why and how women should not do what they promise to do. Yet this is by no means the whole story, for I also want to explore what has been denied.[13]

In what follows my purpose is not to list exhaustively, with genuine or faux disbelief and disgust, laws and stories from the Hebrew Bible that nowadays seem ridiculous. Rather, a synoptic view points to five minor and two major strategies. As for the five, women are punished in various ways, represented as exchange objects, relegated to supporting roles, dealt with violently, and removed from collective blessings. But two strategies stand out: women are made subject to a series of laws covering everything from menstruation through vows to rules of marriage, and time and again they ensure a pattern of inheritance through the male line.

LOCKDOWN

To begin with, the two great punishment stories are those of Eve and Miriam, Genesis 3 and Numbers 12. Both have a similar plot structure: a man and a woman rebel against God and get punished for it. Note that in each story the center of rebellion is the woman. Thus, in Genesis 3 Eve eats from the tree first after discussing it with the serpent. Only then does she give some to Adam. The reward: sandwiched between the curses for the serpent and man, she is locked into childbearing, hardship (*'itsevonek*), pain (*'etseb*), and the rule of her man (v. 16).[14] In Numbers 12, it is remarkable how Miriam suffers *all* of the punishment—she is smitten with a skin disease and must undergo purification—while Aaron gets off without a scratch. Why, you want to ask, is she at the center of the punishment? The underlying "problem" for these texts is the same: a social hierarchy needs to be (re)asserted. While in Genesis 3 the woman comes in between animal and man, in Numbers 12 she is at the bottom of the pile.[15] Woe to anyone like Miriam, let alone Eve, who tries to work outside the hierarchy.

Table. Comparison of Genesis 3 and Numbers 12

Genesis 3	Numbers 12
Yahweh Elohim (vv. 8–9)	Yahweh
Man (vv. 10–11, 17–19)	Moses (vv. 7–8, 13–14)
Woman (vv. 12, 16)	Aaron (vv. 11–12)
Serpent (animal) (vv. 13–15)	Miriam as prophet (vv. 6, 9–10; see Exodus 15:20)

As if being located within a hierarchy and relegated to a minor, supporting role (Exodus 15:20–21) were not enough, women are also identified as exchange objects between men (see Exum 1993: 151). The so-called wife-sister stories (Genesis 12:10–20; 20; 26) operate on this premise. The wives in question, Sarah and Rebekah, may be exchanged between men. In each case the claim by the patriarch "She is my sister" (Genesis 12:19; 20:2; 26:7) sets up the possibility of exchange. The dupes, Pharaoh and Abimelech, bring Sarai/Sarah and then Rebekah into their harems only to find out that the woman in question is not available. Now, while the actual exchange of women may seem to be short-circuited by the information that they are not available for exchange (by a plague in Genesis 12:17, a dream in Genesis 20:3–7, and by a voyeuristic moment when Abimelech sees Isaac fondling Rebekah in Genesis 26:8), the outcome is very much within the exchange logic: Abraham twice ends up with massive gifts of sheep, oxen, silver, asses, servants, and camels, while Isaac finds that a little exercise in deception is the means to God's blessing; he is rewarded with great wealth as a result. The message of these wife-sister stories? Keep your women within the exchange network and you (masculine) will be blessed.

So far we have women as exchange objects and at the bottom of hierarchies. This is when they actually gain a mention: another approach is to deny them any presence whatsoever. While much of the Hebrew Bible operates on this premise, it shows up starkly when a woman is mentioned and then obviously forgotten. I think here of Dinah, the only mentioned daughter of Leah (Genesis 30:21; 34:1). Although in the final tally she would make the thirteenth child of Jacob, she is conspicuously absent from Jacob's blessings in Genesis 49; only the twelve sons are blessed and occasionally cursed.

All of these approaches are but supporting acts for the most consistent modes of dealing with women in these stories: by legislation and by tying them into male inheritance and succession. As for legislation, a suspiciously large number of laws deal with women (Exodus 21; Leviticus 12, 15, 18, 19, 20; Numbers 5, 30; Deuteronomy 21, 22, 23, 25, 27). Apart from the exceptional cases, such as the extraordinary law on how to deal with a woman of whom you (masculine) happen to be jealous but don't have any proof (Numbers 5:11–31), most of them fall into clusters. And these typically focus on anxieties over women and sex. I can't help but wonder at what obsessions kept the lawmakers tossing in their beds at night.

So we find some laws dealing with female virgins (Deuteronomy 19:21–22; 22:13–21, 23–29), female slaves (Exodus 21:1–11; Leviticus 21:10–14), and incest. Indeed, most of them worry and obsess over this last category. Ever since Lévi-Strauss (1968: 31–51), the cluster of incest laws (Leviticus 18:6–18; 20:10–14, 17, 19–21; Deuteronomy 23:1/22:30; 27:20, 22, 23) has a whole new resonance. I hardly need to point out that the incest taboo is a primary requirement for social formation, but let me note a few things about this collection. First, the underlying logic is one of male honor and shame: time and again, sex with a woman is cast in terms of dishonoring a man, penetrating his nakedness, as the text puts it.[16] Hence the traumatic repetition of the law forbidding sex with a man's father's wife (Leviticus 18:8; 20:11; Deuteronomy 23:1/22:30; 27:20). Second, there is the question as to what is included and excluded. The clearest statement of the incest taboo comes in Leviticus 18:6: "None of you shall approach any one near of kin [besharo] to him to penetrate [legallot] nakedness" (my translation). We find the usual suspects—mother, sister, granddaughter, half-sister, aunt (maternal and paternal)—albeit from a purely male perspective. But there are also some conspicuous absences, especially father-daughter incest (see Rashkow 1994). We can also see the social sense of extending the taboo to various in-laws, such as a man's paternal uncle's wife, daughter-in-law, sister-in-law, and mother-in-law. But by now the list has become a little odd, for we find a distinction between mother and father's wife, and other ones between sisters (they can be a daughter of one's mother *or* father) and aunts (maternal and paternal).

Why make such distinctions? Obviously because nuclear families are far from the scene. I cannot help but think of Morgan's syndyasmian family, a collective in which partners come together and break up quite regularly. Hence it is no exception for a man's father's wife *not* to be his mother, or for his (half-) sister to be his father's or his mother's daughter. Only on the assumption of such a larger family structure do these prohibitions make sense. But the list pushes my desire for sense to the extreme, for we also find a taboo on a woman, her daughter, and her granddaughter (Leviticus 18:17; 20:15), as well as taking two sisters as wives (Leviticus 18:18). Finally, in the list of Leviticus 20:10–21, incest mixes with male-on-male sex (v. 13), bestiality (vv. 15–16; Deuteronomy 27:21), menstrual sex (v. 18), and, just for good measure, sex with a man's neighbor's wife (v. 10). What we have here is a massively different sexual economy in which sex with animals, the same sex, and extended relatives are on a par—all in terms of the shame or honor of the man in question.[17]

The second great category surrounds the challenge of the womb and the ability to bear children. Of course, the laws focus on menstruation. In

Leviticus 15:19–24 menstruation is essentially contagious. Time and space come under a woman's spreading uncleanness, whether it is seven days, the places she sits and sleeps, childbirth (12:2, 5), or whomever she might happen to have sex with.[18] But note what happens: these regulations in Leviticus 15 are sandwiched between much longer regulations for a man who has an emission from his body, whether it is a general discharge (15:2–15) or one of semen (15:16–18), and a woman who bleeds outside the time of her period (15:25–30). The pathologization of menstruation is hardly a new phenomenon.

I have been tracking the various modes in which women are locked into place in the Hexateuch. But I have left until last the incessant need to assert the importance of the male line, especially in terms of inheritance. Again and again we find stories in which this is at least an underlying concern (Genesis 16; 18; 19:30–38; 21; 24–25; 29–30; 38; Exodus 1; Numbers 27:1–11; 36; Deuteronomy 21:15–17; 25:5–10). In fact, this drive is strong enough to overturn some of the laws I have just considered. Two examples. First, incest is perfectly fine if it ensures that one's male seed continues, as the two daughters of Lot show by seducing their father one after the other in Genesis 19:30–38.[19] Well, not quite, for the slur on the Moabites and Ammonites can hardly be missed. Second, the ban on a man having sex with his daughter-in-law does not draw the usual penalties if male children result; so Perez and Zerah are born of the union between Judah and Tamar in Genesis 38. All Judah must do is to acknowledge his paternity and that Tamar is more righteous than he (see Ruth 4:18–22).[20]

Elsewhere the text makes no bones about the primacy of male inheritance, as with the tension-filled struggle for Abraham to produce a son: first Ishmael with Hagar, then Isaac with Sarah, and then a whole spate with Keturah (Genesis 16; 18; 21; 25:1–6). Or with the intense focus on Rebekah's womb in Genesis 25:19–29,[21] from which Esau and Jacob emerge. It goes without saying that these boys are the real focus of the story, particularly Jacob's seizing of the birthright from Esau. However, the intriguing story of the daughters of Zelophehad asserts the principle of male inheritance most loudly: "Each man of the sons of Israel may possess the inheritance of his fathers" (Numbers 36:8). The five daughters—Mahlah, Tirzah, Hoglah, Milcah, and Noah—generate this principle by successfully claiming the inheritance of their father in the absence of any son. Now, the law of inheritance in Numbers 27:5–11 clearly makes them an anomaly; inheritance must go, it states, to sons, or *daughters*, or brothers, or father's brothers, or next of kin. They are the only females in the list. But this does not solve the problem of the daughters marrying outside the tribe. Should they marry outside, the father and therefore the tribe would lose his inheritance to the sons of such a union. And so we find the additional law in which the women are free to marry, but only within the tribe of their father (Numbers 36:6–12).

The case of Mahlah, Tirzah, Hoglah, Milcah, and Noah looks for all the world like an astute response to a valid claim, or indeed a fundamental revision to the law on the basis of their claim (Ilan 2000). But why allow it at all? Would it not be easier to stitch up male inheritance by skipping the daughters and going straight to the father's brothers? Here, at the end of this long list of ways to lock women into a distinct order, comes the first glimpse of something denied or repressed. It shows up with these five women in terms of inheritance—specifically the threat of women with inheritance *not* attached to a man—as it does with the two texts that deal with Levirite marriage: those on Onan who spills his seed on the ground rather than father his dead elder brother's child (Genesis 38:1–11) and the shaming of the man who refuses to have sex with his dead brother's wife (Deuteronomy 25:5–10); he must be spat on and his sandal removed by the woman in question before the elders. Extreme punishments suggest extreme concerns.

However, before I explore this denial further, let me close this section with my favorite vignette: the penalty for grabbing a man's genitals while he is fighting with another man (Deuteronomy 25:11–12). This, of course, happens all the time. Or at least one wants to ask, Why are they fighting? Over the woman? Then there must be an assumed shortage of women. Here the often covert violence of the various laws and stories I have considered thus far breaks into the open.[22] The text reads: "When men fight with one another, and the wife of the one draws near to rescue her man from the hand of him who is beating him, and puts out her hand and seizes him by his genitals, then you shall cut off her hand; your eye shall have no pity" (my translation). Why such a violent response? Here a woman not only threatens to crush a testicle or two or perhaps rip off his penis, thereby cutting (!) the man off from the assembly (Deuteronomy 23:2/1), but more importantly, she asserts the role of oath-making restricted to men (see Genesis 24:2, 9). What Abraham and his servant may do, she may not. After all, are not women's vows inherently untrustworthy, as the detailed regulations of Numbers 30:1–5 suggest?

At this point it does seem that Adorno was fully justified in saying that myth is fundamentally about the rationalization and organization of society, that it codifies law and class and gender. Looking over this long run of laws and stories, a litany of techniques for oppression, if you will, it would seem that he is right. As if to reinforce Adorno's point, we find an extended list of reasons in Genesis–Joshua as to why women should be so carefully contained. They are, after all, disobedient and rebellious (Genesis 3; 19; Numbers 12), quarrelsome and competitive (Genesis 16; 21:8–12; 29–30; Deuteronomy 21), mocking (Genesis 18), nostalgic (Genesis 19:26), seductive and tempting (Genesis 20; 39; Numbers 25), deceptive, untrustworthy, and scheming (Genesis 27; 31; 38; 39; Numbers 30), even to the point of being traitors (Joshua 2), wanton and lascivious (Genesis 39), unclean and dangerous (Exodus 21; Leviticus 12, 15, 18, 19, 20; Numbers 5), unfaithful (Numbers 5), who take a man's property when he's not looking (Numbers 27, 36), and generally threaten a man's world (Genesis 24; Deuteronomy 25:11–12).

SHARDS

One would expect that having completed their task, the framers of these texts could now lock the door and throw away the key. But I have already indicated that the story of the daughters of Zelophehad has in itself the hint of something suppressed, blocked out. Why allow a moment of female inheritance only to ensure that it doesn't get out of hand? The reason, quite simply, is that inheritance in the male line must assert itself against female inheritance. It must, in other words, deny the viability of female inheritance. And it does so by showing that female inheritance is perfectly understandable within a pattern of male inheritance. This is a subtle ideological move. It is not even a threat, as it represents no danger; it is merely a legal problem that needs to be addressed. I am by no means arguing for the suppressed memory of an earlier social formation in which inheritance passed through the female line, as we saw with Bachofen, Morgan, et al. This would be to buy the logic of the text itself, an Edenic state of origin that must somehow be recovered. Rather, it may be read as the signal of an ideological contradiction, a rusty spot in the well-oiled armor of the text.

This story of Zelophehad's daughters is in fact a glimpse of a much more consistent pattern in the Hexateuch. For here Bloch's cunning of myth returns: in the very act of rationalizing and ordering women the text throws up a whole series of possibilities, and it does so in the very act of trying to close them down. The first cracks in the textual pavement are formal: every now and then a woman disrupts the fabric of the text. Rebekah does it in Genesis 25:22 and Zipporah in Exodus 4:24–26. Pregnant and with more than one child struggling in her womb, Rebekah asks a question directed at no one in particular: "If so, why then I ['im ken lammah zeh 'anokhi]?" The Hebrew of her question is at best obscure, and it is not at all clear to whom it is addressed. Syntactically it appears that Rebekah asks it of herself, for only after she asks it does she go and inquire of Yahweh. He of course can't be bothered to listen and rushes in to answer before she has time to speak (Genesis 25:23). Elsewhere I have argued that such disruption marks the ideological and economic battle over her womb: every male in the story wishes to control it, and yet it is finally outside their control.

Zipporah, Moses's woman, breaks up the text even more. At lodgings on the road, Yahweh tries to kill an unidentified "him." And then we read, "And Zipporah took a knife and cut off the foreskin of her son and touched his feet, and she said, 'For a bridegroom of blood you are to me'" (Exodus 4:25, my translation). This simply does not make any sense, either in itself or in the context of the larger passage, although more than one critic has tried to unravel it.[23] However, rather than seek to render a meaning at the level of the immediate text, it would be better to think laterally about this. So I suggest that the formal disruption of the text—each time in words spoken by women—signals another process under way. But for that we need to consider three types of texts: those that hint at women on their own, at a demimonde, and at another way of being.

Women on Their Own?

Every now and then in the Hexateuch a snippet of text appears, a phrase or a clause that hints at a world in which women are on their own. Thus, in Genesis 34:1 we read, "Dinah, the daughter of Leah whom she bore to Jacob, went out to look into the daughters [lir'ot bivnoth] of the land" (my translation). Not only is Dinah listed here as the daughter of Leah, with Jacob secondary, but the story begins with her setting out to "look into" the daughters of the land. Is this to make contact with, to get to know, to connect with the circles of women? If so, it is exceedingly rare (see Scholz 1998). Or is it, as later Jewish commentators suggest, a move into the public sphere of men, where she meets her match (Brenner 2005: 25)? Of course, the text doesn't say as much, but the second verse immediately has Shechem appropriating the verb "to look," and Dinah, now subject to rather than of the gaze, is brutally thrown into the world of men from then on (see Kelso 2003).

The smallest of hints also comes with another phrase from another story: "And her young women [*wena'arotheha*] walked beside the river" (Exodus 2:5). It appears in the midst of the story of the daughter of Pharaoh, who goes down to the river to bathe before finding the basket containing the baby Moses floating on the water. Apart from Moses, the rest of this story has only women, albeit with class relations intact:[24] along with Pharaoh's daughter and her young women, the baby's sister, who gets his mother to be wet nurse. A similar glimpse appears a little later with the seven daughters of the priest of Midian: "And they came and drew water, and filled the troughs to water their father's flock" (Exodus 2:16). They must fend off the shepherds who continually chase them off, and Moses, the "hero" who, having fled Egypt, "saves" them from the shepherds. In between, however, they find a small space for themselves. One more moment, with a very similar result: in the midst of a long list of ways to ensure that women's vows are subject to one man or another, comes this verse: "But any vow of a widow or a divorced woman, anything by which she has bound herself, shall stand against her" (Numbers 30:10/9). Again, it is but a hint of women on their own, fighting for space. But there is no man to whom these women— divorced women and widows—are bound, and so their vows float free.

In the Demimonde

I am not after a romantic image of a world of women that is free from networks of power, one that has in an Irigarayan fashion its own social, legal, and religious organization.[25] Nor is it useful to isolate these hints of women on their own from a wider political matrix.[26] For this reason, I want to fold these few verses and the shards they offer into a couple of other texts. I quote the texts first, in order to let another world emerge: "And they came to the house of a woman, a prostitute, whose name was Rahab" (Joshua 2:1, my translation);[27] "He assumed she was a prostitute, for she had covered her face" (Genesis 38:15, my translation); "Anything that pertains to a man shall not be upon a woman, nor shall a man put on a woman's clothing; for anyone who does these things is an abomination to Yahweh your God" (Deuteronomy 22:5, my translation); "You shall not permit a sorceress to live" (Exodus 22:17/18). Prostitutes, "transvestites," and sorceresses—is this not a taste of the demimonde, to borrow a term from the French Revolution? Forced to live on the edges and beneath the dominant political and cultural system, the demimonde is a world of criminals, deviants (sexual and otherwise), sex workers, alternative and suppressed religious practitioners, the physically deformed and mentally unstable. And there are plenty of those throughout the Hexateuch, women and men (e.g., Deuteronomy 23:2/1; Leviticus 13–14; 18:23; 20:15–16). I hardly need to point out that the very use of terms such as "sorceress," "prostitute," "criminal," and "deviant" are crucial to the process of marginalization in question. That nearly all of my examples are women should come as no surprise, for women are of course a major part of the demimonde of the Hexateuch.

The paradigm of such a world comes with Tamar in Genesis 38. The key lies with her clothing. Widowed by both Er and Onan, sons of Judah, and denied the third son, Shuah, Tamar takes things into her own hands. So, in order to seduce Judah himself, she switches from her usual widow's garments and puts on those of a prostitute (Genesis 38:14), and then with the deed done she switches back again on the way home (v. 19). But what of her clothes? At one level they define social roles, constructs of "woman," one acceptable and one not. And by the end of the story she can add another role to her list: mother of sons. But at a deeper level they are also disguises: that Tamar slips from one to the other indicates not so much a passing from one social role to another as that the roles don't quite fit. She uses them for other agendas only half seen. Is this not characteristic of the demimonde itself—a need to move from safe house to safe house, evading the authorities through disguises, and doing so for the sake of survival?

Another Way of Being

I want to take but one text as a slogan of this demimonde, signal of another way of being: "But his wife looked behind him" (Genesis 19:26, my translation). To look behind (*nbt me'ahare*) is also the very act of looking to this other world, the one suppressed and marginalized in so many ways in the Hexateuch. That it is a woman who does so, Lot's wife, should come as no surprise. The text here is normally emended to read "behind her" in light of the prohibition in verse 17: "Do not look behind you," says the messenger, as Lot, his wife, and their daughters flee Sodom. And so it is read as an act of longing for a fallen and corrupt world, and she is punished for her disobedience by being turned into a pillar of salt. But the Hebrew, with no alternative versions as evidence for such an emendation, reads "behind him." She looks, then, to that whole realm that exists behind the man's back, or at least one who stands for all of the organization, rationalization, and codifications of this protracted myth.

This world behind his back, the demimonde, also includes the rebels. Or rather, rebellion is the defining feature of the demimonde. And here we find the rebel Miriam in Numbers 12. I am interested here in the way the text constructs such a possibility, although more than one biblical scholar has fallen into the trap of arguing that Miriam's story reflects an actual state in which women had it far better (Meyers 1994; Trible 1994) or at least had a significant role (van Dijk-Hemmes 1994; Janzen 1994). What Numbers does give us is a more biblical term for the demimonde: "outside the camp." For her troubles Miriam finds herself "shut up outside the camp seven days" (Numbers 12:15, my translation). But the reason is as intriguing as it is common: rebellion is pathologized as a disease. Yahweh afflicts her with a skin disease, and so she must follow the stipulations for such diseases and be banished from the camp until pronounced clean (see Leviticus 13:4, 5, 27). Two further points are worth noting about this text: Miriam does not recant, utters not a word of repentance. Only Aaron does so (Numbers 12:11). Further, while she is outside the camp, "the people did not journey on until Miriam was gathered in again" (12:15, my translation). They wait for her, not setting out until she joins them. A pause for her cause? Or perhaps a way to rope her back into the system? Or is it a signal of the shelter and protection rebels so often find among nomads, peasants, workers, and common people?

This rebellious substratum goes well beyond the women, or rather, they are part of a larger phenomenon. Let me give one example, a foretaste of chapter 3. What we find is a whole realm of alternative religious practices, of which the golden calf episode in Genesis 32 is something of a paradigm. While the story becomes a sinister justification for the brutal compassion of Moses's leadership and the complete abdication of Aaron as an adequate leader (see Boer 2003: 42–64), I am intrigued by who actually instigates the construction of the calf. It is the "people" (ha'am), tired of waiting for Moses to return from his chat with God, who say to Aaron, "Get up! Make for us gods who walk before us; for this Moses, the man who brought us up from the land of Egypt, we do not know what has happened to him" (Exodus 32:1). Someone is giving orders here, and it is not Aaron and can hardly be Moses. From here on the people set the agenda, something Aaron recognizes in his moment of truth, after he has shuffled and dissembled when Moses returns and questions him (32:22–24). But note how the people are depicted: they have "spoiled" themselves (shikheth, 32:7; compare Genesis 6:11–12), they are quick to turn aside (32:8), stiff-necked (qesheh 'oref, 32:9), and evil (32:22), so much so that apart from some collateral damage—about three thousand men in this story and then a few more in the plague (32:28, 35)—they are barely saved. It is not the last time rebels would be characterized in such a fashion.

Rebellion lurks beneath the surface of the Hexateuch, and it tries to deal with such insurrection in various ways. This chapter, especially its second half, has also been an engagement with Adorno's strictures concerning the repressive ordering that myth entails. And the upshot: myth is more cunning than that, for in the attempt to close down the possibilities for women on their own, for a demimonde or a realm "outside the camp," indeed for rebellion itself, these stories and laws give such options plenty of airplay. What, then, of primitive communism? Quite simply, I will use the term for a little longer as a temporary place holder for such a demimonde.

There is one further point that comes out of my discussion of biblical scholarship in the first half of this chapter: the denial of the viability of that rebellion and demimonde is the mechanism by which the text can hang together in the first place. That is, the social and political world that this political myth produces can take place only on the basis of the denial and blockage of that which challenges it. However, to develop this point we need the help of psychoanalysis.

CHAPTER THREE

The Fantasy of Myth

The fantasizing [*fabulation*] of antiquity, mythology as you call it . . .
—Jacques Lacan (1998: 115)

I n this chapter I take on the psychoanalytic hesitation over myth. Simply put, for psychoanalysis myth seems to serve the forces of reaction. It does so as fantasy, which is the way we shield ourselves from the horror or trauma that threatens to tear our world apart. In order to survive we construct fantasies to keep that kernel or trauma at bay. All of which means that fantasy and myth become the means of ensuring a status quo and avoiding its breakdown. Too often myth does indeed become the way a social system legitimates itself, managing dissent and any movement for radical change.[1]

My response to this demur from psychoanalysis is structured in two sections. To begin, I explore how myth may be understood as fantasy. Let me reiterate my take on fantasy from the first chapter on theory: fantasy is *the* way we deal with the psychoanalytic version of the constitutive exception, with what cannot by definition be part of the system and yet is absolutely necessary for that system to operate. I am quite deliberately making use of Lacanian psychoanalysis here against the much broader range of possibilities in fantasy studies.[2] The hapless text that I draw into this discussion is the paradigmatic Genesis 2–3, although I suspect it is more than up to the task. I then move on, in the second section, to expand the notion of fantasy in terms of Lacan's two categories of the Real and the Symbolic. More specifically, I read the binary between chaos and order, or creation and destruction, in Genesis–Joshua as the tension between the Real and the Symbolic. Chaos tends to side with the Real and order with the Symbolic—at least initially—but what interests me is how politics cannot help but rise to the surface. And so the texts that come into play here are the stories of the Flood (Genesis 6–9), Babel (Genesis 11), Korah's rebellion (Numbers 16), and the theme of murmuring that recurs throughout the Hexateuch. In this section I am most interested in the politics of the Real, for rather than the location of a reactionary halt to any subversive movement, the Real turns out to be the subversion that lurks around every corner.

THE FANTASY OF GENESIS 2–3

How does fantasy work in Genesis 2–3? Let me begin by putting it this way: fantasy does not mean that when we desire paradise and cannot get it in reality, we fantasize about it. Rather, the problem is this: How do we know to desire paradise in the first place?[3] I am extracting and focusing on a key feature of Genesis 2–3, namely, the "garden in Eden" (*gan be'eden*; Genesis 2:8), which contains trees that are both "desirable [*nekhmad*] to the sight and good for food" (2:9). However, what is curious about the narrative of Genesis 2, especially verses 4–14, is the way it does not actually say that we are in paradise, in an ideal state. Such an assumption is deduced from various features: God created it, put Adam there among the plants and animals, made sure it was watered with rivers, and so on. That it is an ideal prelapsarian state has to be deduced, loaded onto a text that makes little of the garden itself. The question then becomes: Why is the "garden in Eden" desirable? What constitutes that desire? How does it begin? The answer is that fantasy provides not so much the object of desire itself as it teaches us *how* to desire. How it does so will unfold by means of four strategies of fantasy that are crucial to Genesis 2–3: narrative occlusion, the paradox of loss, the inherent transgression, and the empty gesture.[4]

Narrative Occlusion: The Fantasmatic Gap
A weary commonplace of theories of myth is that myth is fundamentally a narrative, particularly a foundational narrative with the usual features of plot and characters. Genesis 2–3 would seem to be no exception. Or more specifically, Genesis 2 is a narrative of origins—of the man, garden, trees, rivers (with a few precious metals), domestic and wild animals, birds, and then woman. In short, it is a narrative about providing somewhere reasonably comfortable for the man to live. So we find that the god, Yahweh

Elohim, first shapes (*weyitser*) man and gives him the breath of life (2:7) hard on the heels of the inaugural Flood, or at least the first moisture (2:6). There follows the planting of the garden (2:8), making the trees to sprout out of the ground (2:9), and the river that goes out from Eden to become the four rivers Pishon, Gihon, Tigris, and Euphrates (2:10–14). The narrative then turns to the search for a helper (*'ezer;* 2:18), whether shaped (*wayitser*) by Yahweh Elohim out of the ground like the animals on foot and wing (2:19–20), or constructed (*wayiven*) from Adam's side (*hatsela'*) like the woman (2:22). At a stretch we might see the origins of male-female relations or, as some would like it, marriage (2:24), as well as human disobedience (3:1–7). But on a more curious note we also have the origins of the legless serpent, the fear of snakes, toil, childbearing, hierarchy, thorns, thistles, and the hard work of the daily production of food (3:14–19).

The catch with all of this—and I am hardly pointing out something new—is that Genesis 2–3 is not the only narrative of origins in this text. For in Genesis 1 we have a very different narrative, indeed, an alternative universe created by an alternative deity. This time Elohim creates (*bara'*), makes (*'asah*), and divides (*hbdl*) light and darkness, the firmament of the heavens that separates the waters, dry land in the midst of the waters below (earth and sea), plants and trees, the various lights in the heavens, creatures of sea and then land, and then finally the man and woman—in this sequence.

Just in case we might doubt the differences between the two, it is worth noting that the man is created at the end (Genesis 1) and then the beginning (Genesis 2) of the two stories. Further, in contrast to the six days of creation in Genesis 1, all we find in Genesis 2 is one day (2:4). The world created in Genesis 1 is good, whereas in Genesis 2 it is "not good that Adam should be alone" (2:18). Genesis 1 has many elements—light and darkness, firmament, the sea and the creatures that live therein—that do not appear in Genesis 2.

I could go on with the differences between these accounts, but the point is that there are two quite distinct narratives, with their own narrative chronologies and contrasting features. The very fact that we have more than one narrative here is the signal of a problem—and I hardly need to add that the story of the Flood (Genesis 6–9) is yet another creation story. The problem, however, is not that we have multiple narratives of creation, but that these multiple stories are cast *in narrative form.* For a fundamental feature of fantasy is that the very need to offer a narrative signals a deft effort at camouflage or concealment.

This particular element of fantasy—its coherent narrative form—was first formulated by Freud (2001, vol. 5: 488–508; see Lacan 1991a: 213–14) as "secondary revision," an element of the "dream-work." Secondary revision is the process that makes coherent narrative sense of the illogical content of dreams. It provides the links between disparate and confusing elements and reorders the dream's elements so that we remember them as narratives. Although it is part of the four elements of the dream-work—the other three are condensation, evading censorship by displacement, and modes of representability (Freud 2001, vol. 4: 279–338)—it is also something Freud attempts to move past in analysis in order to find out what goes on before secondary revision does its work. This secondary revision for Freud is fantasy, closely related to daydreams and the conscious desire for order and sense. By generating narrative, it conceals the incoherent and unrelated elements of the dream.

As far as Genesis 2–3 is concerned, therefore, the very existence of narrative functions as an indicator of fantasy. Or rather, these multiple narratives of origin are an effort to conceal what may be called the fantasmatic kernel. What is this kernel? It is the horror or Void that we dare not and cannot tackle. It is, in other words, the trauma we must confront, and yet if we come face to face with it, it threatens to destroy us. One of the best examples comes with Freud's (2001, vol. 17: 175–204) essay "A Child Is Being Beaten." He traces back the adult masturbatory fantasy of witnessing a child or children being beaten by an indistinct adult to the primary moment of early childhood: my father is beating the child whom I hate, for he loves only me. The real point here is that it applies both to girls and boys, for both have an incestuous attachment to the father. This is the unbearable horror that must undergo repression or regression if it is not to lead to adult perversions and neuroses. For the later Lacan, this is a signal of a more fundamental trauma that has various shifting names: the Real, or that little piece of the Real known as *objet petit a* which gives us "the basis of being" (Lacan 1998: 95) and then infamously the universal "Woman" as the fantasmatic support of "Man," not to speak of God (71–81). The function of fantasy is to conceal this core of our being that we dare not face.[5]

It is one thing to assert an unbearable fantasmatic kernel and the effort to conceal it, but another to say why. Let me bring in here a second theoretical point: the possibility of fantasy relies on a necessary gap between our everyday reality and a deeper, unknown fantasmatic kernel or origin of that reality.[6] For psychoanalysis, fantasy is *the* way of dealing with the horrible kernel or unbearable truth that we dare not face. Fantasy mediates between our mundane, everyday lives and that unbearable truth. To put it another way, fantasy conceals the unbearable truth so that we may live out our everyday lives at all, as mundanely as possible.

Further, *narrative* is the specific mechanism by which fantasy throws a rope between the fantasmatic kernel and what it sustains (mundane reality, the text, etc.). There is, however, one further step: fantasy attempts to mediate the horror "beneath" the explicit details of the text by means of a narrative that simultaneously conceals that horror *and* creates it in the process of concealment. In other words, the dialectical catch is that in the very act of concealing it, fantasy creates the kernel or horror it purports to conceal. That there are profound political consequences for such a function of fantasy will gradually become clearer in what follows.

The Paradox of Loss

I want to explore what that kernel might be, but let me do so by picking up another feature of fantasy: the paradox of loss. Here we encounter a prime instance of the logic of the fantasmatic kernel that I identified earlier: the narrative of fantasy *creates* the kernel in the very process of concealing and mediating it. Let me go a step further here. The horrible kernel is not a prior thing that the narrative of fantasy then seeks to conceal: the horror is constituted by the narrative itself.

Genesis 2–3 is overlaid with multiple narratives of loss, but there is always a catch: in each case the object in question emerges or is created in the story and is then lost. Or rather, the object emerges only at the moment of its loss. The cherubim placed by Yahweh Elohim along with the multidirectional or perpetually turning sword blade (Genesis 3:24) have much to answer for, it seems to me, but they also signal the paradox itself: none of these items will ever be recovered; no one may return to Eden, except perhaps Eve, especially to the tree of life, for the way is forever barred. Before the ever-vigilant gatekeepers the possibility that any of the items existed in some prior, pristine state (I speak here of the narrative only) dissipates like smoke.

But let me track a few of the paradoxes of loss in this text. For starters, it is not that the fruit of the trees is freely available (Genesis 2:16; 3:2) in the garden only to give way to the sweat and toil of agricultural work after the curse (3:17–19). Rather, the fantasy of fruit available without toil emerges only when the thistles and thorns threaten agricultural labor—hence the danger of the free fruit, epitomized by the tree of the knowledge of good and evil (2:17) and the tree of life (3:22, 24) that constitute a tainted and impossible dream. A second paradox is that of living forever (3:22): eternal life is not a state barely lost (3:22–24), squandered in a moment of indulgence, but rather a wish in the face of death (3:19). Only from this perspective can endless and thoroughly mind-numbing bucolic bliss look attractive. Who in their right mind would want to live in such a garden?

Third, the question as to why Adam also eats of the fruit may be cast in terms of the tension between a man clinging (*davaq*) to his woman and a woman's desire (*teshuqah*) for the man who rules over her (Genesis 2:24; 3:16). The two texts should be read together. Thus, Adam's disobedience in eating of the fruit becomes a radical version of "clinging": "And she also gave some to her man and he ate" (3:6b). But in doing so Adam thereby loses what he most wants. We should read his act as the radical outcome of Genesis 2:24—"Therefore a man shall leave his father and mother and cling to his wife"—but the very process destroys the relationship. He no longer clings to her, but she to him, now for reasons of desire and subordination: "Yet your desire shall be for your man, and he shall rule over you" (3:16b).

Shame, choice, disobedience, and the law follow the same logic: nakedness as such emerges only at the moment of the awareness of shame and not in some prior state of innocence (Genesis 2:25; 3:7, 10). The freedom to choose by the woman and then the man can appear only after the decision to eat from the tree, for the act of choosing establishes choice itself (3:1–6). Or disobedience can be such only in the act itself, for it cannot be a prior possibility, or the Fall would already have happened. In other words, the proscription of Genesis 2:17 already assumes transgression, for the law is itself based on an inherent transgression. Or fantasy provides not a realization of desires prohibited by the law, but in the process of expressing those desires installs the law itself.

Then there is the garden in Eden, which becomes a possibility only when it is lost, when the entrance is barricaded and eternal bouncers are on duty. In fact, the garden in many respects stands for the sum total of the paradox of loss: rather than a state given and then squandered, the garden is possible only at the moment one postulates its loss. Except that I want to suggest another aspect of the paradox at this point, namely, that it speaks not of a past state forever lost but of a state never yet realized. This is where the political dimension kicks in, for the paradox of the simultaneous loss and emergence of the garden is also the paradox of utopia. This possibility—that the system of political economics under which we live will in fact disintegrate with the chance of something better to follow—can arise only when it is felt to be no longer possible. Thus, when the gate to utopia seems blocked, when the path is overgrown with thorns and thistles, then utopia emerges as a possibility.

I can now add some complexity to the argument that myth may be understood in terms of fantasy. Not only does fantasy mediate and conceal the unbearable fantasmatic kernel, not only does it do so in narrative form, and not only does it produce the kernel through such a narrative, but the pattern of emergence and loss illustrates another feature of fantasy. Let me put it this way: the fantasmatic kernel is constructed at the very moment of its concealment and denial.

How does this work? As far as emergence and loss are concerned, the crucial point is that they constitute one moment and not two in narrative sequence. As Joni Mitchell sang in "Yellow Taxi," "You don't know what you've got 'til it's gone." Fantasy attempts to separate the two into a temporal sequence characteristic of narrative. In other words, fantasy attempts to put in narrative, diachronic format what is in fact a synchronous antagonism. Since the tension between emergence and loss is absolutely synchronous, it is the form of narrative itself that is the means of repression. Thus, fantasy provides a narrative of both emergence and loss: something (free fruit, living forever) first appears and is then lost. Through its diachronic arrangement, narrative obfuscates the radical synchronicity of emergence and loss. They are one and the same, for the object appears at the moment of its apparent loss; it is not something that existed prior to its loss.

So also with the fantasmatic kernel: it is not that the narrative of fantasy mediates and conceals the kernel itself; rather, it hides the fact that it creates the kernel at the very moment that it sets out to tell the story. I am now in a position to hazard a definition of myth as fantasy: *fantasy produces the fantasmatic kernel in a radically synchronous fashion, a fact that it conceals by means of a diachronic narrative.*

The Empty Gesture

There is, however, a final feature of myth as fantasy that emerges from Genesis 2–3. Not happy with merely concealing the synchronous production of the kernel, fantasy teases us: it offers us a glimpse of that kernel, or at least makes us believe that we have indeed caught sight of it out of the corner of our eye. And that tease comes through what may be called the empty gesture: it is an offer that can never be fulfilled, a forced choice that has all the appearance of a genuine offer or choice. For instance, when a distant relative offers you accommodation should you happen to be in his town, you can tell by the tone of voice, the offhand way the offer is made, that you are expected to decline it graciously.

Genesis 3, then, generates the false impression that the man and woman have a choice, especially through the persuasive dialogue of the serpent (Genesis 3:1–5):

> Now the serpent was more subtle than any other wild creature that Yahweh Elohim had made. He said to the woman, "Did Elohim say, 'You shall not eat of any tree of the garden'?" And the woman said to the serpent, "We may eat of the fruit of the trees of the garden; but Elohim said, 'You shall not eat of the fruit of the tree which is in the midst of the garden, neither shall you touch it, lest you die.'" But the serpent said to the woman, "You will not die. For Elohim knows that when you eat of it your eyes will be opened, and you will be like Elohim, knowing good and evil." So when the woman saw that the tree was good for food, and that it was a delight to the eyes, and that the tree was to be desired to make one wise, she took of its fruit and ate; and she also gave some to her man, and he ate.

What if they hadn't eaten from the tree? What would have been the consequences had the woman said no to the serpent? Most hearers and readers of this mythical fragment have entertained such a thought, whether in an existential moment replicated millions of times in one's life, or purely in terms of the narrative itself. What would the narrative have been like if they had stayed in paradise? Would the relations between the sexes have been just and ethical? Would there have been an absence of exploitation? Would they have remained vegetarians? And so on. Of course, in light of the fact that the narrative itself requires the eating of the tree in order to proceed, such a possibility is false. They never had a choice, and so the gesture is empty.

The text maintains what might be called "the false opening" (Žižek 1997: 29). It gives the impression that the woman may have actually said no to the serpent and that the man may have said no to the woman, or at least that there was an element of choice in the matter. But then it simultaneously "closes the actual span of choices" (29): they are in a no-win situation, a forced choice. Further, if they had actually made the other choice, refused the fruit and its promise, stayed in the garden, then the whole system would have come crashing down around their ears. There would be no narrative, no Hebrew Bible, no . . .

This is where the whole thing collapses around us. Should we actually grab the beast on our shoulder and stare it in the face, the world as we know it would collapse. Such is the fate from which fantasy protects us: the showdown with the fantasmatic kernel. For instance, in order to ride a bicycle, or perhaps fly in an airplane, we protect ourselves from the knowledge that with all their intricate working parts these machines could and do fail to operate on a reasonably regular basis, that they might fall to pieces beneath us, that the extra turbulence may be the first shock waves of a terrorist's bomb. If we did operate in this way, with the constant awareness of some horrible underside or disaster, we would begin to suffer from paranoia, or psychosis more generally, for the world would become nightmarish and treacherous, conspiracies abounding in every action and word. Oh wait—since the attack on the World Trade Center in New York on September 11, 2001, many people do in fact live this way.

The last example is not fortuitous, for I want to give a political spin to this disastrous confrontation with the fantasmatic kernel. It is not merely some psychic horror, a personal psychosis or breakdown in the coordinates of one's personal existence that is at stake here—or rather, these things point to, or indeed act as, a code for something else. What would bring the social and political status quo crashing down, at least as far as our text is concerned? Let me explore a few hints.

On the Track of the Kernel

To begin with, the sliding scale of blame blurts out more than it intends to. Challenged by Yahweh Elohim, who is out for his evening stroll, Adam says, "The woman whom you gave to me, she . . ." (Genesis 3:12). And the woman says, "The serpent . . ." (3:13). The serpent says nothing, despite its garrulous nature. Is this because the buck stops with it? Do we have a convenient shifting of blame from man to woman to serpent? I suspect that the serpent does not need to say anything, for Adam has already said it: "whom *you* gave to me." I can picture man, woman, and serpent all nodding in quiet agreement. But I am saying nothing new by pointing out that Yahweh Elohim is to blame in this story from the moment he created this flawed gem. Even the structure of Genesis 3 suggests so. The text works overtime to reinforce the impression that the sum total of waywardness resides with the three other characters. So it moves from serpent to woman to man in recounting the deed (3:1, 6), in reverse with the blame shifting of 3:9–13, and then back again from serpent to woman to man in the curses (3:14–19). The crucial hinge comes in verse 8. Its very nonchalance betrays its central role: "And they heard the sound of Yahweh Elohim walking in the garden to catch the breeze of the day [*leruakh hayyom*]." This is the calm act of someone in complete control. He is calmly and carefully looking for someone else to blame, focusing first on the man: "Where are you?" (3:9). And then it begins.

However, the blame does not stick to all three in equal measure. Note the phrase in Genesis 3:17: "Because you listened to the voice of your woman . . ." Adam's sin, it seems, is to have listened to a woman. For *this* reason, and not because he ate from the fruit of the tree, is the ground cursed with thorns and thistles so that he will eat only with the sweat of hard labor. The serpent gets a direct "Because you have done this" (3:14), but the woman is given no reason at all. There is no relationship to the deed: she is just cursed. Or is her error to have spoken to her man?

The serpent takes it on the chin and slithers away, it legs now uselessly piled up and left behind. But the reason given to the man takes on a deeper resonance if we look back over the story one more time. For at the moment when he gives himself completely to the woman, just after she has been created from his side, she misleads him. Thus, after waking from his divine anaesthetic he cries out in recognition, "This finally is bone of my bones and flesh of my flesh" (Genesis 2:23). And then *he* leaves his father and mother and clings to her and they "become one flesh" (2:24). What happens immediately afterward? The serpent and the woman have a chat about the tree, and before he knows it the man eats of the fruit (3:6). What rotten luck! No wonder he blames Yahweh Elohim (3:12). But Yahweh Elohim skips aside and lays the blame on the woman (3:17).

The woman, it seems, is becoming a distinct problem. And it gets worse. For just when it looks as though a schizophrenic Yahweh Elohim has carefully sewn up the case and secured the garden by banishing the human beings from it, the woman slips out of his grasp, dressed in her new skins. Note what happens: when Yahweh Elohim gets around to closing the garden indefinitely for renovations, only Adam is banished. Since Adam had become like one of the gods, "Yahweh Elohim sent him out of the garden of Eden, to work the ground from which he had been taken" (Genesis 3:23). Just in case we are not quite sure of what we have read, the text comes to our aid: "He drove out Adam" (3:24a). Who knows where the woman is? She rejoins Adam in Genesis 4:1, but does she still have access to the garden?

It seems as though the woman has gotten through the police cordon. Well, not quite, for she has already been trapped. The key verse is "The man called his wife's name Eve, because she was the mother of all living" (Genesis 3:20). At first we might think that the verse is chronically misplaced:

should not the "mother of all living" ('*em col khay*) make a grand entrance in the martial regularity of Genesis 1 or at least the earthy potter's tale of Genesis 2? For in these chapters we find the fecund creativity of the gods, man, ground, earth, and even sea. But by Genesis 3:20 the phrase "all living" rings hollow, for there is nothing left for her to create. Belated, misplaced, all she can do is give birth to the miscegenated: Seth, Cain, and Abel in Genesis 4. The name Eve—*Khavvah*, from the word for "living"—becomes a cruel joke, especially when Eve is the only one in the story given a proper name.[7] But is this not the whole point? All Eve can be is the mother of human children. In fact, if we look at the text again, the verse is exceedingly well placed. It comes after the curse of pain and hard labor in bearing children (3:16) and before the ominous banishment of Adam from the garden. As Mieke Bal (1987: 128) points out, this is a story of the origins of the prison of motherhood. But this is not all, for Eve is doubly trapped. Whereas Adam's curse means that he must leave the garden for the relative freedom of the open fields, Eve's curse carefully ensures that she is not only caught in motherhood, but is also confined to the claustrophobic flawed crystal of the garden. I hardly need to point out that here the garden stands in for domestic space where she must bear and raise children.

Is the woman, Eve, the fantasmatic kernel of this text? It would appear so, especially if we follow Lacan's (1998: 71–81) liking for verbal play. The verse that intrigues me is "She is to be called woman ['*ishah*], for out of man ['*ish*] she was taken" (Genesis 2:2). The verbal play—a real labyrinth of language—is crucial. The woman has something extra, quite literally the *ah*, since she came out of the man, who is now something less, just '*ish*.[8] It is as though the side (*hatselah*) of the man from which she was constructed (2:22) now appears in the text as the *ah* added to '*ish*. This is where I want to bring in Lacan's objet petit a, the little object "a": *autre*, other. This little object is the small chunk of the fantasmatic kernel that makes me who I am, like a small stone in my shoe that I cannot find but that reminds me of its presence with every step. At a purely verbal level, woman is precisely that objet petit a: being made from the man's side (*hatselah;* 2:22), she is man plus *a*: '*ishah*. He has lost it (the side, object petit a, the *ah*), or rather had it taken, and she has gained it. Woman, then, is the objet petit a, as Lacan argued. Now for the final step in this little wordplay: if the objet petit a is a little piece of the fantasmatic kernel, then woman herself is also a piece of that kernel.

Yet she is a *piece* of the kernel, and not the horror of the fantasmatic kernel itself. For, as I argued in chapter 2, along with Miriam in Numbers

12 Eve is one element in a much more widespread rebellion by women in the stretch of text from Genesis to Joshua. In other words, Woman is not the fantasmatic kernel; the rebellion in which she takes part is. Is this not Freud's point in *Moses and Monotheism* (2001, vol. 23: 1–137), namely, that the ultimate trauma of these texts is the rebellion against Moses? As for the woman, her real rebellion is not merely to break a prohibition: she breaches a social hierarchy that locates her somewhere between animal and man. Into this hierarchy she is forcefully returned. Quite simply, then, the woman is a problem in this text because she is the one who rebels. Or, in psychoanalytic terms, she is a real problem because she is the little piece of the fantasmatic kernel called *objet petit a*. The whole notion of fantasy now takes on a distinctly political edge.

Let me return to my earlier definition of fantasy and see what it looks like now. To begin with, fantasy conceals the fantasmatic kernel by constructing a narrative. Now I can add that what really needs to be concealed is political insurrection. But I went on to argue that fantasy is responsible for creating the kernel in the first place. Thus, if we move one step further, the very telling of the fantasmatic story produces the rebellious kernel. This act of production is in fact what fantasy attempts to hide by means of a narrative that moves forward in time, a narrative of the many ways rebellion must be repressed since it threatens the system itself. So what happens to my earlier definition of myth as fantasy? It reads: fantasy produces the fantasmatic kernel in a radically synchronous fashion, a fact that it conceals by means of a diachronic narrative. Now, in light of the political twist that I have given to it, the definition should read: myth (as fantasy) produces the possibility of political insurrection (the fantasmatic kernel) in a radically synchronous fashion, a fact that it conceals by means of a diachronic narrative in which such insurrection is systematically repressed.

Bloch's cunning of myth returns with a vengeance, for here we have the very construction of political uprising in a myth of reaction. It is not merely that such rebellion somehow escapes the hand of the censor, surviving in bits and pieces that must be retrieved, nor even that such remnants survive only because of their reactionary contexts. Rather, the repressive myth we have here produces the possibility of insurrection. No wonder that coming face to face with the fantasmatic kernel brings everything crashing down.

Now, in concluding this section, I can return to my initial point regarding fantasy, namely, that it teaches us how to desire. As I argued earlier, fantasy is not the desire for something I cannot have, something I have lost or do not have access to. Rather, fantasy teaches us how to desire *since it produces the object we desire.* The catch is that it will always turn out to be something "we" did not expect. And what is that object? Nothing other than the fantasmatic kernel I have been tracking in Genesis 2–3. As with fantasy, so also with political myth.

Thus far I have worked around two key concepts from psychoanalysis: fantasy and the fantasmatic kernel. But now I would like to add three others: the Real, the Symbolic, and the constitutive exception. Simply put (if that is possible), the constitutive exception is what I have been calling the fantasmatic kernel: it is the exception that constitutes the text, a social and political order, an ideology. Further, it must be an exception—excluded, denied, and blocked—in order to take on its foundational role. For example, the existence of a small but active Communist Party in Australia during the 1950s, 1960s, and 1970s produced a structure of mainstream politics unimaginable without the Communist Party. Understood as the vanguard of the global communist movement, the Australian Communist Party became a massive threat. Endless measures were put in place, from political policy to secret police to community spying, to keep the Communist Party in check. It was, in other words, the crucial exception that constituted post–World War II politics as such.[9]

A more specifically psychoanalytic way of viewing this relationship is in terms of the Real and the Symbolic. Now the fantasmatic kernel and the constitutive exception morph into the Real. The Real is the set to which all of these other elements belong. At the risk of stating the obvious, the Real for Lacan is not reality as we know it. It is a far deeper reality that simply cannot be represented in any adequate way. All we can do is attempt to come close with partial efforts. The reason: the Real is so crucial and all-pervasive that we cannot know how it functions in any direct fashion. It is like the foundation for every aspect of our existence, and yet no matter how deeply and systematically we dig we can never uncover it. Perhaps Lacan's most crucial category, it is a wholesale reworking of Freud's (2001, vols. 4–5; see especially Lacan 1998: 90–95; 1993: 8–10) great discovery of the unconscious.

In contrast to the Real, the Symbolic is the world as we know it: the complex web of language, social structure, the law, belief systems, and so on (Lacan 1991b: 156–59, 173–74, 177–79).[10] Without going into the details of the Oedipus complex, the gate through which the Symbolic is attained, it may be obvious that the Real is the foundation—to sustain the building simile a little longer—of the Symbolic. Now things become interesting: in order to sustain the Symbolic, the Real must remain out of sight. And it must remain so because it threatens at any moment to bring the Symbolic crashing down. It is, then, both an indispensable structuring feature of the Symbolic *and* thoroughly destabilizing. For example, should the writhing mass of desires and drives from our unconscious, which must be repressed in order for us to survive, actually come to the surface and take absolute control of our conscious lives, our psychic selves and social structures would collapse in an incestuous, murderous free-for-all in which we gleefully celebrate the disasters of our closest friends.

Onto this grid of the Real and the Symbolic I want to map a traditional distinction within biblical scholarship between cosmos and chaos.[11] It is in fact a commonplace in dealing with ancient Near Eastern texts in general. Thus, in the case of the early chapters of Genesis, creation involves the systematic imposition of order against a background of chaos. In Genesis 1 order manifests itself as the differentiations between light and dark, firmaments and waters, the various groups of animals and plants, human beings—all in the martial order of six days. In Genesis 2 cosmos is established with the creation of the garden, with its carefully demarcated boundaries. No creative conflict here, nor the battle to the death with the forces of chaos that we find in other ancient Near Eastern creation myths, such as the Babylonian political myth *Enuma Elish* (see Boer 2006). Or rather, the violent threat of chaos is delayed, at least in narrative terms, until the story of the Flood in Genesis 6–9, to which I now turn.

Naturalizing Rebellion: The Deluge

The Flood story begins by seamlessly splicing together both moral and social chaos with natural chaos. Ominously it begins, "And Yahweh saw that the evil [*ra'ath ha'adam*] of Adam was great in the earth and that every formation of the thoughts of his heart was only evil [*ra'*] all day" (Genesis 6:5). But what in the world is Adam doing here? Commentators quickly point out that "Adam"—ha'adam—at this point is a collective term for humanity, and then translate it as such. But they jump a little too quickly, since it is worth considering why Adam might be here. He does seem to have a knack of turning up at unexpected moments. This cameo appearance at the very beginning of the story of the Flood effectively ties this text of Genesis 6–9 in very tightly with the earlier material of Genesis 1–3 on creation, transgression, punishment, and procreation. And just to hammer home the point, we find that Noah was the *first* "man of the soil" (*'ish ha'adamah;* 9:20). A new beginning indeed, for was not Adam made from the same substance (*ha'adamah*), and was not Cain a "worker of soil" (*'adamah;* 4:2)? But things have not gone well since Adam set out from the garden—or perhaps from Adam's perspective they have gone rather too well. For Adam and evil, the two key terms of the text I quoted a moment ago, are now engaged in a close little dance. In this text, evil *ra'(ah)* is both a moral category and intrinsic to Adam's being, as two key phrases indicate. The first—the evil of Adam, *ra'ath ha'adam*—now has them in the intimate form of the Hebrew construct, so much so that the two make virtually one word. But it gets even better with the second phrase: "every formation of the thoughts of his heart" (*wekhol yetser makhshevoth libbo*). In other words, everything that takes shape, everything that he devises in his innermost thoughts, was "only evil" (*raq ra'*). Evil is for this verse intrinsically human and moral. Genesis 6:5 bends over backward to make sure we get the point: humans are evil. In other words, they are rebellious.

The second key text from the opening of the Flood story is Genesis 6:11–12: "And the earth was spoiled [*wattishakheth*] before Elohim and the earth was filled with violence. And Elohim saw the earth, and behold, it was spoiled [*nishkhathah*], for all flesh had spoiled [*hishkhith*] their way upon the earth."[12] If in Genesis 6:5 the point is that human beings are evil, then here we have the *naturalization of evil*. That is, evil spreads its fingers to draw the natural world into the domain of human evil. And it does so in a very underhanded manner. The key lies in the conjunction of "earth" (*'erets*) and the various forms of "spoil" (*shakhath*), which may also mean "ruin" or "destroy." Three times they circle each other: the earth was spoiled (twice), and then "all flesh had spoiled their way upon the earth." The first two uses are passive (*Nif'al*) and the last active (*Hif'il*): the shift is crucial. In the first two the "earth" is the subject of the verb, but the catch is that earth can mean the ground or soil, as well as Earth (capital E) as perceived political unity and the realm of human existence; the English "world" is closer to this sense. So we might translate this phrase either as "the ground was ruined" or as "the world was spoiled." Or rather, we should take both senses on board, for the ambiguity is central. Indeed, the possibility of both senses sets up the slippage between human evil, "the world was spoiled," and natural ruin, "the ground was ruined."

Before we know it, human evil is a perfectly natural category that includes the whole of nature. Human evil slides into natural chaos, so much so that nature now becomes the sole locus for chaos and destruction. The text becomes a classic rendition of the Real, full of those inchoate and chaotic human fears of flood, fire, disease, famine, earthquake, and the odd large—or small—predator that may bring one to a swift and painful end. Or rather, the fear that one's life may come to a meaningless bloody halt classically finds expression in such ways, for the Real may break in at any moment and spoil everything. As a dangerous foundation, providing the basis of life and the means for its destruction, it is not for nothing that the Real can make one of its few appearances only in mythical material like this.

How does chaos turn up here? Obviously as a flood, or rather a flood of waters (*hamabbul mayim*), which will kill everything on Earth (Genesis 6:17). Most of the text concerns the various preparations and modes of dealing with the destruction caused by the Flood, but chaos does get a run in Genesis 7:11–24. I am less interested in the relatively boring rain, even though its forty days and forty nights are proverbial (7:12). Far more intriguing is the following: "On that day all the sources of the great deep [*tehom rabbah*] split, and the windows of the heavens were opened" (7:11b). The deep (*tehom*) is of course the primeval abyss over which God's face passes in Genesis 1:2. If we thought that it had been tamed and ordered in the first creation narrative, then here it returns with a vengeance: cosmos is undone and chaos returns. Is this not the Real—ultimate chaos surrounding and swamping one on all sides? Like the unconscious, it surges forth from above and below. Further, the description of the rising Flood is a masterly piece of writing (7:17–20). With each verb the Flood rises ever higher: the waters increase, bear up the ark, prevail, increase again, prevail mightily, and prevail once more. And each time something marks their unstoppable rise: the ark rises high above the earth, it floats on the face of the waters, the mountains are at first covered and then covered by as much as fifteen cubits. When the last levees and sandbags have given way, then the mayhem really begins. In a way comparable to the waters building up verbally in the text, so also is the text saturated with gasping, flailing, and drowning animals and human beings. The reader is almost swamped with the repetition: "all flesh died . . . everything died . . . he wiped out every living thing . . . they were wiped out . . ." (7:21–23; see also 6:7; 7:4). The roll of the dead does the same thing—birds, cattle, beasts, swarming creatures, Adam, in short, all that existed on the face of the Earth—twice.[13]

The Flood, then, is an overwhelming naturalization of chaos. But it could be so only with the earlier bridge constructed between human and natural evil, between moral evil and the spoiling of nature. Human rebellion, the story tells us, leads to natural chaos. In fact, the point is even stronger: human rebellion *is* chaos.

By contrast, the ark is cosmos in this text—a speck tossed about in a vast flood, without sail or other form of propulsion. I am reminded of Ursula LeGuin's famous novel *The Dispossessed: An Ambiguous Utopia*. At one moment Shevek, a scientist from the anarchist planet Annares, stands by a painting of the first spacecraft that made its way to their new planet. Between the two planets, old and new, it is barely a sliver on the canvas. Yet in the story of the Flood, that small sliver of an ark gets most of the attention. Compared to the short, sharp burst of the deluge's chaos, cosmos is a detailed and painstaking process. Here we have the Symbolic in all its glory: as cosmos, as order and organization, as the structure of the psyche and of society. Slowly but surely it beats back the irruption of the Real, carefully boxing it in and closing it down. The Symbolic appears in a range of forms: the instructions for building the ark (Genesis 6:14–16); what to bring on the ark, whether human beings (6:18; 7:6, 13), land animals (6:19–20; 7:2–3, 8–9, 14–16), food (6:21); the reassuring rhythm of the organization of time by means of calendar calculations (7:4, 6, 10, 11a, 12, 17, 24; 8:3–7, 10, 13–14; 9:28). On top of what are nothing else than the various elements of creation, we also find the reverse of chaos as the waters subside: the closing of the sources of the deep and of the windows of heaven, the gradual appearance of dry land, the flights of the raven and the dove (8:1–12), and then their emergence from the ark in an orderly reversal of their embarking (8:15–19). But we are not done yet, for along with the covenant (6:18; 8:20–22; 9:8–17) we also find the establishment of the patterns of life, of "seedtime and harvest, cold and heat, summer and winter, day and night" (8:22). Before Noah can rest and grow his vineyard in the fulfillment of this pattern (9:20–21), the bureaucratic program continues: instructions for food and the reassertion of the need to be fruitful and multiply (9:1–7) and the mark of its fruition in the genealogies (6:10; 9:18–19; 10:1–32). In fact, the full genealogical list of Genesis 10 is not usually counted as part of the Flood narrative, yet it is the final structural assertion of cosmos and order after the chaos of the deluge (see also 4:17–26; 5:1–32).

Let me sum up: the Flood story gives us a thorough exercise in the naturalization of rebellion. Once the connection has been made between human evil and "nature," this evil shows up in the natural chaos of the Flood. Or rather, chaos is the riot of nature, so against it order must be imposed—in terms of chronological time, the categorization of animals, of seasons, and of human generations. To put it in terms of Lacanian psychoanalysis, the

Real is, for this story, the domain of natural chaos and the Symbolic is the realm of the order and cosmos of human activity.

The Subversion of the Real

I have left one question begging: Where does the deity belong? The initial impression is that Yahweh or Elohim side squarely with cosmos: creation and order must be imposed over chaos, and the gods are the ones who do so. Indeed, in the Flood story, nearly all the instructions, from building the ark to repopulating the earth, come from heaven. In other words, Yahweh/Elohim is at home in the Symbolic. Standing in opposition to this is the chaotic realm of the Real, manifested in human rebellion that brings about natural destruction.

Yet there is a catch: the ultimate source of this chaos is none other than the doppelgänger deity, Yahweh and Elohim (for they are in fact two names brought together at certain points in the pieces of myth I have been considering). For if we look a little more closely at the Flood story, we see that Elohim is the one who, in a massive case of overkill, decides to destroy the earth. The mosquito is splattered with a sledge hammer. But as far as the text is concerned, it is a perfectly fair response. In the same way that Earth is spoiled, and all flesh has spoiled their ways, so also will God spoil them along with Earth (Genesis 6:13, 17: the same verb, *shakhath*, is used here as in vv. 11–12). After all, with human and natural corruption all rolled into one, Earth in all its senses is already ruined: all Elohim need do is push the teetering edifice with his little finger.

The Flood is thus *punishment* for rebellion. So much is fairly obvious; less obvious is the way punishment becomes a means of appropriating chaos by the forces of order. Or, along with the Symbolic, Yahweh and Elohim join forces to become the driving force behind the Real as well. (For Lacan [1998: 68–77] this is in fact where God should be located.) Yahweh and Elohim seem to occupy all the possible spaces. They are both the source of cosmos *and* the threat of chaos.

What we find is that the forces of order also occupy the space of rebellion. The logic goes as follows. Rebellion triggers the threat of chaos against cosmos, of the Real against the Symbolic. But before this can get out of hand, rebellion is appropriated by reaction in two steps: first as naturalization and second as punishment. Now the story of the Deluge naturalizes rebellion: the act of rebellion by human beings produces the chaos of the Flood. Chaos, in other words, belongs to the realm of nature and human sin; opposed to it is cosmos. But then the Flood is also punishment for that rebellion. In other words, the realm of natural chaos is appropriated by divine power as a means of punishment. Suddenly, the divine figures occupy both cosmos and chaos, both Real and Symbolic. Human rebellion simply gets squeezed out of any viable place.

This process shows up in three other moments: the story of the Tower of Babel (Genesis 11:1–9), the rebellion of Korah (Numbers 16), and the theme of murmuring. Beginning with Babel, we see that in contrast to the Flood narrative, rebellion in this story is quite clearly a human one. None of the seepage into the realm outside human society takes place here, so it becomes a useful contrast to the Flood story. Let me highlight some key points of a narrative that, not unexpectedly, has been worked through again and again.

To begin with, it is the fourth major story of the repression of human rebellion, after the forbidden fruit of Genesis 2–3, the murder of Abel by Cain in Genesis 4, and the evil of humanity in Genesis 6–9. Further, it is the most collective story of rebellion out of the lot: no individual is named here. There is no Adam or Eve, no Cain or Abel, and no Noah. Finally, what the "sons of Adam" (bene ha'adam) do here is not marked as problematic until after the fact. There is no warning or law; it is all retrospective. In Genesis 3 a prohibition is broken; Cain's act is marked as sin before it happens (4:7); the reason for the Flood is evil (6). But there is none of that in the story of Babel. All we find here is that Yahweh is frightened by human potential: "This is only the beginning of what they will do; and nothing that they propose to do will now be impossible for them" (11:6). It is, quite simply, a collective challenge to the powers that be: together the people make bricks and mortar, build a city and tower—basic acts of a civilizing process.

If there are any doubts as to the collective nature of this rebellion, the modes of dealing with it speak all too loudly. Yahweh sows division. Note how often terms for confounding, confusion, and scattering appear: "Let us confound [wenovlah] there their language" (Genesis 11:7); "and Yahweh scattered [wayafets] them" (11:8); "Yahweh confounded [balal] the language of all the earth . . . Yahweh scattered them [hefitsam]" (11:9). The result: "They ceased building the city" (11:8). It is of course a paradigmatic narrative of divide and conquer, of setting one's opponents against each other.

But what happens in this story is that Yahweh embodies the Real opposed to the Symbolic. For the people make two significant moves in terms of the Symbolic. They form an ordered society whose mark is the city, and they speak a language. Social order, with all of its associated elements of organization and sanction, come together with the central role of language in the Symbolic. Has Yahweh now switched sides to become the embodiment of the Real over a very human Symbolic? Is rebellion really a moment of the Symbolic, in contrast to the Flood story? At one level this is indeed the case, except for one moment. The language that the people speak is all too simple: "And the whole earth had one language and few words" (Genesis 11:1). The key lies with the "few words." It is less language than some primal form of speech, like a child learning its first words or perhaps an adult a new language. What Yahweh must then do is bring into being the crucial element of the Symbolic, namely, the complexity of mature language. In the name of the Symbolic he must then break up this collective rebellion, for it is a sign of social immaturity. In case we had any doubts, the rest of Genesis 11 shows the Symbolic coming back with a vengeance. For in Genesis 11:10–30 comes the genealogy of Shem, which will lead eventually to Abram. Here the text is on the same wavelength as Genesis 6–9, where the regular beat of the genealogy marks the establishment of cosmos over chaos. Both the Real and the Symbolic, chaos and cosmos, are Yahweh's turf.

The narrative of Korah's rebellion produces a similar result. As the text is now it tells of a priestly rebellion, centering on the issue of ritual and incense, which is crushed through divine intervention. It is, in other words, a story of a "premature palace revolution" (Bloch 1972: 80) within the priestly upper class. However, there are two moments in the story that hint at something deeper: the initial moment of insurrection and the mode of dealing with it. As for the opening, the text reads, "And they rose up [*wayyaqumu*] before Moses" (Numbers 16:2). And then they say, "You have gone too far! For all the congregation are holy, every one of them, and Yahweh is among them; why then do you exalt yourselves above the assembly of Yahweh?" (16:3). *They* of course are Korah, Nathan, Abiram, and On. But note that it is quite specifically a rising up, a rebellion, and that its motivation is not to usurp Moses but to assert that no one is superior, that all are holy before Yahweh, the name of the deity used in this text. Not quite democratic, not even egalitarian—these terms are a little too anachronistic—but an assertion of a collective against an elevated ruler with some divine right.

The second intriguing feature of the story is the way the revolt is handled: Yahweh splits open the ground, which swallows up Korah and his conspirators and their households as an example to anyone else who would rebel (Numbers 16:31–33). Here I follow Ernst Bloch in espying a signal of popular rebellion, for the God who emerges here is one of "white-guard

terror" (Bloch 1972: 80), one who acts to quell an uprising in as spectacular a fashion as possible. But Bloch's point—that here we have a story of
political uprising—is really only a beginning. For the punishment is yet
another manifestation of chaos: the ground splits open, fires break out,
and the rebels are swallowed live by the open ground. In other words, the
insurrection against the established order (signaled by Moses's special
status before Yahweh) triggers the threat of chaos. Challenge the Symbolic, in other words, and you risk the Real breaking in and destroying
the Symbolic. Further, that threat or risk takes on the form of natural
chaos, for it is the earth itself that becomes chaotic and dangerous. Or,
as I put it earlier, rebellion is naturalized. But then it all becomes a little
more complex with another layer: the threat of the chaotic Real is in fact
a punishment Yahweh visits upon the rebels. Yahweh therefore becomes
the manifestation of the Real, the agent of chaos who threatens to tear
apart the Symbolic. But—and here is the final twist—Yahweh is also the
upholder of the Symbolic: Moses has a special status because Yahweh has
chosen him, and *this* cosmos must remain in place. By this time the rebels
have nowhere to go: they are not an alternative Symbolic, nor are they the
Real that structures and undermines the Symbolic. Denied a space in the
text, not even able to dispose of Moses and elevate him into a god (Freud
2001, vol. 23: 1–137), the earth comes in as an all-too-convenient disposal
unit for these troublesome revolutionaries.

Let me close this discussion by tarrying with chaos—the Real—a little
longer, which will then allow me to draw in my earlier discussion of fantasy. In the stories of the Flood, the Tower of Babel, Korah's rebellion,
and sundry murmurings, time and again the Real is appropriated by the
forces of reaction. Of course, "reaction" is shorthand for those who wish
to preserve their power within the narrative of the text, or rather those
who seek to assert their power: Yahweh and his doppelgänger Elohim,
Moses and Aaron and the social and political orders they embody. In each
story, the trigger for chaos or the first rumblings of the Real is some form
of human rebellion. But before the rebels can even think about organizing
themselves, Yahweh swoops in and claims chaos for himself, using it as a
means of punishment for what then becomes disobedience and sin.

But what happens if we block this appropriation of the Real by reaction? For Yahweh is distinctly reactionary, patrician even, but one who is
subject as much to the unknown original authors as to subsequent readers.
What we are left with is the Real as the domain of chaos (minus Yahweh).
But the Real both underlies and destabilizes the Symbolic; without it the

Symbolic could not exist, and yet the Real perpetually threatens to bring it crashing down. So also with chaos, which both underlies and destabilizes cosmos; without it cosmos could not exist, and yet chaos perpetually threatens. There is enough in the stories I have considered to add rebellion and insurrection to the mix, which now become necessary support for and perpetual threat against the political and ideological status quo of these stories. Or rather, we don't just add insurrection and stir, for insurrection is the central concern of these narratives. As *constitutive exception*, insurrection must be outside the viable zones of these stories, and yet it is crucial for the possibility of the stories in the first place. Yahweh's appropriation of all viable spaces, especially with the Real, ensures that insurrection is systematically blocked from any space whatsoever.

Murmuring

The final instance of this logic comes with the oft repeated murmuring stories throughout the wilderness wanderings. Ernst Bloch first argued that they should be read politically and positively: the people murmur against Moses, God, and any other leader not because they are sinful whiners, but because it is a trace of a popular, revolutionary consciousness. Indeed, in what follows I read Bloch with Freud's (2001, vol. 23: 1–137) *Moses and Monotheism*, for Bloch gives a political edge to Freud's own myth of the primal rebellion and patricide. The murmuring stories are the story of the bitter waters of Marah (Exodus 15:22–25); the manna and the quail in the wilderness (Exodus 16); the contention and strife over water at Massah and Meribah (Exodus 17:1–7); the response to the report of the spies (Numbers 14; Deuteronomy 1:27); Korah's rebellion and its aftermath (Numbers 16–17); and Aaron's rod as a way to settle discontent (Numbers 17). The key word is the verb *lavan*, translated as "murmur," and the substantive *telunnah*, "murmuring."

I am interested in the larger pattern of these stories, which is that something goes wrong with the wilderness journey—thirst, hunger, the land of Canaan looks far less promising than the propaganda suggested, or the leaders act in an authoritarian and stupid way—and the people murmur against the figures of authority. Note the targets: Moses (Exodus 15:24; 17:3; Numbers 14:36; also Numbers 17:20/5), or Moses and Aaron (Exodus 16:2, 7; Numbers 14:2; 17:6/16:41), or Yahweh (Exodus 16:7, 8; Numbers 14:27, 29; 17:25/10). Occasionally they just murmur in general, a groundswell of discontent (Exodus 16:9, 12; Deuteronomy 1:27). One last occurrence in this stretch of text, after Moses and Aaron have finally disappeared, comes in Joshua 9:18. Here the congregation murmurs against "the leaders" (*'al hanniesi'im*). This final mention brings out the point of the murmuring stories: they challenge, question, and attack the leaders in general.

By and large, the responses to these murmurings escalate from a relatively simple response—supplying drinkable water and food (Exodus 15:22–25; 16:1–21; 17:1–7)—to full-scale punishment. Indeed, after the murmuring that follows the negative report about the "Less-Than-Promising Land" from the spies we find nothing less than a Deluge-type punishment: all but Joshua and Caleb are to die before they can enter the land (Numbers 14:20–38). It is a mitigated punishment, one that Moses achieves in a desperate last-minute bid to stay Yahweh's hand (Numbers 14:13–19), an act that positions him very carefully as the compassionate, caring one. Yahweh had just wanted to wipe them out there and then (Numbers 14: 11–12), but now he will do so slowly, over forty years, and save a couple of faithful ones. Mitigated? Except perhaps for Caleb and Joshua, but a quick death is far better than a slow one in the wilderness, although at least their children get to enter the land. The story of Korah and company (Numbers 16) is the first spectacular installment—after the original spies die of the plague (Numbers 14:36–37)—of this slow death, although now with some fireworks and plague thrown in.

The difference in responses to the murmurings—between a simple Here you are, then, to Wipe them out!—marks another feature of these stories. They cluster around two crucial moments in the overarching narrative of Genesis through Kings. The first cluster comes immediately after the crossing of the Reed Sea and escape from the Egyptians (Exodus 15–17),[14] and the second on the threshold of Canaan (Numbers 14, 16, 17). The first involves issues of water and food at the outset of the wilderness wanderings; the second focuses on lack of trust and outright rebellion. In both cases the leaders are ultimately responsible. And in both cases we get variations on the same complaint: "Would that we had died by the hand of Yahweh in the land of Egypt, when we sat by the fleshpots and ate bread to the full; for you have brought us out into this wilderness to kill the whole assembly with hunger" (Exodus 16:3). Or "Why did you bring us out of Egypt, to kill us and our children and our cattle with thirst?" (Exodus 17:3). And then, on the verge of Canaan: "Would that we had died in the land of Egypt! Or would that we had died in this wilderness! Why does Yahweh bring us into this land, to fall by the sword? Our wives and our little ones will become a prey; would it not be better for us to go back to Egypt?" (Numbers 14:2).

So far, then, we have a uniform series of protests against the triumvirate, Moses, Aaron, and Yahweh; an increasing scale of punishments; and a bunching around two central moments in the narrative: the first steps into the wilderness and the final step before Canaan. I want to ask one more question: Who murmurs? It is "the people" (*ha'am*) in Exodus 15:24 and 17:3; "the sons of Israel" (*bene yisra'el*) in Exodus 16:12 and Numbers 14:27, 17:20/5; "all the sons of Israel" (*kol bene yisra'el*) in Numbers 14:2; "the whole congregation" (*kol ha'edah*) in Numbers 14:36 and Joshua 9:18; and "the whole congregation of the sons of Israel" (*kol a'dath bene yisra'el*) in Exodus 16:2 and 9 and Numbers 17:6/16:41.

But this is hardly a demimonde anymore: the whole people in whatever form now systematically murmurs, grumbles, and disrupts the basis of power. I am, however, intrigued by one phrase that is a continuation and variation on this: *bene meri*, "the sons of rebellion." After Korah's rebellion and at the end of the story of Aaron's rod—that assertion of authority and power via a flowering and almond-producing rod (!) over those who murmur in discontent—we find the whole congregation of the sons of Israel has become a motley bunch of *rebels*. The verse is worth quoting in full: "And Yahweh said to Moses: 'Put back the rod of Aaron before the testimony, to be kept as a sign for the rebels [*bene meri*], that you may make an end of their murmurings [*telunotam*] against me, lest they die'" (Numbers 17:25/10). The text is not talking here of Korah and company, for they have already been swallowed and digested by the earth, or some other revolutionary cell that could fit in the proverbial phone box, but of the "sons of Israel," as verse 27 (English translation, v. 12) makes clear. Indeed, the competition over Aaron's rod operates at the top level of organization, at the level of the father's houses: while his rod represents the house of Levi, the other eleven come from each of the other tribes (see Numbers 16:17–18; 17:2–3). This is a contest that involves the whole people, and Aaron's budding rod turns them all into rebels.

SUMMARY

It is time to summarize my argument to this point. I began with the women in chapter 2. In part of my discussion of "women first" I argued that Genesis–Joshua systematically seeks to contain women in a series of *unoriginal tales*. Eve in Genesis 3 and Miriam in Numbers 12 are the key: their rebellions are shown to be profoundly threatening and therefore thoroughly unviable. Both Genesis 3 and Numbers 16 insert them back into a distinct social hierarchy. But once these two have put the spark to the gunpowder, the text explodes both with rebellious women and an almost obsessive concern to keep them in place: as exchange objects in the wife-sister stories that circle around Sarah and Rebekah (Genesis 12:10–20; 20; 26); by slicing them off lists of descendants due for blessings, such as Leah, daughter of Rachel (Genesis 30:21; 34:1; 49); by a spate of legislation (Exodus 21; Leviticus 12, 15, 18, 19, 20; Numbers 5, 30; Deuteronomy 21, 22, 23, 25, 27); by tying them into male inheritance and succession in as many ways as one could imagine and a few one probably couldn't (Genesis 16; 18; 19:30–38; 21; 24–25; 29–30; 38; Exodus 1; Numbers 27:1–11; 36 Deuteronomy 21:15–17; 25:5–10).

Now, out of all of this, I argued that the story of the daughters of Zelophehad—Mahlah, Tirzah, Hoglah, Milcah, and Noah in Numbers 27:1–11 and 36—shows a glimpse of something else. Quite simply, the threat and possibility of female inheritance must be roped back into the system of male inheritance. Hints of another world also come with Rebekah's question in Genesis 25:22 and Zipporah's foreskin act in Exodus 4:24–26, and those texts that open the possibility of women on their own, as with Dinah in Genesis 34:1, Pharaoh's daughter's slaves in Exodus 2:5, and the vows of women not attached to any man (Numbers 30:10/9).

This overbearing concern with locking women into a system and denying the possibility of anything different is hardly occasional or isolated within this text. But we get only so far by arguing that some patriarchy or other is to blame here, whether that is the result of some inherent fear of women by men or perhaps an inbuilt misogyny that turns up with sickening regularity. We need to widen the terms of reference, something I began to do with the suggestion of a demimonde.

More of that in a moment. I already suggested in that earlier discussion that locking women into the system was perhaps necessary for the world of the text to hold together and make sense. But here psychoanalysis came to my assistance, particularly with the notion of fantasy and its function in concealing the fantasmatic kernel. In my more detailed reading of Genesis 2–3 as fantasy, it turned out that although the hints of the fantasmatic kernel initially pointed to the woman as the culprit, in the end it was rebellion itself, for which the woman is camouflage. But there was a double edge to this: what seemed to be an existing fantasmatic kernel mediated and concealed by fantasy turns out to be something produced by fantasy itself. And the mode of concealing it is to construct a diachronic narrative for what is radically synchronous. Or, to put it in more concrete terms: Genesis 2–3 on the surface is about the rebellion of a woman and then a man against authority, who are then suppressed and punished. What this narrative conceals is the fact that the possibility of this rebellion against Yahweh Elohim is produced at the very moment the story begins.

So now we find ourselves in a dialectical bind: not only does the system exist by blocking the possibility of what doesn't even exist, but it also produces that possibility in the first place. There is, however, a little sleight of hand in the preceding statement, for I have too rapidly connected rebellion with system. That connection is in part the agenda of this chapter: thus far I have explored various modes of insurrection and subversion within Genesis–Joshua.

This is where the subversion of the Real comes in handy. I argued that Lacan's Real in the Hexateuch is the overarching set into which all the other terms fit as subsets. Through a series of readings—of the Flood story in Genesis 6–9, the Tower of Babel (Genesis 11:1–9), the rebellion of Korah (Numbers 16), and the theme of murmuring—the Real took on much more of a political scent. And it appears here in these texts as a chaos that perpetually threatens order and cosmos. It turns up variously as flood, the confusion of language, and a gaping earth. But what has happened in these stories is that human rebellion has been naturalized—it brings on natural disasters—and the zone of the Real has been occupied by the deity. Not content with ordering the cosmos of the Symbolic, God decides to occupy the Real as well. Before we know it, chaos has become punishment of human sin in the hands of God. Human rebellion has nowhere to go.

I have, however, left out a phrase in my return to the Real here: chaos is not merely the threat to order, it is also *the support of cosmos*. Without chaos, cosmos would be nothing; without the Real, the Symbolic could not function. By now it should be clear that these phrases have a distinctly political sense, especially one in which we block the appropriation of the Real by chaos. The Real becomes a zone of subversion, but subversion with a structuring role: the cosmos of the text is structured precisely to deal with political subversion which menaces that cosmos with collapse at any moment; yet that cosmos could not exist without that danger. But we are not going to get away without one more twist: that threat is produced by the text in the first place (the logic of fantasy). Insurrection is then the constitutive exception of the Hexateuch.

Yet the Real is far more than this in the Hexateuch. Not merely the cells from which the rebels launch their raids into the world of the text, it signals a systemic alternative. The first hints of this come with another element in my earlier discussion: the suggestions of a demimonde. "Demimonde" has of course all those associations with the French and Russian Revolutions: the realm of rebels of all stripes, criminals, sex workers, pornographers, and sundry unsavory types. Much better than the associations that now hang around "underworld." In Genesis through Joshua we find prostitutes (Genesis 38:15; Joshua 2:1), "transvestites" (Deuteronomy 22:5), sorceresses (Exodus 22:17/18), and zoophiles and other deviants (e.g., Deuteronomy 23:2/1; Leviticus 13–14; 18:23; 20:15–16). Before we know it, the ranks of the rebels have expanded well beyond women and occasional figures such as Korah or even the builders of Babel to include a widespread demimonde. In fact, it threatens to include pretty much the whole of humanity, barring one or two, in the story of the Flood.

The move from being a rebellious demimonde to becoming the people as a whole takes place with the murmuring stories. Clustering around the crossing of the Reed Sea out of Egypt and the Jordan River into Canaan, the stories grow until the whole people are in fact "sons of rebellion." The text works overtime to present them as whiners and grumblers, disobedient, slow and somewhat stupid—all convenient labels to stick on political rebels to deny them any legitimacy. Here I can bring in the insight from my reading of Genesis 2–3 in terms of fantasy, and that is that political myth produces the possibility of political insurrection in the first place. Rather than a diachronic narrative in which rebellion is suppressed—the Flood, Babel, Korah, and the murmurings—these stories create the possibility of rebellion in a radically synchronous fashion. In my earlier discussion I tracked down the kernel as insurrection, but after Korah and Babel and Co. it takes on the contours of the constitutive exception and the Real as well.

That Real is starting to become somewhat politicized. But nothing politicizes the Real more than its own central function: its perpetual threat to bring the Symbolic cosmos crashing down. Thus far I have read this threat in terms of women such as Eve and Miriam, of an underground that must be suppressed, of insurrection that lies at the heart of the stories of the Garden, the Flood, Babel, and Korah, and of the whole people as rebels in the murmuring stories. One question remains: What do the people rebel against?

CHAPTER FOUR

The Sacred Economy

Marxism finally gets its chance to speak in this chapter. Feminism and psychoanalysis have had their say, although with a Marxist lilt that the attuned ear may have picked up from time to time. But any discussion of political myth in relation to the Hebrew Bible can in the end not shirk its responsibility to speak of political economics, which, if you look (perhaps for the first time) at the subtitle of *Capital*, is another way of indicating the fundamental role of economics in any Marxian discussion of history.

The major concern of this chapter is: What is the relationship between the dynamic I have been tracking and historical reconstruction? Or rather, what connection does the tension between the status quo and rebellion have with a real social and political context? In answering these questions I undertake a reconstruction of the underlying economic patterns of ancient Israel. It may come as a surprise to find that there is no such reconstruction. To be sure, there is any number of garden-variety efforts that fall into the usual traps: confusing politics for economics, being mesmerized by the scant references to trade, applying terms from capitalist economics to ancient Israel, and feeling comfortable with a day-to-day analysis that confuses chronicle with diachronic history. What I am after, however, is the deeper logic of the economy, something that must be more synchronic than diachronic, more theoretical than analytic. And that will lead me to a new model of such an economy that I call the *sacred economy*.

Before I get there, however, I must answer a prior question. In the previous two chapters I focused on drawing out the patterns of subversion and insurrection that lie embedded in the text of the Hexateuch. I have reached the point where the occasional glimpses of female dissent, or the hunt for the fantasmatic kernel, or indeed the hints of a subversive demimonde have now overflowed their hidden corners to become an inescapable feature of the whole people. So much so that by the time we get to Numbers 17, the people themselves are rebels. In other words, persistent and widespread rebellion is an inescapable element of the text itself, cast as disobedience and outright sin. I have even argued that rebellion is produced by the construction of the status quo in the text. But I have not answered the prior question: What precisely do the people rebel against?

A STATE-IN-WAITING: THEOCRATIC TYRANNY

The answer is the state. Not just any state, but a particular one. This is where we need to shift gears and move to another level, to the overarching patterns of the text as a whole. What I am after, in other words, is the nature of the master narrative from Creation to Promised Land. But since this master narrative is really part of the complex political myth I have been tracing, I would rather speak of a *master myth*. At this level the myth concerns the way the people become a state as they cross the wilderness. By the time they reach Canaan, they are a sovereign state, named Israel, ready to take over the land. The problem, however, is that the state and its various institutions that first appear in the wilderness narrative never seem to have existed as it is represented. What we have, in other words, is a political myth of origin that is never realized, that never actually legitimated anything remotely resembling itself in reality. Or rather, if the myth did and does legitimate anything, then it is nothing like what we find in the myth.

For the remainder of this chapter I argue two things. First, the master myth of Genesis through Joshua unfolds before us a "State-in-waiting." Second, the perpetual rebellion against this state within the text is both an attempt to deal with the impossibility of realizing this state in reality and a signal of a political and economic contradiction. As for the first point, I track the way the state comes together in the Hexateuch and then contrast it with a very different historical reconstruction. On the second problem, I ask why the text deals in such extensive and complex ways with rebellion against a state that will never exist. And my answer to that question is twofold. To begin with, it marks the effort to provide a story, or a series of stories, as to why that state cannot be realized and yet simultaneously maintains the hope that it might be if that opposition can be removed. Further, I make use of Lévi-Strauss's idea that myth is an imaginary resolution to a real social contradiction. In short, what shows up in the text as a profound tension between the state and various groups of the people is in fact a literary effort to respond to a very different political and economic tension. What that tension is must await my argument.

So let us see how the State-in-waiting is assembled in the Hexateuch. Athalya Brenner succinctly outlines what is at stake at the level of the master myth. In tracing out what she calls a multidimensional theme of passage, she finds

> a passage through painful transformation from loosely-defined population into ethnicity; a passage from a "religion of the fathers" (Genesis) to a communal covenant-bound, legally grounded, exclusive monotheism; a passage through the axis of space, from one country (Egypt) to the threshold of another (Canaan); a passage through the axis of time, represented by the typological forty years in the (mythic) wilderness; a passage from disorganization and confusion into institutionalization. (Brenner 1994a: 11)

However, in order to provide some political and social specificity to Brenner's outline, I would like to use the heuristic categories of Althusser's ideological state apparatuses (ISAs; 1971: 121–73). Out of Althusser's list,[1] the passage through the wilderness from Egypt to Canaan produces four crucial state apparatuses: religion, family, a legal system, and a political system. On top of these we find what Althusser calls the repressive state apparatus (RSA) of an army and indeed a police force (see Boer 2003: 14–41). The difference between repressive and ideological apparatuses is that whereas the RSA operates by means of direct violence and its threat—especially with the police, courts, prisons, and army controlled by the government—the distinct characteristic of the ISAs is their predominantly ideological function. In contrast to the RSAs, the ISAs are not directly repressive, which means that they become the site for ideological and class struggle between the ruling classes and those ruled.

The religion instituted in this myth is that of Yahwistic monotheism based on what Jan Assmann (1997) calls the "Mosaic distinction," with its own system of religious professionals, ritual, and physical structures. The family structure that emerges, especially in the backbone genealogical lists, is that of the gens or clan and then the tribe. The judicial system comprises both judges appointed by the leader and the pervasive body of religious professionals. And the state is a theocratic tyranny: one leader is appointed by Yahweh, with whom that leader relates in symbiotic dependency. The priests do pervade the other institutions, such as the judiciary and the RSA of the police, but they are also a distinct tribe, the Levites, and thus separated (made sacred, set apart) from the people. The other RSA, the army, is not a professional standing army but a militia, drawn from the adult males in times of conflict.

The book of Exodus is the site for the mythic origin of exclusive monotheism, and its structuring features are the initial vision to Moses in the burning bush, the appearance at Mount Sinai, the perpetual assertion of Yahweh's singular claim from an apostate and rebellious people, and the elaborate construction of the material requirements for worship. Thus we find Yahweh's introduction to Moses in Exodus 3:14: "I am who I am" ('ehyeh 'asher 'ehyeh) or simply "I am" ('ehyeh). The context for this singular claim is the rousing call to rescue the people from bondage in Egypt, a claim that also takes the form of "the God of your fathers, the God of Abraham, the God of Isaac, and the God of Jacob" (3:15)—a little piece of narrative glue that happens to be Yahweh's singular emergence.

From Exodus rises Mount Sinai, literally and figuratively. Here is enacted the most interesting feature of this story's monotheism: the Mosaic distinction. Simply put, the Mosaic distinction is between what is true and what is false, rather than what is sacred and profane. That is, in the first of the Ten Commandments, "You shall have no other gods before me" (Exodus 20:3; see Deuteronomy 5:7), we find the difference between true and false gods, true and false religion, a distinction that overrides that between sacred and profane. That second distinction now becomes a consequence of the first, as with the command for Moses to remove his shoes when he tromps too close to the burning bush (Exodus 3:5), or the wavering debate as to who might be able to climb the mountain and how close the people might come (19:21–25). But what are the implications of the Mosaic distinction? First, the other gods become false gods—no gods at all—and not other gods with whom Yahweh is in competition. Second, Assmann (1997) argues that Yahwistic monotheism, like Akhenaten's Egyptian monotheism with which it shares so much, is a "counter-religion" that sets itself up by trampling over earlier religions. I am less interested in Assmann's tendency to see these earlier religions as some actually existing system (what he terms "Egypt"). I am much more interested in the following observation: "This monotheism derives its crucial semantic elements from a construction of the rejected other, and these semantics have continued to exert their influence to the present day. Mosaic monotheism is an explicit counter-religion which depends on the preservation of what it opposes for its own definition" (Assmann 1997: 211). For Assmann Mosaic monotheism must preserve what it usurps for its own coherence, hence the perpetual pattern of apostasy and the worship of false gods that we find throughout the Hexateuch and beyond. But this goes only so far and begs the next step: Mosaic monotheism is a mythic construction that *creates* the other denied system in order to define itself.[2] This is the logic of the master myth of the Hexateuch as such, for the state being constructed in this myth is unthinkable without the creation of systematic opposition, an opposition that must be denied and blocked for that master myth itself to exist.

How does the narrative of Sinai create the denied other? The story of the golden calf of Exodus 32 (see also Deuteronomy 9), in which the whole people rebel, provides an answer. This is the only story of rebellion or murmuring in the sojourn in the wilderness of Sinai that runs from Exodus 19 to Numbers 10, but it has two distinct features: it is a religious rebellion, and it comes in between two crucial assertions of the Mosaic distinction. The episode takes place while Moses is on Mount Sinai and when the Mosaic distinction is first made in the narrative. But when he encounters the apostate Israelites, Moses throws the two tablets of the law down in anger (Exodus 32:19), and so, once the worship of the golden calf has been dealt with, he must take two other tablets upon which Yahweh will write the words once again (34:1). But are they the same words? For Exodus 34:27 suggests that now we have a different set of words on the tablets: "Write these words; in accordance with these words I have made a covenant with you and with Israel." Which words? It would seem that "these words" actually refers to the alternative ten commandments in verses 11–25: a ban on the worship of other gods; a ban on making molten images; the feast of unleavened bread; dedication of the firstborn; observing the Sabbath; the three feasts of weeks, first fruits, and harvest; and four instructions for sacrifice (no blood sacrifice with leaven, no Passover leftovers, dedicating first fruits to Yahweh, and not boiling a kid in its mother's milk). These are the "ten words" Yahweh writes on the tablets of stone (34:28). There are three overlaps with the more well-known ten: the ban on other gods, the prohibition of images, and the observance of the Sabbath. More important, in these alternative ten commandments the Mosaic distinction is asserted even more strongly. No other means of worship and no items of worship are to be tolerated (Exodus 34:11–16; see Deuteronomy 7:1–5). Why? "For you shall worship no other god, for Yahweh, whose name is Jealous, is a jealous God" (Exodus 34:14).

Once Mosaic monotheism has created its other, and once the people actually leave Sinai in Numbers 10, the rebellions come thick and fast, from the craving of meat (Numbers 11) to the worship of Baal of Peor (Numbers 25). And Deuteronomy will obsess over the religious rebellion of worshipping other gods (Deuteronomy 7:1–5, 25–26; 11:26–32; 12:29–31; 27:15; 28–30). But if the other, "false," religions are not to be permitted their material basis, then Yahwistic monotheism must have it. Indeed, the whole Sinai episode (Exodus 19–40) is an interior designer's delight. Here we find detailed instructions—from Yahweh—for the construction of the tabernacle and its rituals all the way from the color of the curtains to the cut of the priests' robes and the perfumes they should wear (see Boer 2001). The instructions take up the bulk of the information Moses receives on Sinai (Exodus 25–30), and a good section of Exodus itself is taken up with building the thing (35–40). Of course, there is no evidence whatsoever that such a tent ever existed. But the machinery of religion and its all-important collection of religious professionals receive far more attention in the stay at Sinai than they might have hoped for, whether it is the spelling out of sacrifices and rituals of ordination (Leviticus 1–9, 16), priests and feasts (Leviticus 21–24), and altars (Numbers 7) or exemption from military service and indeed any other productive work for the tribe of Levi (Numbers 1:47–54; 3; 9).

As far as the second great ideological state apparatus—the family—is concerned, I have already explored some of its contours in my discussion of primitive communism in chapter 2. Here, however, I am interested in three features of the Hexateuch: the family stories of Genesis, the genealogies as narrative backbone, and the wholesale tribalization that takes place. Thus in Genesis family intrigues and interactions dominate. So we find Adam and Eve and Co. (Cain, Abel, and Seth); Noah and his sons; Abraham and his women (Sarah, Hagar, Keturah) and children (Isaac, Ishmael, and Keturah's sons); Isaac and Rebekah; Jacob and Esau; then the whole complex of Jacob and Leah and Rachel and Bilhah and Zilpah and their thirteen children (including Dinah); Joseph and Asenath and their sons, Ephraim and Manasseh; and finally the story of Judah and his daughter-in-law Tamar and their sons, Perez and Zerah. Too often these are pared down to the patriarchs—Noah, Abraham, Isaac, Jacob, and Joseph—so it is worth reminding ourselves how deeply they are stories of complex families. I am tempted to make the comment that strikes me whenever I hear the woes of one family or another: same story, different family. But in their homely and foibled familiarity, these stories establish far more strongly the ideological state apparatus of the family.

Interleaved with these stories of kin comes the rhythm of the genealogies, with their strident assertion of the dominance of male descent against which the stories of women come to grief. Less the fill-in between major story units, the genealogies are in fact the backbone of Genesis (Crüsemann 1996). Thus, hard on the heels of the first creation stories and the banishment from the garden, we find the first genealogy in Genesis 4:17 and the last note in Genesis 47:23. If the long sojourn at Sinai has little in the way of genealogies, concentrating as the narrative does on other crucial ISAs, then the censuses of Numbers 1 and 26 make up for the absence. But it is Genesis that sets in place the family, with its entwinement of familial stories and genealogies, almost as the groundwork for what follows. I am tempted to invoke Althusser's (1994: 105) comment here, made as he reflects on the effect of his own family: "It is an irrefutable fact that the Family is the most powerful ideological State apparatus."

Indeed, Genesis also gives us the third feature of this institution: the tribes. Not only do we get the first story of the sons of Jacob (minus Dinah), born of either Leah and Zilpah or Rachel and Bilhah, beginning in Genesis 29:31, but the whole narrative builds up to the blessings and curses of Jacob in Genesis 49. The act of blessing is then repeated in a grand moment of inclusion by Moses in Deuteronomy 33. But in between there is a constant process of reinforcing the tribes, whether in the census of Numbers 1, the organization of tribal camps in Numbers 2, the long list of offerings for the new altar in Numbers 7, the order of tribes when leaving Sinai (Numbers 10:17–28), or in the list of those responsible for dividing the land (Numbers 34:16–29). The actual allocations of Joshua follow tribal patterns (Joshua 13–21). In fact, the whole master myth from Genesis through Joshua would hardly make sense without the structuring role of families and then tribes.

I can pass through the judicial ideological state apparatus rather quickly. At the most obvious level there are the 613 laws of the Pentateuch, the bulk of which appear in the long stay at Sinai and many of which obsess about women and a half-seen demimonde. Despite the fact that many of the laws do indeed deal with religious matters, and despite the fact that in some cases priests act as arbiters (see Deuteronomy 17:9), the establishment of a judicial system is separate from that of the religious professionals. But note that it happens at the last moment before the people arrive at the mountain of Sinai (Exodus 18): Jethro, Moses's father-in-law, suggests that Moses should lighten his stress level and appoint "rulers of thousands, of hundreds, of fifties, and of tens" (18:21), who will then "judge the people at all times" (18:27). It is, if you like, a series of lower courts to deal with petty cases, while Moses remains at the highest judicial level. With the system neatly in place, the laws can now roll out from the top of the mountain. But two things are worth noting: these men are appointed by Moses, and they are "rulers" first, judges second. Or rather, they are appointed as rulers over the people much like military commanders, and part of their task is to judge. The judiciary, in other words, is entwined with the political system.[3]

That political system is, as I mentioned earlier, a theocratic tyranny. Although the priesthood comes close to being the ruling body, Aaron is never more than second in command: the Hexateuch presents neither a hierocracy nor an oligarchy. From the moment Yahweh appoints him in Exodus 3:7–12 until his drawn-out death in Deuteronomy 34 (one wishes that he might have keeled over just a little earlier),[4] Moses is the divinely appointed leader and the form of government a tyranny. Here many of the rebellions in the text aim their energy, from Miriam through to the murmurings of the people. Many commentators have pointed out how much the figures of Yahweh and Moses are wrapped up in each other in the Pentateuch, how one can hardly do without the other. And it is not for nothing that Moses is Machiavelli's (1988: 19–20, 88) first example of the ideal Prince. Joshua, carefully appointed by Yahweh (Deuteronomy 31:23), follows on in exactly the same vein (34:9–12).

We have, then, four arms of the machinery of a State-in-waiting: exclusive monotheism with its system of religious professionals and material basis, the family and tribal structure, a judiciary, and a form of government. These four elements combine to produce that crucial element of a state: a sense of collective identity. That identity is the "sons of Israel." Although the four elements of this state are distinct in the text, they also overlap in so many ways, especially with the repressive state apparatuses of the military and the police force. Abraham sets the agenda here, with the 318 personal thugs from his household functioning as a mafia to carry out some necessary dirty work in rescuing Lot (Genesis 14:13–16). This will go in two directions, one to the personal police force of Moses and the other to the popular militia. The first, in which the Levites slaughter a few brothers and neighbors and companions as an ordination in blood (Exodus 32:25–29), deals with internal policing, and the Levites double very handily for such a chore. The militia, from which the Levites are exempt (Numbers 1:47–54), is called up to deal with external threats, such as that of the perpetual Amalekites, who seem to get wiped out time and again only to return for one more round (see Exodus 17:8–15), or the Midianites (Numbers 31) and others. Here the institution of the family—in terms of tribal structure—becomes the bedrock for the army. For the censuses of Numbers 1 and 26, along with the departure from Sinai in Numbers 10, comes through as a roll call for war. This State-in-waiting, it would seem, is a highly militarized one.

Against this state the various murmurings and rebellions I traced out in chapters 2 and 3 rumble and then break up. The women run afoul of the judicial (note how many laws obsess about women) and challenge the political (Miriam), the family (assertion of a male line), and the religious (Eve). The chaotic challenge of the Real, along with the rebellion of the people as a whole, threatens to break the hinges between all of these apparatuses, beginning with the theocratic tyranny of the Moses-Yahweh nexus and then running all the way down the scale.

HERE COME THE RUSSIANS

Let us pause for a moment and see where my argument has come. The master myth of the Hexateuch provides the lineaments of a theocratic tyranny with interwoven institutions of religion, family, judiciary, a militia, and a police force provided by the priests. This tyranny faces perpetual and widespread rebellion that must constantly be suppressed. Not only is the opposition to this State-in-waiting necessary for the narrative construction of that state, but the story itself produces the opposition. The catch with this master myth's State-in-waiting is that it does not resemble any known reality for ancient Israel.

Now I arrive at a point in the road where many have stood before: to show how the text does not tell us anything much about history, proceed to a historical reconstruction, and then, perhaps, account for the production of the text. These are the age-old concerns of historical criticism, namely, the desire to produce a history of the text and of the history behind the text, all the while agonizing over the historical reliability of the text. My interests are different, for three reasons. First, I do not need to enter into futile debates over the historicity or otherwise of these texts, since no reputable biblical scholar any longer argues that the Hexateuch gives any direct and reliable historical information, unlike the heated debates concerning the historicity of the monarchy and indeed exile to Babylon. But this depends on what one means by "historical information," and that question leads to my second point: rather than rewrite the annals of Israel, focused on crucial political events and moments, as so many biblical scholars still do, or argue about the existence or otherwise of some person or other, I am interested in economic history. Third, I am not blinkered by purely historical concerns, a condition that seems to afflict so many biblical scholars. For any Marxist study worth its salt takes not only history as a crucial concern, but also literature, religion, culture, politics, ideology, and economics. Above all, it assumes and explores the ways these areas are intimately related.

So I too will engage in a spell of historical reconstruction, with one glaring difference from the established historical-critical history of ancient Israel: I make use of a wealth of material from the former Soviet Union over some sixty years, material that is still off the radar of most biblical studies.[5] The catch is that whereas much of this work was dismissed in the context of the cold war, especially in biblical studies, Soviet scholars worked readily and comfortably with Western scholarship in a properly ecumenical scholarly agenda.[6] Since this work is barely known in biblical studies, I will track some of the major items of the Soviet research.

These Soviet debates ranged all the way from the intricacies of grammar to the overarching frameworks of modes of production, whether Asiatic, Ancient (slave-based), or Feudal. They begin with the much-debated texts by Marx and Engels on precapitalist economic formations, texts with which, astoundingly, biblical scholars have rarely engaged. This material, however, lies scattered in various pieces by Marx and sometimes Engels over a thirty-year period that includes newspaper articles, letters, critiques of political economy, and ethnological research.[7] The key item in the debate, however, was the Asiatic mode of production (AMP), whose features were soon distilled as common rather than individual private property in land, often personified in the figure of the god-ruler; the centralized control of public works by government (irrigation, building, roads, and so on); the decentralized and self-sufficient economic world of villages, with their resilient combination of agriculture and handicrafts, as opposed to the imperial state; and the social division of labor in terms of usefulness.[8] However, for reasons that will become clear, the most intriguing sections of Marx's work on the AMP are those that investigate the economic complexities of that mode of production; instead of the widespread notion of a "stagnant" economic form, Marx traces the way exchange, surplus, rent (in labor and in kind), and tax operate within the village community, between communities, between communities and the state, and between the state and the limited long-distance trade generated by manufacturers.

A strange feeling soon descends on anyone who reads through the Soviet material, for nearly all the positions taken in Western debates on the reconstruction of the ancient Near East and biblical societies are prefigured in these discussions, in some cases by more than forty years! Thus, apart from versions of pan-Feudalism and pan-slavery and debates over the viability or otherwise of the Asiatic mode of production, we find questions over the reliability of data, the appropriateness of terminology such as "mode of production" and "class," the nature of historical theory and reconstruction, and the danger of multiplying hypotheses (especially modes of production) against the danger of lumping everything together in an overarching category or two, such as Feudalism. All these points were made in the first years of debate in the 1930s.

The debate over the best model for ancient Near Eastern political economy followed some reasonably clear stages:[9] the AMP gave way briefly to Feudalism, which then fell beneath the sweep of the slave-based mode of production, which in its turn begrudgingly allowed the return of a revived AMP. The "anti-Aziatchiki," as the opponents of the AMP were called, swept the field early in the debate, and the AMP disappeared as a viable category. For a few years Feudalism became the preferred descriptor—a position that long held sway in non-Marxist scholarship on the ancient Near East (see Schloen 2001: 187–89)—but it soon fell away. Thus, in a profoundly influential lecture of four hours delivered in 1933 at the Academy of the History of Material Culture in Leningrad, V. V. Struve sidelined Feudalism as a viable term: "If we say that everything is feudalism, then we get a feudal porridge in the literal sense from Babylon to Napoleon" (quoted in Dunn 1981: 44; see Struve 1969a). In a broad sweep that covered all of the key documents in the histories of Mesopotamia and Egypt, he went on to persuade most scholars that the evidence pointed to a slave mode of production. Even though slaves were numerically inferior to various other classes, such as free laborers and landholders, these slaves were owned collectively by the state and temple complex, worked the year round, and were therefore the dominant means for the extraction of surplus. Apart from arguing in favor of a slave-based mode of production, Struve's interest lay in the internal contradictions that generated the periodic rise and collapse of the various ancient Near Eastern empires: Sumerian, Babylonian, Assyrian, Persian, and so on.

What we find after Struve's decisive intervention are those who refined his argument for almost three decades (Tyumenev 1969a, 1969b), with debates over the nature of labor and class through detailed exegesis of the available documents (Struve 1969b; Dandamaev 1984); others who held onto the notion of Feudalism (such as I. M. Lur'e [see Dunn 1982: 47]); others who began to distinguish between an early, primitive or immature form of slaveholding society and its mature form in Greece and Rome (even old Struve himself); yet others who pointed out that the means of coercing large parts of the population into slavery did not exist in the ancient Near East (D'iakonoff 1974), that the bulk of produce was created by free laborers, that we do indeed have the rise of a despotic state and all its religious appurtenances with Sargon and the Akkadians (D'iakonoff 1969b, 1991b);[10] and others who argued for a fundamental difference between the ancient Near East and the Graeco-Roman world (Melikishvili [see Dunn 1982: 63]). Gradually, under the weight of further evidence, debate, and a thousand qualifications—including a bold effort by Tyumenev to argue that, apart from the rulers, everyone in the whole Ancient East was in fact a slave and that Greece and Rome constituted aberrations!—Struve's position crumbled. As the slave mode of production began to falter, the AMP, now decked out with an impressive array of new data, reemerged from the wings refreshed and revitalized after a long rest.[11] This took place precisely when, in the 1960s and 1970s, it suffered a series of attacks in the West. For instance, biblical scholars who are aware of these debates (e.g., Simkins 1999) see the criticisms of Hindess and Hirst (1975: 178–220) as the final nail in the coffin of the AMP. Their criticisms are *theoretically* telling given the assumed framework within which they operate, for instance, that no mode of production can be developed from the tax-rent couple and that the so-called stasis of community-based production is a feature of other modes of production, such as the Feudal, as is tax and tribute. But what intrigues me is not merely that the criticisms of Hindess and Hirst were already rehearsed in the 1930s in the Soviet Union, but also that when Hindess and Hirst were seeking to lay to rest the AMP in the 1970s the AMP was returning to the Soviet debate.

However delectable this material is (and I will have occasion to return to it), let me cut to the chase and identify a few points relevant to my concerns. To begin with, one (unwitting) achievement of the 1970s debate in the Soviet Union was to separate the ancient Near East decisively from China, India, Peru, and elsewhere; they had been lumped together by Marx. This distinction emerged in the debate over the (dis)continuity of the ancient Near East with Greece and Rome. The closer the ancient Near East came to the slave mode of production of Greece and Rome, the further it traveled from any common ground with other so-called AMPs. But by the time the AMP made a comeback, it had taken on a life of its own in the ancient Near East.

Further, a crucial issue is whether the state can be considered a class. In conventional Marxist theory the state is distinct from class and is indeed generated out of class conflict; this is one of the fundamental criticisms of the AMP by Hindess and Hirst. Others have pinned their arguments to a different formation of class and state in which the two can be one, without explaining how (Krader 1975: 292; Tyumenev 1969a). This is a significant confusion, as I will argue in more detail below. The state is not identical with the growth of a temple-city complex, that is, with the concentration of power and wealth in a small ruling elite. Rather, the state emerges in a deep tension between the temple-city complex and the resilient village commune.

Finally, what emerges from these discussions is not merely the value of ever new philological and archaeological data from the ancient Near East, but also the continual debates over and refinements of the heuristic models used to make sense of the data. It is too often forgotten that the key lies in neither an ostrich-like empiricism that prefers to believe theory is a hindrance,[12] nor the pure theory of which Hindess and Hirst are the best example. These Soviet debates from the 1930s to the 1980s provide a good example of the dialectical interplay between data and theory of which Marxism is one of the best examples.

Theoretically, my debts in what follows are to regulation theory, one of the most promising branches of Marxist economic theory, that derives ultimately from Althusser (see Boyer 1990). In taking up Marx's example of being attentive to data along with sophisticated theoretical reflection, regulation theory argues that Marx's key terms and ideas are in fact ad hoc constructions, put together for a specific purpose but never meant to become an eternal template or recipe. Thus, if Marx's terms and concepts were developed in his analysis of capitalism, then it may be necessary to rework those concepts as well as develop new ones in noncapitalist contexts and even within capitalism. One example will suffice: regulation theory is not bound to the traditional idea of mode of production, preferring instead "regimes of accumulation"; thus we find in the recent past Fordism, Toyotism, and regimes led by services, knowledge, export, competition, information and communications, and finance, with perhaps the last beginning to dominate in the early twenty-first century (Boyer 2000). The categories of Marxism become a series of problems that need to be rethought, reworked, or replaced.

Let me make it quite clear: the most viable historiography for the ancient Near East is one that deals in terms of economics. But it is not just any economics, nor indeed "political economics," but a sacred economics. For what we find in the ancient Near East is what may best be described as a *sacred economy*. By sacred economy I mean a system in which the economy operates and is understood in terms of the sacred rather than the political. In what follows I begin to spell out what this means.

In dealing with a sacred economy I take on two tendencies in biblical studies. The first is, as I commented earlier, an overwhelming tendency to regard history as the record and reconstruction of major events, usually of a political nature. For instance, much still attaches to the date of the exile to Babylon, if it happened; or to the events of the united and then divided monarchies, if they existed; or to the Hasmonean uprising (at least no one doubts this). Valuable to an extent, it is also a self-defeating exercise, since so little information concerning such events is available. The simple fact that biblical scholars can rarely pin anything down to less than a couple of centuries suggests a very different sense of history; hence my interest in the broader sweeps of economic and social history. Second, in those studies that do focus on social and economic history, there is a tendency to see a nascent capitalism at work, or at least to retrofit terms from capitalism to the ancient Near East. So we find references to "market economics," "trade balance," and "free market." This tendency is simply misguided and at times ludicrous. Worse, it perpetuates a myth of capitalism, namely, that everywhere we look we find capitalism—which is, after all, the deepest expression of human nature—in various stages of its long path to maturity. Here the value of the Soviet studies is even greater.

As for the reconstruction itself, the key nodes are the village commune, the temple-city complex, the formation of the despotic state, labor and class, mediations between empire and village commune, and what I call theo-economics, or regimes of allocation.[13]

The village commune, as both a kinship and an economic unit, persists through a series of economic and sociopolitical crises. The village commune was first identified by Marx as a key feature of the Asiatic mode of production, and then became the focus of Soviet studies (Jankowska 1969a; D'iakonoff 1974; Kozyreva 1991: 108–11). It is really what is at stake in the debate over the domestic, household, or familial mode of production that I followed in chapter 2, with one significant difference: the village commune has nothing to do with any notion of primitive communism that lies at the basis of these biblical studies. Without reference to the Soviet work, Western studies have belatedly picked up the importance of the village commune (see Leemans 1982; Liverani 1982; 2005: 21–24). Indeed, Liverani's (2005: 21; see also Thompson 1999: 120–24) description, based on evidence from Ugarit and Alalakh (Syria), is as good a description as any: "While the political and cultural centrality of the palace is beyond doubt, the majority of the population (about 80 percent . . .) lived in villages, relying on its own means of production: family-owned lands and flocks of sheep and goats." Both Soviet and later Western descriptions of the village come closest to the syndyasmian family of Lewis Henry Morgan that I discussed in chapter 2: an extended family of perhaps twenty to twenty-five couples who constitute the basis of a tribe.[14] At least until the Persian era (537–303 BCE) there was no substantial change in the structure and nature of the village commune, except for a significant reduction in the number of village communes in Persian Yehud (Carter 1999: 249).

As for the *temple-city complex*, the term is self-descriptive, for it designates the way the city (what we would call a town) is unthinkable without the structuring role of the temple and indeed the palace, which is an add-on to the temple. There is one point concerning the temple-city complex that I cannot emphasize enough: *the temple-city complex is not the same as the state*. Rather, the state arises in a tension between the village commune and the temple-city complex. The confusion between temple-city and state has led to many dead ends in studies of this period.

In contrast to the village commune, the temple-city underwent a constant process of change from Sumer to the Hellenistic era. The two are inextricably connected, however, much like a wheel: the village communes comprise the multiple points at the ends of the spokes, all of which have some connection to the axle. Again, Soviet studies (see Sarkisian 1969) preempt Western studies, although on this matter Soviet studies have had a skewed influence through the translation of Weinberg's (1992) work. He argues that the exile to Babylon (587–33 BCE) marks a change from the "father's house" (bet-av) to a citizen-temple community typical of the Achmaenid period.[15] Apart from uncritically taking the data in Kings and Ezra through Nehemiah at face value, especially the statistics, he makes a diachronic sequence of two items—what I have called village commune and temple-city complex—that were in constant relationship with each other.

The third item concerns the *formation of the state* (see D'iakonoff 1969b; 1991b; 1991c: 27–43; Kozyreva 1991: 103–7). It continues to surprise me that an essentially Marxist narrative for the emergence of the state has entered into mainstream biblical studies. It goes like this. Under certain conditions (soil fertility, rainfall, trade or booty) the differentiation of wealth and power sets in and is concentrated in the hands of certain individuals. This is the beginning of class, in which a certain group is disconnected from the production of essential items for survival, such as food and clothing. This class then relies on those who do produce these essentials and must extract it from them in some fashion, whether by coercion or persuasion or some mix of the two; the technical term for this is *exploitation*. With further concentration of wealth and power we get chieftains and towns, and then, at some vague point when the extraction of essential items becomes sufficiently complex and requires some form of defense for such wealth, we get the city and the state and its ruler, whether a king, despot, or tyrant. Such a narrative, with minor variations, turns up in the work of Niels-Peter Lemche (1988: 22–24; 1998b: 94–95), Philip Davies (1998: 59–73), Norman Gottwald (2001), and, not to be outdone, William Dever (2001), but also the work of Karl Kautsky (1953) and Perry Anderson (1974), to name two others in a whole panoply. However, rather than the assured result of a thousand repetitions, a few questions remain unanswered: What is the trigger that gets the process of differentiation under way? Does differentiation grow out of an earlier, undifferentiated state? And what is that earlier state? Primitive communism?

The major problem, however, concerns the direction of the narrative itself. It leads inexorably to the conclusion that this concentration of power in the chieftain or at least a small group is the development of the state. In other words, the exploiting class is the same as the state.[16] But as I have already pointed out, this is a confusion of the first order. From here a series of confusions follow: the state-cum-exploiting class then exploits the village communes, or tribes, and from this point state-versus-tribe becomes an irresolvable tension (e.g., Lemche 1998b: 98–100; Simkins 1999; Yee 2003: 60–63; Liverani 2005: 75–76). At this point Marxist and non-Marxist studies stand side by side, which can lead Hindess and Hirst (1975: 192–93) to argue that such a theory—the state is one with the exploiting class—is simply nonsensical within Marxist theory. But let me go back to the initial point in this series of confusions: the state is not the same as the city (temple-city complex), nor indeed is the state the same as the chieftain or tyrant and his small group of exploiters. Rather, following the insight that the state arises only in the tension between classes and is not a conglomeration of individuals, my argument is that the state arises in the conflict between this group and the village commune, which may then be described as "classes."

The fourth node concerns *labor and class*, especially the nature and variety of labor and the implications for any notion of class. Class arises in the conflict between village commune and temple-city complex, although the former far outweighs the latter in terms of the amount and variety of labor. In discussions of class, we move between efforts at broad typologies and an awareness of the sheer diversity of types of labor.[17] Thus, while D'iakonoff (1987: 3; 1991c: 39) attempts a typology for the whole ancient Near East that distinguishes between those who own the means of production but do not produce (government agents and religious professionals in the temple-city complex), those who own and produce (members of the village commune), and those who do not own but produce (slaves, day laborers, corvée laborers), Klengel (1987) shows how much variety there was for just one period (Old Babylonian):[18] independent householders, public labor service, merchants, workers possessing but not owning means of production, recipients of crown land, workers whose labor is consumed directly by the owner of the means of production, personnel of large economic units, and various types of indenture and slavery such as debt slaves and those either captured in war or born into slavery.

It is important to remember that juridical distinctions, however loose and slippery they might have been, between groups of people in the literature from ancient Israel and the ancient Near East do not necessarily match class distinctions (see Zel'in 1968; D'iakonoff 1987; Giorgadze 1991: 281–83). For instance, Liverani (2005: 17–18) notes a basic distinction in Ugarit and Alalakh between king's men and free men, but he points out that the distinction is political, judicial, and functional, while there was much economic variation. This is vitally important for biblical scholarship, since the text looms large in any reconstruction. Juridical distinctions between people, such as those in the Hebrew Bible between Israelite and foreigner (Moabite, Ammonite, Canaanite, etc.), women and men, widow, orphan, forced laborer, and slave, are not necessarily class distinctions. Such fluidity may reflect the instability of social structure (Jakobson 1969: 295), but it seems to me that juridical and functional distinctions effectively divide people who are in a similar class position. It prevents them from unifying and gaining what we might call class consciousness. The law, administered by the state, therefore becomes a direct instrument of compulsion. Marxist economic theory calls this extra-economic compulsion for economic reasons.

Fifth, we have *mediations* between empire and village commune. Some despotic states became empires, such as the Sumerian, Babylonian, Achaemenid, and Persian. What the studies thus far do not consider sufficiently are the various mediations of the relationship between despotic empire and village commune. This is especially true of small vassal states such as Israel, and indeed cities like Jerusalem, that stand between empire and village commune. Here Dandamaev's (1969: 296–97) point is crucial:

> It is known that side by side with a common code of laws, gold currency, royal measures of weight and the use of Aramaic as the official language throughout the entire territory of the empire, there continued to exist in every satrapy of the Achaemenid state old local laws, customs, traditions, religions, measures of length and weight, systems of currency, local writing systems, and spoken languages. In other words, each satrapy of the Achaemenid empire remained an independent socio-political unit with social institutions and an internal structure of its own.

Not only is the vassal state a crucial mediator between empire and village commune, but it may also act as a buffer.

THEO-ECONOMICS

Finally, there is what I call *theo-economics*. After a detailed analysis of available archaeological data, Charles Carter (1999: 285) comments, "A new study of the economic patterns within Yehud [the Persian province of Judah] is still to be written and will require new data or new methods of interpreting the existing data." In response I propose that we speak of the sacred economy of the ancient Near East (including Israel) in terms of a tension between allocation and extraction, or between an allocative economics and an extractive economics.

This distinction arises from a rather simple fact that is all too often forgotten in any economic analysis of ancient Israel: the overwhelming dominance (95 percent or more of the population) of village-based agriculture for the production of the necessities for human existence, namely, food, clothing, and shelter. The idea of a system of regimes of allocation is my effort to provide some sophistication to this simple point. By contrast, an extractive economics, based on tribute and trade, was a relatively minor business, especially in a marginal zone such as ancient Israel. This has not stopped more than one scholar becoming mesmerized by scant evidence of trade and tribute. Even though trade was very limited and carried out spasmodically by only 2 to 3 percent of the population, somehow it becomes in such work the economic motor of the whole system. Needless to say, such a view is mistaken, importing the assumptions drawn from capitalism into the ancient Near East.

As far as an allocative economics is concerned, the primary problem was twofold: accounting for production outside human control and knowledge, and ensuring adequate allocation of such production.[19] The key issue then becomes the allocation of what produces on its own. How does one account for production outside human control? By the action of the deity, who is responsible for fertility of the soil, rains, open wombs, and so on. How does allocation take place? Through the decisions of the deity, which now stands in as a code for those with power to make decisions concerning allocation—chieftains, foreign emperors, and sundry other tyrants. Since the deity is central to the process of accounting for productive capacities and to the allocation of such producing items, I suggest we use the term *theo-economics* as the economic logic behind the sacred economy. This theo-economics is the dominant form of economy in the ancient Near East, and so we should speak of "regimes of allocation" to describe the various ways allocation operated.[20]

By contrast, a minor role was played by extractive economics, which is the process of extracting something from a producer by someone or some group that has not produced it. Here we are on more familiar territory, where the technical Marxist terminology of exploitation—the process of acquiring from those who do labor by those who don't—and surplus value may be relevant. But we need to be very wary about using such terms, for what we do not have in the ancient Near East is a market economy. Thus, there is no complex and widespread scheme of production, distribution, and consumption that is necessary for a market economy. Above all there is no process of commodification in which an endless series of very different items become equivalent through their exchange value as commodities. Given the minor status of an extractive economics, it was often understood in allocative terms, as I discuss in a moment in regard to tribute. However, in light of my introduction of the term "regimes of allocation," in regard to extractive economics I suggest that there also were "regimes of extraction."

We may distinguish six regimes of allocation: allocation in terms of land, fertility, family, war, patron-client relations, and the judiciary. There were two regimes of extraction: tribute and trade.

Regimes of Allocation

1. Land and agricultural technology: While Western scholarship has tended to assume that "private property" in land was a viable concept on the basis of such descriptions as Abraham's purchase of a burial plot for Sarah from Ephron the Hittite in Genesis 23, it is questionable whether we can speak of private property in land at all, especially when the legal concept of absolute private property was not developed until the time of the Romans (Anderson 1974: 65–67). The closest we may come is some notion of the village commune holding land in common, or perhaps the state, but this is a very different sense of ownership. Rather, we need to speak of the allocation of land. Thus, in the political myth of the Hexateuch, Yahweh allocates land to Israel in the long delayed promise of a land that runs as a thread through the whole story.

2. Fertility: Closely related to but distinct from land allocation is the allocation of fertility, which includes land but also animals and women. At this level the overriding metaphor is of a receptacle for seed, whether that is a woman for a man's seed, the ground for crop seeds, or female animals for the seed of male animals. God in his various names ultimately controls and thereby allocates such fertility, as the narratives of opening and closing wombs of both women and animals indicate, as well as the fear of famine and celebration of plenty.

3. Family: In a family-based regime of allocation the structures of kinship determine the allocation of a whole series of items, including land, women, and animals. Kinship patterns determine the allocation of women in terms of endogamous or exogamous partnering, and thereby the allocation of children, especially sons. But kinship also sets the way inheritance passes on through the clan, in terms of land and animals, as well as other items such as the booty of war. Indeed, as I pointed out earlier, kinship structures are intrinsic to the nature of the militia. The census lists of Numbers 1 and 26 are war lists, but they also determine the allocation of plunder. The whole kinship structure, no matter how shifting and artificial it might be, is determined by the deity. He is, after all, the God of Abraham, Isaac, and Jacob, or the "God of our fathers."

4. War: The militia, which we may call the regime of the war machine, is another mode for the acquisition and allocation of land, animals, and women. The narrative of the conquest of Canaan, however fictional it might be, indicates the way such allocation was understood. Of course, it requires the dispossession and conquest of land originally allocated to another people. Thus we find the long list of reallocation of the land to the various tribes (Joshua 13–21). The notion of the ban in its various modes is an indicator of this regime, for in the divine command to exterminate all men, women, children, and animals, we find the need to eliminate everything except the land for reallocation. Thus in Joshua 6:21 the story depicts the invaders utterly destroying "all in the city, both men and women, young and old, oxen, sheep, and asses, with the edge of the sword." At other times, spoil and cattle are the only items allowed to be taken, as with Ai (Joshua 8:2), and then reallocated. However, the war machine as a professional army of the imperial center overlaps with extractive economics, for its task then includes ensuring the payment of tribute to that center.

5. Patron-client allocation: Along with kinship and the war machine, the patron-client regime is another, overlapping way of dealing with the distribution of land, women, animals, and booty, but also more intangible items such as protection and service. Although Simkins (1999) has argued that patronage is a mode of production all on its own, it is far better understood as one element in a larger economic system, for patronage is found in other economic systems apart from the sacred economy.

6. Judiciary: In contrast to the judiciary under capitalism, which turns on the two poles of sustaining the institution of private property and the private individual, and in contrast to Feudalism, in which the judiciary functioned to ensure the class structure of Feudal society, the role of the judiciary in the ancient Near East was to oversee the workings of allocation. It is not for nothing that many of the laws in the Hebrew Bible deal with the allocation of land, the control of women, the patterns of kinship and inheritance, and the nature of patron-client relationships. The fact that these laws are presented as given by the deity is yet another signal of the dominance of the sacred in an allocative economics.

Of course, an economic system is not determined by a unique item or two. Rather, it is the nature of the combination of the elements, or regimes, as I have called them here, into a whole that is important. Thus, while kinship, war, patronage, and the judiciary are found in other systems, it is their combination as modes of allocation that makes the sacred economy unique.

Regimes of Extraction

1. Tribute: That tribute existed—as extraction by a local state from the peasants and by an imperial center from subject states—is beyond doubt, but its function is open to endless debate. On the one hand it led Norman Gottwald to develop his famous and influential notion of the tributary mode of production, since tribute, he argued, was the primary mode of exploitation (the extraction of surplus). But it was also one of the main points of Hindess and Hirst's similarly influential argument against any notion of an Asiatic mode of production: tribute is tax, which is not unique to the ancient Near East, nor does it function as the prime mechanism for the extraction of surplus. Tribute, however, is not the determining feature of the sacred economy. It is a crude mode of extraction, extending the plunder of war into a system of tribute gatherers, a bureaucracy, the accumulation of treasure in temples and palaces and its ostentatious display. Indeed, its primary role was the maintenance of the temple-city complex and the larger imperial state. However, even though it is not the determining feature, tribute is the point at which the main tension of the sacred economy shows up. We can now see that the tension I noted earlier between the village commune and the temple-city complex manifests itself in the tribute extracted by the latter from the former. Yet the fact that tribute was a problem within a sacred economy shows up in the way it was justified in terms of an allocative ideology. Thus the deity was the one who sanctioned tribute, most notably in the notion of the temple tax or tithe, a reallocation of produce for the sake of the priests and the material structure of religion.

2. Trade: The existence of trade has led more than one historian of the ancient Near East or of the Bible into paroxysms of capitalist delight, finding market economics at work in every nook and cranny. The Soviet studies are again instructive (see Jankowska 1969b; D'iakonoff 1991a), for they stress how basic and limited such activity was. The tendency in Western scholarship has been to find nascent capitalism, coded as "market exchange," in the smallest hint of trade. So we find anachronistic categories such as "privatization," "rate of interest,"

"trade balance," "free market," and "international market economy" (e.g., McNutt 1999: 195; Warburton 2003; Thompson 2000: 233; I. Finkelstein 1989; Silver 1983). This is simply an anachronism, for trade does not mean a market form of exchange; such a form requires an extensive network of market relations before it becomes market exchange (Wallerstein 1983), a network that simply did not exist in the ancient world. The appearance of the odd merchant or two and trade between them does not a market economy make. One key example will suffice. During the period of the Roman emperor Diocletian, when transport was much more efficient than in the ancient Near East, it was cheaper to move the same quantity of wheat from one end of the Mediterranean to another, from Syria to Spain, than it was to transport it 120 kilometers (or 75 miles) overland (Anderson 1974: 20). In the earlier periods of the largely landlocked empires of Sumer, Babylonia, and Persia, where the only cost-efficient mode of transport would have been along the rivers, trade was relatively minimal, engaging only two people out of every one hundred. While there is no doubt that money (at least as tokens or weighed metal) and trade certainly did exist, we do not find commodification and the crucial metaphorization and totalization of the market that is necessary for a market economy (see Jameson 1991: 260–78). To attribute either some innate capitalist impulse to human beings, or to suggest that we find market exchange in Jerusalem in the Babylonian and Persian periods (McNutt 1999: 195),[21] either buys into the myth of capitalism or lapses into severe anachronism. Trade, then, was a minor item in the total economy, and certainly nowhere near a driving force. What passes for trade was a very small circulation of luxury goods among a small ruling class facilitated by merchants. What we do find is the limited barter of basic goods between local village communes (Thompson 1992: 179–80; 1999: 118–19),[22] but this turns out to be the reallocation of products of animals and the soil. It can hardly be called trade in the sense of market exchange. Like tribute, however, trade is an indication of a limited extractive economics, one that contributed to the tensions within the sacred economy.

The overarching system was one of allocation, which may be understood as theo-economics. By this I refer to the theological metaphorization of allocation. The first six categories I have outlined, and even tribute at times, are spoken about in theological terms; or rather, it is not possible to imagine such a system without the language of the sacred. This language of the sacred, speaking of everything with reference to Yahweh or God or whomever, is *the* language of this worldview. It is the code in which everything makes sense, to which everything refers. This means that not only are the gods attributed with the powers of production—of land, wombs, seasons, rains, and so on—but they are also the ones who allocate, who are at the center of each regime of allocation. Thus Yahweh, Asshur, or Marduk chooses a people, allocates them land (more to the tyrant and his apparatchiks and less to others), opens and closes wombs, calls the war machine into action and is responsible for its successes and failures, determines kinship structures and the modes of patron-client relations, and establishes and sanctions the collection of tribute (tithe) in the temple.

Succinctly, the sacred economy looks something like this. The fundamental tension existed between the village commune and the temple-city complex. The village commune was an economic and kinship unit, a gens, engaged in agriculture. While the vast majority of the population (some 95 percent) lived in village communes, a much smaller ruling elite, comprising tyrants, religious professionals, and other hangers-on, was based in the temple-city complex. However, in contrast to many reconstructions, the temple-city complex is not the state: the state arose in the tension between village commune and temple-city complex. Indeed, this is the primary form of class conflict, although within this opposition a large variety of types of labor may be found. This relationship was compounded by the existence of a few imperial centers, such as Babylon, Egypt, and Asshur, and in between the village commune and the imperial center the local temple-city complex acted as a buffer and intermediate exploiter. The economy may be described as primarily allocative, operating in terms of regimes of allocation: land, fertility, kinship, war machine, the judiciary, and patron-client relations. The major contradiction of the system lay with the existence of some extractive economics, most notably in tribute and trade. This tension manifested itself directly in the long-running feuds between village commune and temple-city complex. However, the underlying logic was theo-economics; that is, political, social, juridical, and above all economic relations were expressed in terms of the sacred. This sacred economy was remarkably persistent from the Bronze Age until the Roman period (Carter 1999: 255), when a major socioeconomic shift to a slave-based system began.

What I have provided is very much a broad sketch of an economic model that needs to be fleshed out in greater detail. It is also, to begin with, a synchronic analysis that requires a discussion of the various changes that a diachronic analysis is able to provide. However, it seems to me that economic modeling necessarily begins with a synchronic approach since such models cover vast periods.

THE CONTRADICTIONS OF THEO-ECONOMICS

What remains is to ask why the master myth of Genesis–Joshua arose in the first place, especially when the State-in-waiting reflects no known reality in the ancient Near East. Needless to say, this is not the first time such a question has been asked, albeit in different forms. Answers are often some version of a propaganda theory. For instance, for Liverani (2005) it provides the ideology of the returnees from Babylonian exile for a claim to the land, while for Lemche (1998a: 86–132) it is in fact part of a double myth that links exile and exodus in order to provide political propaganda for the Hasmoneans. A second option comes from Philip Davies (1998): because the Hasmoneans created the canon that created "Ancient Israel," this might be called the "clerical fantasy" position, in which a clergy or scribal class dreams of an ideal Israel as a way of expressing their own political aspirations. Another possibility is the more sophisticated "resistance" position of Mark Brett (2000), where the text (at least Genesis) becomes a subtle criticism of an exclusivist imperialist position.

I could go on, but the common point of these and other options is a *conscious* and intentional political and ideological—if not religious—agenda. It is a simple point, but I am interested in the *unconscious* dimension of the text and its relation to its context, as my earlier use of psychoanalysis should have made clear.[23] In this respect I make two points. To begin with, the master myth of Genesis through Joshua is like a dream in which the elements of the sacred economy are rearranged as a fantasy. Further, the tension between the State-in-waiting and its widespread opposition is at a formal level the imaginary resolution of a real contradiction within the sacred economy. If on the first point I rely on Freud, readers will recognize Lévi-Strauss in the second.

As for the first point, rather than the "rationalistic paraphrase" characteristic of so much biblical historiography (Lemche 1988: 7; 1998a: 163), we find that the elements of the sacred economy are rearranged like a fantastic dream. Note that nearly all the regimes of allocation turn up in the master myth in another fashion, but the regimes of extraction are absent. In terms of family and kinship, all I need to do is recall the lengthy discussion of women and the domestic mode of production in chapter 2, as well as the crucial function of tribalization in the Hexateuch. The land is always present, held up as a carrot that seems to swing back and forth between Egypt and Canaan until it is realized in Joshua's conquest and allocation of the land. The war machine is nothing other than the militia that I tracked a little earlier (Althusser's repressive state apparatus). The patron-client regime of allocation shows its face at the level of the tribe, particularly in stories about the leaders of the tribes, in the arrangement for rulers-as-judges in Exodus 18 and in the relationship between Moses and the people. The only form of tribute is one that is understood in terms of allocation, namely, the tithe for the priests; every other form of tribute does not rate a mention. Of course, the overarching role of theo-economics shows up in the figure of Yahweh throughout the master myth.

The interesting question now is this: Why do all the regimes of accumulation turn up and none of the regimes of extraction? Here it is worth noting another absence: the village commune and temple-city complex in the context of empire. The reason for the absence of both groups—regimes of extraction and the tension between village commune and temple-city complex—is because they are both marks of the primary economic tensions of the sacred economy of the ancient Near East. Here I make use of Lévi-Strauss's formula, already noted, that cultural products such as myth are imaginary resolutions of real contradictions. The master myth of the Hexateuch then becomes an effort to deal with this primary social, political, and economic tension, and it does so by excising it from the story. All we have in this master myth are regimes of allocative economics. Everything that generates tension with this structure is absent.

The final question I need to ask is why this tension between allocative and extractive economics, which manifests itself in the conflict between the village commune and the temple-city complex, is a problem that needs to be resolved. The answer is that extractive economics undermine the economics of allocation. Here we come up against the necessary limit of the sacred economy, a limit that enables the sacred economy to function but also hobbles it from full realization: the imposition of control over and extraction of vital necessities from the village commune by the temple-city complex, and then a similar mix of control and extraction by a much larger empire, undermined the logic of the regimes of allocation at the heart of theo-economics.

The master myth then becomes a fantasy in an effort to deal with this tension. It is an attempt, if you like, at a pure theo-economics without its limit, an unfettered allocative economics. But, as Lévi-Strauss has made clear, such a conflict cannot be excised so easily, for an imaginary resolution carries traces of the contradiction with which it deals. In other words, these traces are what we would expect, for no real social and economic contradiction can be removed without leaving such traces. So the contradiction shows up at other levels: it is the assumed background of so many laws and instructions delivered in the wilderness and at Sinai. Above all, it appears in the rebellion by and conflict over women that I explored in chapter 2, and in dealing with a demimonde that will turn out to be a widespread and systematic rebellion against a theocratic tyrant, Moses, as I found in chapter 3. The systematic and widespread rebellion that runs through the Hexateuch is *the formal trace of the excised extractive economics.* The conflict between the theocratic tyranny of the State-in-waiting and rebellion is the displaced trace of the tension between allocative and extractive economics. In the same way that extractive economics is the tension and limit of allocative economics, so also the systematic rebellion of the Hexateuch is the necessary limit of the theocratic tyranny found there.

We can go one step further. It seems to me that the perpetual effort to close down the unending rebellion against the State-in-waiting is also the mark of the impossibility of this myth's realization. Here I want to uncover a deeper logic at the heart of political myths that is still with us today. Each system operates in terms of an ideal or utopian projection of what it might be. The key to realizing that ideal is overcoming some obstruction or other. The catch is that the obstruction or limit is precisely what makes the system work, its necessary limit. Should the ideal be realized, the system would in fact collapse. For this reason the myth attempts an impossible resolution: in order to maintain the belief in the possibility of realizing the ideal, it represents the blockage in narrative form as something that prevents the ideal from being realized (rebellion). Yet at the same time it must represent this blockage rather than just exclude it, for that blockage is the very reason for the existence of the ideal in the first place. This is the contradiction at the heart of the political myth of Genesis–Joshua: its function is to maintain the hope for the realization of the ideal, and yet that hope relies on what blocks that hope from being realized. Should an unfettered theo-economics be realized, the system would collapse.

CHAPTER FIVE

Foreign Policy and the Fantasy
of Israel in Australia

And it is never ending. You never reach the finish line. It keeps getting moved
further ahead. . . . It's like one of those experiences you have and you dream . . .
and you are trying to reach something and you never get there.
—John Howard (quoted in Metherell 2005: 1)

Now it is time for the present to have its say, although it has wanted to
do so for some time. Indeed, the reader will not have missed the way
such present concerns underlie my argument concerning the political myth of the Hebrew Bible. The political myth of Creation to Conquest,
from Paradise to the Promised Land continues to be one of the most powerful political myths, from providing the ideological underpinnings of the
modern nation-state to the passionate battles over Israel and Palestine. In
this chapter and the next two I am interested in the use and abuse of this
political myth, particularly what I call the fantasy of Israel in the foreign
policy of Australia and then the United States. The final chapter steps over
the line and dares to undertake some mythmaking for the Left.

This chapter takes on the negative side of political myth as it manifests
itself in the issue of foreign policy. I am interested in the way the deeper
logic of the political myth of Genesis–Joshua, what I call the fantasy of Israel,
has emerged in Australian foreign policy statements regarding Islam, Judaism, and Christianity, or, in concrete foreign policy terms, majority Muslim
states, majority Christian states, and Israel. I have called it the fantasy of

Israel because it projects a certain fantasy that must not be realized, for its realization would be disastrous. Yet it keeps alive the hope that the fantasy may indeed be realized by means of generating opposition and rebellion; if only that opposition could be overcome, it tells us, the fantasy will become reality. My specific concern is the baleful way in which this logic of the fantasy of Israel has been used in Australian foreign policy and how that policy touches on, or reveals, other dimensions of foreign and domestic policy.

My argument has three stages. The first is to peer closely at a number of foreign policy statements by the former conservative Liberal-National government of Australia.[1] Then I move to some key texts in the later part of the political myth of the Hexateuch, particularly those that wrestle with the tension between a peaceful ideal and the perpetual threat of being knifed in your sleep. The fact that we find the very same tension in the foreign policy statements of the Australian government as we do in the later part of the Hexateuch leads me to suggest that the deep connection between the biblical texts and those statements may well be found in the psychoanalytic notion of fantasy, which is itself the key to the theory of political myth that I have developed in this book. Fantasy, which in this context has both limit and promise, is not the final word, and so I close by exploring what fantasy does not allow us to see and hope for.

FOREIGN POLICY

Given my propensity for diving straight in, let us see what the Australian government papers have to say. I need to point out for those readers fortunate enough not to know too much about Australian politics that most of these statements and papers come from the foreign minister, equivalent to the secretary of state in the United States and the foreign secretary in the United Kingdom. I have selected some by the rather pedestrian former foreign minister Alexander Downer (who requested his speech writers to write each sentence as a paragraph so he doesn't get confused or lose his way) and his more erudite predecessor, Labor's Gareth Evans, (who has long fancied himself as a future U.N. secretary-general).

Apart from the fascinating dross of economic relations—more prominent since the Department of Foreign Affairs was merged with the Department of Trade in 1988, which is itself revealing as to the ultimate concerns of Australian foreign policy—what soon emerges is a distinct bifurcation. Here is Gareth Evans, Labor's foreign minister until 1996, speaking in Jerusalem at a dinner hosted by Foreign Minister Shimon Peres on July 10, 1995:

As I come to the end of what has been a welcome return to a country which means so much to many Australians, I feel reassured that the idealism which gave rise to the birth of Israel has not diminished among this country's present leaders. The present Israeli government has demonstrated a strong commitment in principle to the peace process, and I hope that commitment can be sustained in practice through all the trials that lie ahead. (Evans 1995a)

And then again, a few months later in the same year at the Sam Cohen Memorial Lecture in Melbourne on September 10, 1995:

But Rabin knows with his head, as David Ben Gurion did so many years before him, that Israel had to trade land for peace—that it could not be simultaneously Jewish, democratic and occupy the whole of Biblical Israel. And he had believed that land *could* be traded for peace, albeit slowly, cautiously, and giving away at each stage no more than absolutely had to be given away. (Evans 1995b)

Already the tension between an ideal Israel at peace and a very different image of continuing tension begins to show itself. Of course, I am not going to let the reference to biblical Israel pass me by. Now let us hear from Alexander Downer almost ten years later (note the paragraph structure):

Above all, we admire the strength and courage of Israelis, for these are attributes Australians see in ourselves.

Australians share the hopes and aspirations of Israelis for a better, secure and prosperous future and we are prepared to stand by our friends, do what we can, to ensure we reach this goal. (Downer 2004a)

Then also from 2004:

I have just completed a series of high-level meetings in Jerusalem with the leaders of Israel.

I reaffirmed to Israeli President Moshe Katsav, Prime Minister Ariel Sharon and Foreign Minister Silvan Shalom, and to other Israeli leaders, the abiding strength of Australia's friendship with Israel and our commitment to its right to live in security and at peace with all its neighbours. (Downer 2004b)[2]

An ideal, peaceful Israel? Australia's solidarity with their close friends, Israel? Well, the very same website, the same government department, the

Department of Foreign Affairs and Trade headed by Alexander Downer until 2007, also had the following advice for travelers to Israel on July 9, 2004:

In view of continuing tensions in the Middle East, the ongoing risk of terrorism and the level of violence in Israel and the Occupied Territories, Australians should consider carefully their need to travel to Israel at this time.

Australians in Israel should exercise extreme caution particularly in commercial and public areas, and should take into account the overall security situation when planning their activities.

The overall security situation in Israel remains tense and the risk of indiscriminate terror attacks remains high. Targets in the past have included areas where large numbers of people gather, such as hotels, pedestrian promenades, street shopping malls, restaurants, cafes and other places of entertainment, as well as buses and bus stations.

Australians should avoid non-essential travel to Israel's border areas where security incidents have also occurred. There are live minefields in the border areas with Lebanon and Syria, and in the West Bank. Some minefields may not be clearly marked. Australians are advised to travel only on established roads or trails.

Australians should not travel to the West Bank or the Gaza Strip. Australians in the West Bank and the Gaza Strip should take the opportunity to leave as soon as possible where it is safe to do so.

Australians in Israel, the West Bank or Gaza Strip are urged to monitor closely local media reporting of developments in Israel, the Occupied Territories and the region. If instructed by local authorities to take measures that will remove them from harm, Australians should heed this advice. In the event that your locality is threatened directly by military action, terrorism or civil disorder, Australians are advised to maintain a low profile, stay away from strategic locations, and in the absence of other advice remain indoors.

Israeli military operations in cities and towns in the West Bank and Gaza continue to occur at short notice and prolonged military incursions are possible. Checkpoints may be set up or closed at any time. During any military operation it is possible for the Israeli Defence Forces (IDF) to declare the area a closed military zone. Any civilians found in the area in breach of this order can then be arrested, detained in prison and, where considered appropriate, deported.

The capacity of the Australian Embassy to assist Australians who choose to enter or remain in the West Bank and Gaza may be limited by circumstances beyond the control of the Embassy. (Department of Foreign Affairs and Trade 2004)

You get the picture: the idealism of the birth of Israel that is so important for many Australians versus indiscriminate violence and terror of which Australians must be wary; the shared aspirations of both Israelis and Australians for "a better, secure and prosperous future" versus "prolonged military incursions"; a strong commitment to the peace process versus "indiscriminate terror attacks" in shopping malls and bus stations; "the hopes and aspirations" of Israelis and Australians versus live minefields. In other words, we have a contradiction: while the various statements and speeches from Evans and Downer have stressed the solidarity of Australians with Israelis in the aspirations for an ideal and peaceful Israel, the travel warnings depict Israel as a violent mess.[3] As long as the threat of violence can be contained as an external threat, the ideal of a peaceful Israel remains in place. At this level, Evans and Downer, at least when they were speaking, seem to be on safe ground: if it were not for that external violence, Israel would be at peace. This is where the text I emphasized in the travel warnings becomes significant, for here we find an implicit recognition that the violence and disruption come not from outside Israel, but are just as much internal to Israel itself.

BIBLICAL ISRAEL

Let me now juxtapose the tension between these texts from DFAT, as the Department of Foreign Affairs and Trade is affectionately known, with a few passages from the last part of the political myth of Genesis–Joshua, stitching them into the preceding quotations through Evans's reference to "biblical Israel." After the grand narrative in Joshua of crossing the Jordan River and systematically conquering the land of Canaan, the tribes gather (or at least the remaining seven do so) in order to divide up the land.

> Then the whole congregation of the people of Israel assembled at Shiloh, and set up the tent of meeting there; *the land lay subdued before them.* (Joshua 18:1, emphasis added)

> Thus Yahweh gave to Israel all the land which he swore to give to their fathers; and having taken possession of it, they settled there. And *Yahweh gave them rest on every side* just as he had sworn to their fathers; not one of all their enemies had withstood them, for Yahweh had given all their enemies

into their hands. *Not one of all the good promises which Yahweh had made to the house of Israel had failed; all came to pass.* (Joshua 21:43–45, emphasis added)

"The land lay subdued before them. . . . Yahweh gave them rest on every side. . . . Not one of all the good promises which Yahweh had made to the house of Israel had failed; all came to pass." Yet, just when we think we have an image of a peaceful Israel, one in which the land is subdued and may be calmly divided between the tribes, we find another picture, that the danger of being knifed in your sleep has not abated, that there is tension: "But the Jebusites, the inhabitants of Jerusalem, the people of Judah could not drive out; so the Jebusites dwell with the people of Judah at Jerusalem to this day" (Joshua 15:63).

Note where this text comes: not after the preceding two quotations, with their images of a subdued and restful land, but before, in the narrative of conquest itself. And if we think this is but a glitch in the total picture, that Jerusalem in some way remains exempt from the statement that there was rest on every side, then an even earlier text spikes such a compromise assessment. In Joshua 13:1–7, when the man himself is already "old and advanced in years" (13:1),[4] we find a long list of peoples who remain in the land, who remain to be driven out: Philistines (in all of the five traditional cities of Gaza, Ashdod, Ashkelon, Gath, and Ekron), Geshurites, Avvim, Canaanites, Sidonians, Gebalites, and all the inhabitants of the hill country from Lebanon to Mis'rephothma'im.

However, when we turn from the last lines of Joshua, barely passing across the border into the book of Judges (which I will now rope into the political myth of the Hexateuch), we find that the first verses of Judges come in for what at first appears to be a chilling reality check. For just when the book of Joshua finishes with the image of rest and peace after a grueling conquest, the first chapter of Judges doles out a telling refrain in a partial roll call of the tribes: "But the people of Benjamin did not drive out . . ." (Judges 1:21); "Manasseh did not drive out . . ." (1:27); "And Ephraim did not drive out . . ." (1:29); "Zebulun did not drive out . . ." (1:30); "Asher did not drive out . . ." (1:31); "Naphtali did not drive out . . ." (1:33); until we get to the final item in the list: "The Amorites pressed the Danites back into the hill country" (1:34). Note the inversion: syntactically the Danites have shuffled over to become the object of the verb, the Amorites pressing them rather than the Danites failing to drive them out.

Apart from the Amorites, who are not driven out? The inhabitants of the plain of Judah with their iron chariots (Judges 1:19); the Asherites, particularly in Acco, Sidon, Ahlab, Achzib, Helbah, Aphik, and Rehob (1:31–32); the inhabitants of Bethshemesh and Bethanath (1:33); but mostly Canaanites in a list of named towns and their unnamed but connected villages: Bethshean, Taanach, Dor, Ibleam, and Megiddo (1:27); Gezer (1:29); Kitron, and Nahalol (1:30). Of course, I did not really need to repeat the list in all its detail, but it does hammer home the contrast with the image in Joshua of peace and rest all about, following a victorious "conquest."

I must admit, however, that I am guilty of some selective reading, for I have focused on the second half of Judges 1, where the tide of Israelite dominance of the land ebbs noticeably. If we read back through the chapter, we will notice that it begins with all of the huff and puff of armies marching about the countryside driving out various peoples. Or rather, Judah, with the assistance of Simeon, does so under the aerial support of a divine promise (Judges 1:2), and they systematically clear their respective territories. Given the closing picture of rest in Joshua, the continued conflict is in itself a problem, but what sticks out is how quickly flow turns to ebb, for even with Yahweh's support, Judah can't quite overcome the chariots of the plain: "And Yahweh was with Judah, and he took possession of the hill country, but he could not drive out the inhabitants of the plain, because they had chariots of iron" (Judges 1:19).

The tension, in other words, between rest and conflict that I identified in Joshua is, if anything, intensified in Judges 1, with the weight shifting perceptibly to internecine conflict. However, there are a couple of verses that epitomize the tension that is by now becoming inescapable, so let me quote them:

> And the men of Judah fought against Jerusalem, and took it, and smote it with the edge of the sword, and set the city on fire. (Judges 1:8)

> But the people of Benjamin did not drive out the Jebusites who dwelt in Jerusalem; so the Jebusites have dwelt with the people of Benjamin in Jerusalem to this day. (Judges 1:21)

The verse I quoted earlier from Joshua now comes back to haunt the text: "But the Jebusites, the inhabitants of Jerusalem, the people of Judah could not drive out; so the Jebusites dwell with the people of Judah at Jerusalem to this day" (Joshua 15:63).

What we have in the text, in sequence, is that Judah did not take Jerusalem and then it did, but then somehow Jerusalem and the Jebusites survived the smiting and burning to defy the Benjaminites a few verses later. Now we could do a number of things here, such as take a vote (two against and one for the taking of Jerusalem), or resort to sources and their problems, or read the contradiction as the hint to an alternative history of Israel, or read it as the trigger in the text for an allegorical interpretation, or as further signs of the dialogic voice of the Deuteronomist, or as the first marks of the tension between coherence and countercoherence, or perhaps even the beginnings of a Greimasian square in which the only option not covered is that Benjamin did indeed drive out the inhabitants of Jerusalem. Needless to say, in a text as overdetermined as the Hebrew Bible, these and other options have in fact been pursued at various times.[5]

I want to suggest that something else is going on here, that the sharp tension between a Jerusalem conquered and one that resists conquest reverberates throughout the texts of Joshua and Judges. But the surprising thing, for me at least, is the way a very similar tension appeared in the statements I quoted from the Australian Department of Foreign Affairs and Trade, between an ideal of peace and rest after the present battles and an image of continued and unresolved violence.

THE FANTASY OF ISRAEL OR A CHRISTIAN FANTASY?

I want to stress that *both* are images, ideals even: a restful peace *and* unresolved violence. For we all too readily assume that one is an ideal (guess which one) and the other brutal reality, one a dream and the other a fearful waking from that dream. This point is crucial for my final argument concerning the fantasy of Israel, which will unfold in a moment. What I am after here is the deeper structure that makes some sense of the surprising similarity between the tensions in the biblical material I have discussed and the statements from DFAT, specifically their function in the Australian political context.

First, however, my usage of the term *fantasy of Israel* relies on my earlier discussion of fantasy. Without revivifying that discussion in all its gory detail here, let me repeat my definition: fantasy produces the fantasmatic kernel in a radically synchronous fashion, a fact that it conceals by means of a diachronic narrative. So in what follows I am after the way fantasy works in Australia's foreign policy regarding Israel, the fantasmatic kernel, and its concealment.[6]

The first take on the fantasy of Israel looks rather straightforward: violence very easily becomes the fantasmatic kernel, the unbearable trauma that generates an ideal Israel. The notion of an ideal Israel, at peace and rest, necessarily relies on the trauma of continued violence in order to be an ideal at all. To put it slightly differently, the ideal of a peaceful Israel is a fantasy since it necessarily hides the fantasmatic kernel of structural violence on which that ideal is based. While there is some truth in this argument—and it may well be extended to any notion of peace (the infamous Pax Romana or indeed the joke of the current Pax Americana)—it is a horrible truth: peace as we know it builds itself upon a whole range of concealed and structural forms of violence, whether in terms of race, class, gender, sexuality, or environmental degradation.

This argument is valid as far as it goes; however, we can go a good deal further, for one of the catches with my rapid connection to the fantasmatic kernel is that the kernel itself cannot in fact be represented so easily, and the sad truth is that violence and conflict are all too readily represented—in fact overrepresented. But what if peace itself were this kernel, this unbearable truth that cannot be faced at the risk of coming to pieces? For peace is, properly speaking, unrepresentable, beyond our experience, knowledge, and even imagination. Is this not what the Garden of Eden and its politicized double, the Promised Land, stand for? Is it not a peaceful state without tension, contradiction, and conflict, in short, an antinarrative space? For this reason, for the sake of the narrative itself, the transgression of the first human beings is absolutely necessary. We can put this question quite directly in relation to the fantasy of Israel: What if the perpetual warfare were to come to a halt? What if the military incursions in Lebanon, Syria, the Palestinian Occupied Territory were to cease? What if the Palestinian insurrection were to end, with all its acts of guerrilla warfare? What if the opposition to Israel from states such as Iran and Syria were to dissolve into coexistence? Would not the tensions internal to Israel brutally surface, between Jews and Arabs, Ashkenazi and Sephardic Jews, ultra-Orthodox and liberal and so many shades in between, working and ruling classes, Left and Right, rich and poor, those who wish to leave Israel and those who wish to "go up"? Such a peace would bring Israelis face to face with the unbearable truth of internal tension and violence.

Thus far, to put it in terms of the opposition between form and content, I have been more concerned with the formal links between the fantasy of Israel in the Hebrew Bible and the unwitting tensions of Australian foreign policy statements. As far as content is concerned, I will risk stating the obvious: the content of the fantasy of Israel in the hands of Australian politicians is not the same as the fantasy of Israel in the Hebrew Bible, nor indeed is it the same as the fantasy within the hopes of modern Israel itself.

So what is the nature of that fantasy in Australia, or at least among its politicians? On the surface, it appears to be a sharing in the struggle of modern Israel to exist in the face of immense hardships, a close friendship that is cast in personal, political, and economic terms. So, for instance, during his long and divisive reign, the conservative prime minister John Howard (2001a) described himself in the Australian parliament on February 7, 2001, as "a longstanding friend of Israel," assuring himself that many others would accept the same label. During his visit to Israel from April 29 to May 2, 2000, he said, "[The] personal affection I have for the state of Israel, the personal regard I have for the Jewish people of the world, will never be diminished. It is something I hold dearly, something I value as part of my being and as part of what I have tried to do with my life" (quoted in Rubenstein 2000). Again, before the Australia-Israel Chamber of Commerce on August 18, 1999, he spoke of "[my association,] long pre-dating my entry into public life, with the Jewish people of Australia and the profound admiration that I've had for the State of Israel and what that country has achieved since its formation in 1948 in such adversarial and difficult circumstances" (Howard 1999). Alexander Downer went one further, suggesting on his visit to Israel in early 2004, "I could almost be an honorary Jew" (quoted in Tommer 2004). Indeed, though his status as an "honorary Jew" may have been a matter of contention, later in 2004 Downer was declared an "honorary Zionist" by Gurion Meltzer, chairman of the Israel-Australia Chamber of Commerce (O'Loughlin 2004). In these statements Howard and Downer pushed well beyond a simple friendship: "profound admiration" and "longstanding" friendship become "part of my being" to the point of being an "honorary Jew" or at least an "honorary Zionist."

This existential identity translates into economic and political issues quickly enough, the most significant mark being Australia's move away from its previous practice of abstaining from voting for United Nations resolutions against Israeli aggression. From the late 1990s, under the direction of the Howard government, Australia's representative at the United Nations began to vote with the handful of nation-states, clustered around the United States, that opposed such resolutions. Let me give one example among many: when the United Nations in 2004 endorsed the opinion of the International Court of Justice condemning the barrier being built in the Occupied Palestinian Territory, only Israel, the United States, Australia, the Marshall Islands, Micronesia, and Palau voted against the endorsement (Overington 2004). Indeed, John Howard (1999) has said that he is proud his government opposed such measures in the U.N., claiming his record on this to be "profoundly sympathetic and understanding towards the Government and the people of Israel."[7]

In this light Chanan Reich's (2002) book *Australia and Israel: An Ambiguous Relationship* comes as a welcome reminder that the relationship has not always been so chummy (see also Levey and Mendes 2005). Although Reich's book often falls short—for instance, with the cheap argument that personal gain was the motive for not supporting crucial Israeli interests— he does show how the Conservative Menzies government of 1939–41 was not in favor of Jews fleeing to Palestine from Europe in increasing numbers. On paper at least Australia supported the establishment of the state of Israel, and yet in the 1950s the Australian government tended to follow the lines of British and U.S. foreign policy that were concerned also with Arab interests and not so much those of the new state of Israel. Only in the Suez War of 1956 did Australia, along with England and France, begin to develop a distinctly pro-Israeli policy that has been characteristic of Australian governments since. In fact, going beyond the scope of Reich's book, before Howard's Liberal-National government, the Labor years of Bob Hawke (1982–91) exhibited the strongest pro-Israel stance of any Australian government.

Reich's book is a useful counterweight to texts such as Howard Nathan's "Bonded by History" (2000), which argues that there has been a long commitment to Israel by Australia in light of its commitment of troops to the area since 1885 (before federation). Some 12,000 dead and many more injured out of 210,000 troops ensured a bond of flesh-become-soil, suggests Nathan, that makes Australia both a friend of Israel and a voice to be heard in the region. His passing comments to Australian interests obscure the fact that Australian policy was very much tied to that of Britain. Indeed, many epitaphs to the Great War—in churches, at the center of small country towns, and in the major cities—still have the slogan "for King and Empire" etched into their stonework. Early in the third millennium such allegiance has shifted decisively to an aggressive pro-U.S. policy, as the voting patterns in the United Nations show. For all its shortcomings, Reich's book reminds us that the picture presented by John Howard and Alexander Downer of a deep, long-lasting, and heartfelt friendship with Israel began only a decade after the state of Israel emerged.

However, all of this scratches only the surface, it seems to me, setting in historical context at least the repeated affirmation of a close friendship with Israel, a sharing in the fantasy of Israel. I am more interested in what lies beneath the surface, however close to the topsoil it might be, and here I need to consider closely a few comments by the longtime troika of the conservative government from 1996 to 2007: John Howard, Alexander Downer, and the treasurer for many years, Peter Costello. Let me begin with John Howard at a press conference on October 8, 2001, soon after the destruction of the World Trade Center's twin towers in New York on September 11 by two hijacked planes:

> We should never forget the obscenity, the evil of the attack on New York and Washington on the 11th of September. We should never forget the deaths of thousands of innocent people. We should not forget the fact that hundreds of those who died were of the Islamic faith and in no way is the American attack an attack upon Islam. It is an attack on terrorism and an attack on evil and I know that Islamic people around the world, not least Australians of Islamic faith, to whom I again extend a hand of fellow Australian citizenship and mateship as united as other Australians of different faiths and indeed of no faiths are in wanting this country to stand beside our American friends and Americans allies in an hour in which, despite their immense power and immense authority, they need the support and the understanding of their friends. . . . *It is not a fight between Christianity and Judaism on the one side and Islam on the other side.* I've said in the Parliament and I repeat it again that barbism [*sic*] has no ethnicity and evil has no religion and this is a contest, fight, between those who oppose the evil of terrorism where ever they live, whatever country they are loyal to and whatever faith they follow and those who do not. (Howard 2001b, emphasis added)

Now, for all his tumbling, unstructured sentences, for all his futile efforts to suggest that neither religion nor even ethnicity was an issue in the so-called war on terror, in this speech Howard fell foul when he stated that "evil has no religion." It is all too easy to respond, Well, is not evil itself a religious term, one loaded with an inescapable theological content? But in this respect, Howard has always been an easy target, and his well-known fear and dismissal of the "elites"—journalists, intellectuals, and the like—was predicated on the fact that his arguments rarely fared well under scrutiny (his appeal for many years lay precisely in this "ordinary Joe" image). But what intrigues me in this quotation is what lies on the other side of the negative: "It is not a fight between Christianity and Judaism on the one side and Islam on the other side." What is interesting here is not so much the negative itself, but the way it is cast: Christianity and Judaism somehow team up—the oft-cited and highly problematic Judeo-Christian tradition that will appear soon in Peter Costello's speech—against Islam. Why this formulation of the negative? Why not Christianity versus Islam (the position that defined the Middle Ages), or perhaps every religion versus Islam? Of course, what Howard has done is cite the three religions of the book, those that share the Hebrew Bible as sacred scripture in some sense. While there appears to be no squabble between Judaism and Christianity, the odd one out here is Islam, and Howard has trodden carefully without stating the more common formulation of the opposition, namely, the West (Christianity and Judaism) versus Islam (note the quiet disappearance of the old sparring partner, the "East"). We could of course object that the struggle between these Semitic religions shows the unwitting truth of the story of the conflict between Isaac and Ishmael in Genesis, that it is really a struggle between brothers and is therefore the most lethal of such struggles.[8] The problem with this move is that it all too easily becomes a conservative one, turning a limited struggle over land, power, and nationalisms into an age-old religious conflict.

Yet what Howard effectively did in this speech, precisely through his negative, is point to a rift between Christianity and Judaism on the one side and Islam on the other in the contemporary political, cultural, and religious landscape. This was consistent with his avowals of a deep and personal friendship with Israel and the Jewish community in Australia, but it did have profound ramifications for foreign policy. All of which showed up in the voting patterns of Australia in the U.N., the willingness of the Howard government to send troops to invade Muslim majority states such as Afghanistan and Iraq, and the mistreatment of Iraqi and Afghan asylum seekers fleeing from the same regimes with which Australia had gone to war. I would add the fear of Indonesia that resonates in Australian foreign policy, especially since Indonesia is the largest Muslim majority state in the world and barely a spit from Darwin. Domestically, Howard was desperate to avert an anti-Muslim backlash, given the fact that Islam is the fastest growing religion in Australia, with approximately two hundred thousand largely conservative citizens, but internationally it meant an increasing distance from majority Muslim states.

What we had in this speech, then, was an initial separation between Christianity and Judaism on one hand and Islam on the other. Howard could of course protest that I have read more into his comments than is warranted. However, what was implicit in his comments became explicit in those of his well-heeled foreign minister. To begin with, Alexander Downer

(2002) also parroted an avowal of the peace-loving religion of Islam: "It's enormously important that western countries go out and argue the case that Islam is a great force for peace, it's a peaceful religion—a peace-loving religion—it's part of the broader tradition of religions [to] which Christianity and Judaism belong as well."

Well, at least the moderate parts of Islam. For in a presentation at the International Conference on Islam and the West on August 15, 2003 (for the full text, see the appendix), Downer took the obvious and well-tried line of distinguishing between moderates and extremists. This distinction formed the basis of his response in this speech to Samuel Huntington's (1996) thesis of the "clash of civilizations," a clash driven by transnational religious identities that, argued Huntingdon, will become more and more intense. Of course, Downer sided with the moderates, urging cooperation and tolerance. It all sounded wonderfully liberal and calm, but far more interesting was the way Downer characterized each side of his divide. The extremists, he said, are violent, full of hateful rhetoric, willing to sacrifice innocent lives to their cause—terrorists, in short. But then they also become the proponents of the *shar'ia*, Islamic law, of Taliban-style theocracies, indeed of Islamic parties in general, whose vote, thankfully, in Indonesia (his preferred example) is declining. So much was to be expected, but not so the company these Muslim terrorists keep, at least in a historical perspective (and I leave the paragraph format intact):

> It echoes the violent "propaganda by deed" philosophy of some late 19th century European anarchists.
>
> Or like Baader Meinhof or the Italian Red Brigade, Al-Qaeda and Jemaah Islamiyah, don't care that their violence is unlikely to produce immediate results in terms of their political program; it is the act of violence which is important.
>
> All of this serves to underline the fact that what we face today is not some new clash between civilisations.
>
> Rather, it is the age-old clash between moderates and extremists; between tolerance and intolerance; between those who uphold the integrity of their faith and those prepared to kill innocents in its name. (Downer 2003a)

Anarchists, revolutionary Marxists, and Islamic militants all link arms, less for the sake of a cause than for the desire to engage in the act of violence itself (one suspects that this is, for Downer, the definition of revolution). Now, apart from the fact that the anarchists and Marxists would be surprised to find a gun-toting Muslim fundamentalist or two in their midst, I have left one other character out of this motley group: Huntington himself. Here is Downer: "In particular, Indonesia's two largest Islamic organisations were central to the successful transition to democracy—which if you believe *the extremists or Huntington for that matter*, is an alien, western value, incompatible with Islam" (Downer 2003a, emphasis added). And then again: "Certainly much of the rhetoric used by the extremists echoes the [*sic*] Huntington's theme of irreconcilable cultural differences between Islam and West" (Downer 2003a). Huntingdon, it appears, shares with the extremists, that is, the terrorists, the idea that in the sharp divide between the West and Islam (not the East) democracy is of one and not the other, that the frail plant will wither and die in the transition. I do not make this point lightly, for the moderate Downer has set himself up to disagree with Huntington, and so Huntington's position on the clash of civilizations, on the fundamental religious and cultural differences between Islam and the West, must be extreme, or rather extremist. Where it comes to the crunch, at the level of syntax—"the extremists or Huntingdon for that matter"—they are now on the same side of the fence.

Who, then, are on the other side of the fence, on Downer's side? The moderates, of course, but also the pluralists, democrats, and tolerant ones, committed to evolutionary—rather than that dreaded revolutionary—political change. Above all, at least in the context of this speech, Downer (2003a) found himself in the midst of millions of Muslims, since most Muslims are moderates: "By and large the Islam practiced by the majority of Muslims in South East Asia is generally moderate, pluralist in character, and largely tolerant in outlook." Further, in light of the increasing cooperation between majority Muslim states and non-Muslim states, particularly in the fight against terrorism, we find, at least in Downer's vision, a transnational and transreligious coalition. Moderates of the world unite! It is very much a liberal vision of unity in individual difference:

> It must help us to highlight an Islam that we know is practised by the majority of the world's Muslims, including those in Australia; strong in its faith, proud in its traditions, but willing to engage with people of other religions and cultures on the basis of mutual respect. . . . We must recognise that while our prayers might be different our hopes and our fears are more often than not very similar; that values of openness, tolerance, and democratic principles are not things that divide us but thing [*sic*] we share. (Downer 2003a)

This is the true faith of Muslims, at least according to Downer, a faith misappropriated by extremists. But I want to pick up another element that runs against this picture. On a number of occasions Downer somewhat nervously mentioned the evidence of an increasing awareness of Muslim identity, which shows up in greater religious observance and dress codes, particularly among the young. He tried to get away from the implications of his observation, but then he let slip that the extremists might in fact be a "sizeable minority." But just when he was about to be caught in a trap of his own making, he slipped out, suggesting that real moderates, the real democrats, are not so religious after all:

> It is also worth remembering that for many of these countries Islam may be an important characteristic, but it is not necessarily the defining one.
>
> Indonesia, the Philippines, Thailand and Malaysia are also modern, increasingly open economies, with a record of moderate secularism and increasingly vibrant democratic traditions and institutions. (Downer 2003a)

"Vibrant democratic traditions and institutions" are now the result of a moderate secularism that goes hand in hand with an open economy. Here he touched on a very different perception of the development of the state under capitalism, namely, that it is a necessarily secular state for which religion is by no means the cultural dominant. My suspicion is that this is what he would prefer: rather than the increasing devotion and Muslim identity in Southeast Asia, a potential recruiting ground for the sizable minority of "extremists," he would prefer to see Islam fade before the secular drive of modern capitalism, for this is what is modern, open, vibrant, and, of course, moderate. Deep down, Downer was apprehensive of the close link between religion and politics that shows up so strongly with Islam. Implicit here, but quite explicit in the speech I will consider in a moment, is the sense that religion should have no truck with politics, that religious leaders and institutions should keep to their business and leave politicians to theirs.

I have tarried with Downer's speech for a reason: although it appears to espouse cooperation with the moderate majority of Islam, this picture collides head-on with his vision of Christianity. Despite his carefully cultivated image as an "eloquent" moderate, he was (and still is, I presume) an archconservative. The friction is particularly rough at two points: a moderate plural, tolerant, and open—that is, a liberal—Islam, and the more preferable democratic secularism of some Southeast Asian nation-states that signals a move beyond Islam. But for Christianity neither is an option, at least according to the foreign minister. Let me pick up his speech at the Sir Thomas Playford Annual Lecture (August 27, 2003; see appendix). Here Downer made it quite clear that a liberal, tolerant, and plural Christianity is not acceptable; it is, in fact, just a little too close to secularism and the loss of the moral basis for society.

The one point where he did echo the speech on Islam was where he decried the annoying tendency of church leaders to make political pronouncements. Rather than seeking "popular political causes or cheap headlines," they should stick to their central role of "providing spiritual comfort and moral guidance to the community" (Downer 2003b). But it seems that this was a problem only when he disagreed with what they said, when they dared to criticize the Liberal-National coalition government on issues such as the refusal of asylum seekers on the sv *Tampa* (see below), the invasion of Iraq in 2002, or the increased threat of "terrorism" from Australia's slavish support of the so-called war on terror. In fact, it is quite acceptable for the Christian churches to support the government on these matters, as well as to provide the moral underpinnings of society, for "without consistent moral teaching and example from bodies like the churches, how can most Australians be expected to behave selflessly or consider the common good and abide by any kind of social contract?" (Downer 2003b). You may be forgiven for thinking that Downer was commenting on debates of the nineteenth century, when the first signs of secularism caused great concern among church leaders and politicians. But no, this speech took place in the early twenty-first century, when an unusually high proportion of politicians belonged to the Parliamentary Christian Fellowship, listening carefully to what the churches told their political leaders and community as a whole (see Maddox 2005).

The real problem, then, is secularism. It is fine, in fact desirable, for Muslim majority states to become increasingly secular, but not Christian states such as Australia. In this case secularism means the erosion of the moral fabric of society, loss of direction, the abandoning of absolutes in favor of relativity, and, of course, unwelcome political comments from church leaders. In short, it is a kind of "ecclesiastical postmodernism" (Downer 2003b). The cause of the problem lies with the churches themselves, since their leaders are just too far down the liberal theological path for Downer's liking. Or, as he put it, "Uncertainty or disbelief in the fundamental tenets of Christianity are [sic] commonplace among senior clergy" (Downer 2003b). In order to fill the vacuum, these church leaders take up social work, environmental causes, feminist and gay agendas, indigenous rights, and popular politicking—precisely those things that challenged the fantasy of the Howard junta. The result: low church attendance, a significant loss of confidence in the Church, and the eroding of the moral fabric of society. What Downer would have liked the churches to do is precisely what he feared was happening in majority Muslim states: recover their conservative roots and belief in fundamental teachings. In this light, Downer noted approvingly the increase in Pentecostal, Evangelical, and Catholic youth movements, as well as televised services for the old faithful. Such young people are firm, sincere, and proud of their convictions, and their religious observance is notable (although he didn't mention their dress codes). Thankfully, noted Downer, this increased religious observance is closely connected with a growing conservatism among young people, who seem to have gone back to their grandparents' belief systems.

So conservative and proud young Christians in a nation-state such as Australia are fine, but not in Muslim majority states; moderate secularism is welcome in Muslim states, but a lamentable source of moral decline in Australia; liberal, plural, and open religious belief and practice are preferable in Islam, but not in Christianity; the support by clerics of conservative government policies is what we need in Australia but not in Southeast Asia. For all Downer's earlier pronouncements of a "peace-loving" religion, for all John Howard's comments on a common front, they thought and acted with a distinct division between Christianity and Islam.

But what of Judaism? I have left perhaps the most precious statement of Downer's until last. The most telling sign, he suggested, of the Christian churches losing their way is the debate during the past forty years concerning the resurrection of Christ, something he holds as a central tenet of Christianity, an absolute that cannot be gainsaid. And then he catches himself, only to slip further: "Of course it is possible to believe in God in some sense, or other, without believing in the resurrection, *as many good Jewish and Muslim Australians do*" (Downer 2003b, emphasis added). We have come a long way from Downer's claim to feeling like an "honorary Jew" or indeed his adoption as an "honorary Zionist." Now we are in troubled waters, for the resurrection of Christ does indeed mark Christianity off from both Islam and Judaism. Does this mean that all those politicians in the Parliamentary Christian Fellowship cannot at the core of their beliefs see eye to eye with other faiths? What of all those conservative religious young people? Jews and Muslims make it in, but in through the back door, as in some way second-class believers.

What we have, then, is not merely a separation between Christianity and Judaism on the one hand and Islam on the other (as Howard implied), but now the elevation of Christianity above the other two. So far, however, I have relied on just one dreadful statement from Alexander Downer, but we don't need to look too far for an outright statement of the superiority of Christianity, and that came in a speech by the then federal treasurer, Peter Costello, on May 29, 2004, at the National Day of Thanksgiving at Scots Church, Melbourne (see appendix for full text). Here he did three things that bluntly hammered home the slips, strange comments, and half-concealed assumptions of Howard and Downer: he slammed the Muslims through the Islamic Council of Victoria, appropriated Judaism for Christianity, and then peddled his own vision of a Christian Australia that is remarkably similar to the one of Howard I will discuss soon.

The setting of his speech was consciously and overtly Christian, a church with a long Presbyterian heritage, but it was also one that rubbed Muslims the wrong way. Costello was quite conscious of the fact that at the time of his address the Islamic Council of Victoria had a case before the Victorian Civil and Administrative Tribunal under Victoria's Racial and Religious Tolerance Act of 2001.[9] Not one to be diplomatic or even offer some form of resolution of the issues, precisely because he had been criticized before the event for appearing there, he came out swinging: "I do not think that we should resolve differences about religious views in our community with lawsuits between the different religions. Nor do I think that the object of religious harmony will be promoted by organizing witnesses to go along to the meetings of other religions to collect evidence for the purpose of later litigation" (Costello 2004). Further, immediately after making this comment, he raised the issue of violence and terrorism: *that*, of course, should be dealt with swiftly in a court of secular law. But it is the quick shift in the structure of his speech from criticizing the Islamic Council's action to the issue of terrorism that makes the oblique connection. In this context, Costello's earlier observation became all the more sinister. Commenting on the fact that Christianity came to Australia with the first British prison ships, he observed, "If the Arab traders that brought Islam to Indonesia had brought Islam to Australia and settled, or spread their faith, amongst the indigenous population our country today would be vastly different. Our laws, our institutions, our economy would all be vastly different" (Costello 2004). Thankfully for Costello this did not happen; instead, the "single most decisive feature that determined the way it [Australia] developed was the Judaeo-Christian-Western tradition" (Costello 2004).

This is a curious conjunction. Elsewhere he tended to stick with "Judaeo-Christian tradition," but in this case, precisely when he spoke of the possibility that Australia might have been "vastly different"—that is, Muslim—he tacked "Western" on the end to come up with a heavy triple hyphen. And what of that Judeo-Christian-Western tradition? To begin with, the Islamic Council should not seek to address differences through the law courts; rather, it should abide by the values of that tradition, a foreign one that is distinctly Western. And those values, the ones that form the basis of Australia's social, political, and judicial landscape, are "respect for individuals, tolerance within a framework of law,[10] and mutual respect" (Costello 2004). Muslims are then to assimilate into the Judeo-Christian tradition, which, in Costello's opinion, is the only tradition that seems to have these values.

The problem with this phrase, whether we include the "Western" or not, is that it signals an appropriation of Judaism, or at least the Jewish Scriptures, the Hebrew Bible, into Christianity. In many respects the Judeo-Christian conjunction pairs up with that other one between Old Testament and New Testament, which does the appropriation job just as well. It is not so much that Jews and Christians are on the same side of the fence, the Western side, nor even that Jews become honorary Christians (just as Downer may become an "honorary Jew"), but that their scriptures are appropriated wholesale. On this score, Costello didn't disappoint, engaging in some light exegesis, and all the texts come from the Hebrew Bible: Psalm 16:12, Exodus 20:1–17, and 1 Kings 19. The first is the text used by Rev. Richard Johnson at the first Christian service in Australia on February 3, 1788, no doubt to a rapt audience of political prisoners and soldiers who loved being there. The third became the basis of a small illustration concerning the need for faith and perseverance in the face of widespread spiritual and moral decay. This illustration was a loose exegesis indeed of Elijah's flight into the wilderness and the appearance of the "still small voice" (but then, no worse than many a sermon). But it was the use of the Ten Commandments that is most intriguing, becoming the basis in a bold move that throws context out the window—where it joins the Muslims he has so recently tossed out—of *our* law and *our* society" (Costello 2004, emphasis added). The first four commandments become the foundation of monotheism; the fifth and sixth (honoring parents and steering clear of adultery) the basis of marriage and family; the seventh, against killing, the foundation of respect for life; the eighth, against stealing, becomes the root of the respect for property; and the last two (against bearing false witness and not coveting your neighbor's things, including his wife) are the source of respect for others and their individual rights.

At a first, admittedly cursory reading, all this seems somewhat innocuous given Costello's political bent, but when he proceeds to cut them down to the basics the picture becomes decidedly less murky. After pointing out that the Ten Commandments provide the basis for the Rule of Law, objective and unassailable rules to which capricious rulers also were subject and which could be enforced by "Hebrew judges," he went on to summarize: "And so we have the Rule of Law, respect for life, private property rights, respect of others—values that spring from the Judeo-Christian tradition" (Costello 2004). In other words, the foundational creed of liberalism is actually due to Moses! Now, I am thankful to Costello for pointing this out, for up until this point I was not aware that liberalism and its values had such a lengthy pedigree, assuming—mistakenly I can see now—that these arose with the Enlightenment and the advent of capitalism.

Once these values have been appropriated, once what he wants from Judaism has been absorbed, he can then quietly push the Jews out the back door. For "Judeo-Christian" in the mouth of Costello really means just "Christian." A little earlier in 2004 he came clean and asserted that Australia is based not on Judeo-Christian values, but on "Christian values" (Costello 2004; Hamilton 2004). What he really wanted at this point was a "recovery of faith" (Costello 2004), or rather a recovery of *Christian* faith, as the key to the spiritual and moral decay of our society. This is, after all, the great contribution church leaders and members can make. Not to be outdone, late in 2005 John Howard made the same slide from Judeo-Christian to Christian. Thus, in his Christmas address that year, one that repeated a speech in Parliament the day before, he said, "Of all the influences which have shaped Australian life, none has been more profound than the Judeo-Christian ethic," only to go on in the next breath to assert, "We do not deny our own beliefs as Christians, and the contribution of our beliefs to our values and those of our society" (Howard 2005).

The fantasy of Israel has become a Christian fantasy. But it is also increasingly an Australian—assuming we know what values attach to the word "Australian"—fantasy as far as the ruling oligarchy of the time was concerned. Christian values equal Australian values, it seems. And those who do not subscribe to such values should not be allowed in the country, or indeed should be stripped of citizenship and sent elsewhere. In a new low of religious scaremongering, Costello said in a speech at the conservative think tank, the Sydney Institute, in early 2006:

Before entering a mosque visitors are asked to take off their shoes. . . . This is a sign of respect. If you have a strong objection to walking in your socks, don't enter the mosque.

Before becoming an Australian you will be asked to subscribe to certain values. If you have strong objections to those values, don't come to Australia. (quoted in Garnaut 2006: 1)

It is not hard to miss the equation: Muslim equals un-Australian. The similarity of this rising Islamophobia, where it is acceptable to proclaim and publish material that denigrates Muslims, where one can say and do things against Muslims purely because of religious belief and ethnic background, is comparable to the rise of anti-Semitism in nineteenth- and twentieth-century Europe. And in case he should miss out on the competition, Howard has aimed as low as he can. Speaking of "Australian ways" and "our kind of society" (whose, we might want to ask?), Howard has picked on the perceived oppression of women in Islam, signaled by the burqa (see Farouque 2006), and what he sees as jihad-mongering extremists. However, the real problem for Howard was in fact the whole immigrant community: "It is not a problem that we have ever faced with other immigrant communities who become easily absorbed by Australia's mainstream" (quoted in Schubert 2006: 5).

Let us return to Costello. Neither Muslim nor indeed Jewish, the vision or fantasy is a distinctly Christian and Australian one (and I hardly need to point out that the battle also involves claiming a certain sense of these terms). So what was Costello's vision of a society that abides by "Australian" and "Christian" values? It was a fantasy image constituted by the nameless majority:

They will get up tomorrow and go to their places of worship in suburbs and towns across the country, affirm the historic Christian faith, and go to work on Monday as law-abiding citizens who want their marriages to stay together, their children to grow up to be healthy and useful members of society, and their homes to be happy. They care deeply about our society and where it is going.

These people will not get their names in the media. They will not be elected to anything. They will not be noisy lobbyists. But they are the steadying influence, the ballast, to our society when it shakes with moral turbulence. They give strength and stability and they embody the character and the traditions of our valuable heritage. It is their inner faith which gives them strength. Our society won't work without them. (Costello 2004)

This hardly needs further comment.

On four counts, then, Costello has flushed out the assumptions of Howard and Downer: Muslims in fact do not have a place in Australian society unless they assimilate (paradoxically, to values they already hold, which really leaves them no place in Australia); the road to moral recovery is one of inner and private Christian conviction; the vision of Australia, indeed the fantasy of an ideal Australia, is an inescapably Christian one; and in both his wholesale appropriation of the Hebrew Bible and the invocation of the "Judeo-Christian tradition" he has effected a complete effacement of Judaism. Any fantasy of Israel, whether of modern or ancient Israel, is a distinctly Christian fantasy. It is not just that the fantasy of an ideal and peaceful Israel is in some way a transferred ideal of Australia, but that the ideal of Australia involves a complete appropriation of Israel. The narrative of the establishment of the state of Israel—no matter how mythical, or rather, precisely because it is mythical—under Moses in the Hebrew Bible becomes the basis for an Australian Christian society.

Let me return to the initial comment of John Howard (2001b): "It is not a fight between Christianity and Judaism on the one side and Islam on the other side." Well, for Howard and company it looks like it is, or rather, was, except that Judaism, plundered for a Christian fantasy, has been dumped on the way.

THE LIMITS OF PSYCHOANALYSIS

It seems that foreign policy and domestic policy cannot be separated so easily, for the fantasy of Israel becomes all too quickly the Christian fantasy of Australia. In conclusion, however, let me return more directly to psychoanalysis and ask two questions: Lacan's *Che vuoi?* (What is it that you really desire?) and Ernst Bloch's *Cui bono?* (For whose benefit is this fantasy being staged?).

I pick up the second question first. Here we find that domestic policy is inextricably entwined with foreign policy, particularly in relation to four policies during the time of the liberal-conservative coalition government in Australia regarding asylum seekers, the "stolen children," an indigenous-nonindigenous treaty, and the Kyoto Protocol. First, lagging in the polls, days out of an election in November 2001 the Australian government made international headlines by refusing to admit the Norwegian vessel *Tampa*, full of Afghan asylum seekers.[11] The long and troubling echoes of Australian racism surfaced yet again. The liberal-conservative coalition led by John Howard won the election on the basis of a xenophobic wave that was mixed in with issues of "security" after September 11, 2001, and then proceeded to push a whole series of antirefugee bills through the Parliament after the election.[12] Second, the Howard government consistently refused to apologize to Aboriginal people for the policy that remained in place until the 1960s of removing Aboriginal children from their families in order to "assimilate" them into white culture in Australia. The issue is now burned into the national psyche after the *Bringing Them Home*, or "Stolen Children" report of the Human Rights and Equal Opportunity Commission (1997). Third, this liberal-conservative government halted any progress on an indigenous-nonindigenous treaty since it came to power in 1996, systematically closing down one Aboriginal governmental or advocacy body after another, most notably the Aboriginal and Torres Strait Islander Commission in 2004. And finally, Australia was one of the few countries—or rather this government has been one of the few governments—along with the United States that refused to ratify the Kyoto Protocol on the reduction of greenhouse gases (Roarty 2002; Fyfe 2002). On a per capita basis Australia is one of the highest producers of such gases in the world.[13]

On the surface at least there is little that would connect these four elements of domestic policy with the fantasy of Israel in foreign policy statements by the deeply conservative Australian government led by John Howard, but at a deeper level the structure of fantasy works here as well. In terms of positive content, these elements were hardly part of the explicit fantasy of the government of the time in Australia. What, then, is its explicit fantasy? We have already seen a taste of it in Peter Costello's image of the nameless but very moral majority. Perhaps John Howard best summed up this "vision," if we can call it that, of Australia as "relaxed and comfortable." It was one in which men went to work during the week, exercising a little bit of "mateship" on the way (but only to those who were like them), washed the car and mowed the lawn on Saturday, and went to church on Sunday while Mum took care of the kids, supported by a massively skewed tax system in an effort to generate precisely such a reality. I kid you not—Australia as one vast middle-class suburb, full of detached houses on which people devote all their energy, time, and money, without those troublesome and meddling Aborigines, ethnics, gays, greenies, and other "interest groups" who can spoil your evening walk with your dog. And if there was more than a reminiscence of the 1950s here, then it will come as no surprise that John Howard's own model was Robert Menzies, the founder of Howard's Liberal Party who ruled Australia during the 1950s and 1960s. This fantasy really does summarize the notion of a "Christian Australia," albeit with enough wealth to share at least with those genuine "Australian" people who need to buy houses, lawnmowers, and cars, a wealth that comes out of a capitalism that will indeed make us comfortable if only we can get past the various hindrances caused by . . . yes, Aborigines, ethnics, gays, greenies, and other riffraff.[14]

The fantasy of Israel would seem to resonate with a certain fantasy of Australia: an image of peace and prosperity that relies on the covert violence of a series of repressions. Indeed, an initial take on this fantasy of a Christian Australia might argue that it relies precisely on the policies I mentioned a little earlier: the denials, refusals, and repressions characterized by xenophobia, systemic violence to Aboriginal peoples, and environmental destruction. At this level, the fantasy of an ideal Israel based on perpetual and systemic violence is at one with the ideal Australia that builds itself on a long history of ethnic cleansing and environmental abuse. And there is much truth in this, for the realization of a "relaxed and comfortable" Australia for the conservative nameless majority requires the elimination of various racial, sexual, and environmental "interest groups," or at least not pandering to their interests. Yet, as with my earlier point concerning the ideal of peace and the image of continued violence in representations of Israel, I don't think it gets us to the real contribution psychoanalysis can make here.

The catch with all of this is that the fantasmatic kernel is not violence but the image of peace and prosperity. In Howard's case this would mean that the fantasmatic kernel was not some hindrance or other, a repressed violence upon which the "relaxed and comfortable" Australia once rested. Rather, during Howard's reign the unbearable fantasmatic kernel was precisely this "relaxed and comfortable" Christian Australia.

This is where Lacan's question comes to the fore: *Che vuoi?* What is it that you really want? The answer lies slightly off center, and we need to look at it obliquely to find it. It seems to me that what Howard, or rather the liberal-conservative regime in Australia, desired when it was in power and continues to desire today is not so much an endless comfortable suburb with all of its necessary appurtenances. What it really desires is the fantasy itself, the perpetuation of the fantasy of such a "comfortable" Australia, rather than the actual achievement of such a liberal-conservative "utopia." That is, the real force of this fantasy lies not in the realization of the fantasy, for that would be unbearable, but what the fantasy enables the coalition government to do, what it justifies in terms of government policy. This is where the theoretical rubber hits the political road: the fantasy of a "relaxed and comfortable" Christian Australia actually enables a whole series of malicious measures in order to deal with what *seem to be* hitches and hindrances on the way to realizing the fantasy, but are in fact part and parcel of the fantasy itself. It therefore becomes *necessary*, according to such a fantasy, to limit immigration and refuse refugees (thereby generating a "fertility crisis," which then required a baby bonus to encourage women to have more children), to deny any responsibility for the stolen generation and the recompense that comes with such a responsibility, to attack so-called black-armband historiography of Australia that highlights the Aboriginal wars and programs of ethnic cleansing, to close down Aboriginal political advocacy bodies and stall the progress toward a treaty, to persist with practices of environmental degradation, to launch renewed attacks on gays and lesbians (such as an anti–"gay marriage" bill in the Australian Parliament before the 2004 election), and so on. The point here is that should all these hindrances finally be removed, the fantasy of a comfortable Australia would itself disappear, would cease to have its raison d'être. This, I suggest, is the horrible truth, the fantasmatic kernel of such a fantasy: it would cease to exist, would cease to have any appeal, should such a government ever be utterly successful in its domestic policies. Then the whole liberal-conservative agenda would grind to a bewildered halt, anxiously turning this way and that, wondering where their ideal Australia had gone at the moment of its apparent achievement.

This is nothing other than the logic of the political myth of Genesis–Joshua. Not only does the fantasy create its own blockages and hindrances to realization, not only does it rely on precisely those oppositions to be a fantasy at all, not only does it justify a political program that seeks to remove those blockages, but should it actually realize the fantasy the whole system would come crashing down.

Thus far we are well within the logic of Lacanian psychoanalysis, which seems to me to provide explanations for the apparent success of both the fantasy of Israel and the liberal-conservative program that we see everywhere around us in Australia. The question then becomes this: How might the Left gain a grip in a situation where even the hard-won gains of the past are being systematically eroded, where political action seems to be nothing more than a constant pattern of reacting to renewed onslaughts from the Right? I want to offer the beginnings of an answer to this question, but first a word more on the political limits of psychoanalysis.

I have argued that the seeming success of the Right in Australia, at least for a time, was the result of its ability to provide a workable fantasy, a means of keeping the trauma of the Real from crashing into our Symbolic (the realm of language, law, society, and so on). The spin from the Right was and is that if we wish to realize the full potential of capitalism, then we need to resist or defuse the claims of those who question such a dream, those with feminist, socialist, green, and Aboriginal political agendas, among others. However, the net effect of such a myth is that it serves to maintain a particular status quo, that is, one in which we are perpetually striving toward a liberal-conservative utopia, one that seems forever out of reach. Indeed, in a prescient moment, Howard admitted as much in a comment he made to the Federal Liberal Council in 2005, the one I quoted in the epigraph to this chapter: "And it is never ending. You never reach the finish line. It keeps getting moved further ahead. . . . It's like one of those experiences you have and you dream . . . and you are trying to reach something and you never get there" (quoted in Metherell 2005: 1).[15] That such a myth can never be realized I argued above, for it would entail coming face to face with the traumatic kernel of the liberal-conservative agenda: the end of a "relaxed and comfortable" Australia.

Apart from Howard's momentary glimpse, the Right is far more comfortable pointing to such a logic in the Left. In a relic perhaps of the cold war, the Right perpetually criticizes any progressive or emancipatory political movement as doomed to the failures that litter the history of victories on the Left. This position, however unwittingly, taps into the logic of psychoanalysis itself. For the constitutive exception, what both sustains that system and threatens to undermine it at any moment, will also bring up short any movement for political change, any radical program for a thorough restructuring of society, any utopian movement that believes a better world is indeed possible. It will always fall foul to that exception, will always find itself destabilized. Here is one reason for the limited period of the Right's ideological success: while it can effectively point to such a logic in any progressive movement, it simultaneously develops a strategy (fantasy) for obfuscating such a logic in its own agenda.

Is the Left then trapped within such a logic? Let me recall the debate between Slavoj Žižek and Judith Butler in *Contingency, Hegemony, Universality* (Butler, Laclau, and Žižek 2000) that I discussed in the opening chapter to this book. Butler hits the crucial nerve with her questions: "How would the new be produced from an analysis of the social field that remains restricted to inversions, aporias and reversals that work regardless of time and place? Do these reversals produce something other than their own structurally identical repetitions?" (29). This is the logic of psychoanalysis and the taunt of the Right. But it seems to me that the Right and Butler are absolutely correct here. Except that we need to respond with Butler that psychoanalysis is extremely useful in describing the way things are, for the vicious cycle of our political and social lives, indeed in accounting to some extent for the way revolutions have in fact perpetually failed, but not for a radically new possibility: the psychoanalytic cure is not quite a deeply qualitative political change.

For that type of change I suggest that we need to grab the beast from our shoulder and stare it in the face. We need some means of loosening the iron grip of the fantasmatic kernel, of the perverse and vicious cycle of opposition and cooptation. In contrast to the Right, whose fantasy relies on the necessary and perpetual postponement of its ideal in order to maintain Australia "as we know it," the Left must *want* the end of Australia as we know it. My suggestion is that the Left should grasp the traumatic kernel of its fantasy, and that it should never give up in pursuing that kernel. And the best way to do that is call the bluff of the liberal-conservative fantasy.

CHAPTER SIX

Christianity, Capitalism, and the Fantasy of Israel in the United States

By defending the freedom and prosperity and security of Israel, you're also serving the cause of America. (Applause.) Our nation is stronger and safer because we have a true and dependable ally in Israel. (Applause.) I appreciate—(applause)—I'm just getting warmed up. (Laughter and applause.)
—George W. Bush (2004a)

PROLOGUE: JOSEF STALIN AND GEORGE W. BUSH

The United States and the fantasy of Israel are an obvious combination, since the United States continues to be the crucial supporter of the state of Israel. But the United States was not always Israel's best friend. In fact, in the face of British and American opposition, Israel went to Stalin, looking for arms for the "War of Independence." These the Soviet Union supplied, leading to Stalin's epithet, "the grandfather of Israel" (La Guardia 2005).

I have raised this anomaly in the American fantasy of Israel for reasons that will soon become clear—if they are not already so in terms of the dynamics of that fantasy. But before I proceed, here is another: George W. Bush consistently used to oppose the demonization of Islam. Against the Islamophobic diatribes of the Religious Right in the United States, Bush emphasized that Islam is a peaceful religion, highlighted Muslim contributions to the United States, and stressed the similarities between Christianity and Islam.[1]

These are two anomalies in what might at first appear to be a seamless connection between a certain national consciousness of the United States and the fantasy of Israel. Instead, it is a troubled fantasy, with all of the fantasmatic traps that I have traced until now. The building blocks of that fantasy and its anomalies in U.S. foreign policy are what interest me in this chapter.

BACKGROUND

Nothing quite seems to raise political passions as much as the fantasy of Israel, with various gradations of Zionist, anti-Zionist, pro-Palestinian, Islamophobic, and anti-Semitic positions coming to flash points. Throw in the shifting alignments of reactionary and progressive politics over this question and the mix becomes pure gunpowder. Passion is the stuff of political myth, as my initial return to Sorel showed all too clearly.

But let us pause for a moment and take a deep breath or two. If we put the current fantasy of Israel in a longer perspective, it most often takes the form of the Exodus theme, as it is called: the narrative of escape from oppression and arrival in a new, Promised Land. I am saying nothing particularly new in pointing to the long history of the Exodus theme in the national consciousness of the United States, from the pilgrims through the Mormons and presidential speeches to current foreign policy. I do so as an outside observer, as one who is both fascinated and appalled by such a self-perception. Indeed, the Exodus theme has a wide currency. Coupled with Exile it turns up in the founding narratives of the Boers in South Africa, of African American delivery from slavery in the United States, as a key element in liberation theology's biblical interpretation, in postcolonial theory, and in the thought of Deleuze and Guattari. The contrast with Australia couldn't be sharper, for throughout most of the first century of European invasion and colonization the idea of Exodus was not invoked. Australia was instead the land that God forgot to bless at creation, or the land that most obviously showed the results of the curse in Genesis 3. But I have dealt with these appropriations of the Exodus theme elsewhere (Boer 2008). Here I am interested in something different; rather than the appropriation of the content of a story, my concern is with the deeper logic of this particular political myth, namely, that the myth necessarily blocks its own realization since such a realization would lead to total disaster.

I am going to argue that this fantasmatic logic plays a crucial role in the depth of support for the state of Israel within the United States, both at a popular level and in foreign policy. But such an argument comes into contact with two prevailing theories for the popularity of Israel in the United States: the "weak lobby" and "strong lobby" theories (see Larudee 2005). The "weak lobby" theory, championed by Noam Chomsky, among others, argues that support for Israel is really only a minor part—a smokescreen Americans can get behind—for advancing purely U.S. interests in the Middle East. The "strong lobby" theory, supported by the late Edward Said and others, holds that U.S. support for Israel has not advanced U.S. interests and that the support comes about through an effective pro-Israel lobby that has captured the hearts and minds of American legislators and, crucially, the American public. Thus, as Anton La Guardia (2005: 33) argues, "Many Americans see in Israel a reflection of themselves, a settler society born of ideas of freedom and built on the romance of pioneers with a God-given destiny."

BUILDING BLOCKS OF THE FANTASY

As with my discussion of Australia, I focus on various statements, speeches, and other pronouncements—some less astute than others—of key political figures, such as the man with the record for having been the most unpopular president in U.S. history, George W. Bush; the secretaries of state in the Bush administration, Colin Powell and his successor, Condoleezza Rice; the Speaker of the House of Representatives (since the 2006 midterm elections), Nancy Pelosi; Henry Kissinger; and the Democratic presidential hopeful (at least she is so as I write), Hillary Clinton. Out of their statements three building blocks of the fantasy emerge: biblical, cultural, and ideological.

Stepping into the Bible

In contrast to Australia, where the most a politician will dare is some reference to "Christian values" or the "Judeo-Christian tradition" for fear of being too overtly religious, in the United States we find a full-frontal Bible. Ronald Reagan, carrying on a long tradition of "theologian in chief" that may be traced back to Thomas Jefferson, famously made the following observation to the head of the American Israel Public Affairs Committee (AIPAC). It was later leaked to the Associated Press: "You know, I turn back to your ancient prophets in the Old Testament and the signs foretelling Armageddon, and I find myself wondering if—if we're the generation that is going to see that come about. I don't know if you've noted any of these prophecies lately, but believe me, they certainly describe the times we're going through" (quoted in Wagner 2002: 55).

George W. Bush tried to carry the title of theologian in chief as well, although not without some criticism from his support base among the Religious Right ("In the Capital" 2004). But first, let us see what biblical themes emerge. There are, to begin with, the more general statements concerning providence, or the gifts of God that the United States and Israel share. Thus, Bush (2004b) spoke of the beliefs shared by both nation-states, "that God watches over the affairs of men, and values every life." Not to be outdone, Condoleezza Rice (2005) pointed out that the innate freedom and dignity of every human life are "divine gifts of the Almighty," a belief that the two states share. Thomas Jefferson, the first theologian in chief, finds himself rolled out in support, having once written, "The God that gave us liberty and life gave them to us at the same time" (quoted in Rice 2005).

These are really just warm-up exercises before the main show. Far more significant is what may be called *geopiety*, "the curious mix of romantic imagination, historical rectitude, and attachment to a physical place" (Long 2003: 1). Afflicting both large swathes of the American public and its politicians, geopiety is conjured up above all by the phrases "the Blessed Land" and "the Holy Land." Here we begin to see the process of producing and reiterating the fantasy. Colin Powell (2001) hoped for a Middle East "where all the peoples of the region can share in the blessings of the *blessed land* that they occupy." What blessings? Most notably the "fruits of globalization," which turn out to be full participation in one's society, the teaching of peace rather than hatred in schools, a focus on the quality of one's life, but above all a situation where "normal people lead normal lives" (Powell 2001). This is perhaps a little too close to John Howard's nonvision of a "relaxed and comfortable" Australia.

All we need is for such a geopiety to be stitched tightly into the Bible. Reagan's worthy successor in apocalyptic rhetoric, albeit without his slightly bewildered tone, is the Speaker of the House of Representatives, Democrat Nancy Pelosi. While Colin Powell (2001) spoke of "a special friendship" that "involves every aspect of life," Pelosi located the United States deep within the biblical text. For their passion and hyperbole alone, her words are worth considering more closely. Here is part of her speech at AIPAC in May 2005:

As Israel continues to take risks for peace, she will have no friend more steadfast than the United States.

In the words of Isaiah, we will make ourselves to Israel "as hiding places from the winds and shelters from the tempests; as rivers of water in dry places; as shadows of a great rock in a weary land."

The United States will stand with Israel now and forever. Now and forever. (Pelosi 2005)

The biblical quote is from Isaiah 32:2, but what has happened through Pelosi's words is not so much a merging of the United States with Israel as a step by the United States *into the text*. The United States becomes, in other words, not merely the protector of modern Israel but also the protector of biblical Israel. We can sense the deeper wish: had the United States been there in the time of the Bible—"now and forever" goes backward in time as well as forward—Israel would have been saved from imperial incursions. No Egypt or Babylon or Assyria or Persia or Rome would have touched Israel. Nor indeed will their modern successors. For once, Israel has a friendly empire on the world stage.

This is not the first time Pelosi has let loose before AIPAC. Here is part of her speech on April Fool's Day in 2003:

More than a half-century later, our challenge is the same: how can America and Israel together walk the long thorny path and preserve Israel as a special place in the history of mankind?

. . . There are hundreds of college students here today. Allow me to speak directly to the students. Thankfully, you are too young to have witnessed the darkest chapters of the last century—the Nazism, communism, and authoritarianism. But in your eyes I see the glow of one of the brightest stars of the past century—the founding of the State of Israel.

You are the messengers to a future we will never know. It is your charge to build that future in the spirit of *tikkun olam*, the repairing of the world, in the spirit of peace and security.

On behalf of all who cherish freedom, thank you for your commitment to the ideals and values that define our two democracies—the United States and Israel.

My grandchildren tell me that this week begins the month of Nisan, the month of miracles, the month of deliverance. And over the coming weeks, Israelis and Jews everywhere will mark the miracles that have brought us to this day:

The survivors who endured the darkness of the *Shoah* and who braved their way to the light of Israel;

The heroes of Israeli independence who prevailed against overwhelming odds;

And all those who have defended Israel through decades of struggle and sacrifice, including a fallen hero Americans and Israelis mourned together—Space Shuttle *Columbia* astronaut Colonel Ilan Ramon, who literally took the Torah to the stars.

This is the spirit that defines the American-Israeli partnership. America stands with Israel now. America will stand with Israel forever.

We will never abandon Israel. We will never abandon Israel.

God bless you. God bless our men and women serving on the frontlines today. And God bless our special relationship between the United States of America and the State of Israel. (Pelosi 2003)

When I first read the words of Colin Powell I found them strong and explicit. In a perverse fashion I began longing for the bumbling eloquence of the former Australian foreign minister, Alexander Downer. After reading Pelosi's speeches, Powell seems heartwarmingly tame, with his vague comments on sharing in divine blessings and friendship.

Pelosi's 2003 speech was mythic elaboration of the first order. The overall effect of the speech was to universalize and absolutize U.S. support for Israel, to turn the symbiotic partnership into an ontological one. Note the terms: she worked hardest with the temporal register, pushing back into the struggles of the twentieth century that resulted in the founding of the state of Israel and then forward into an eschatological future. But this horizontal register was tied into the mythical calendar, "the month of Nisan, the month of miracles, the month of deliverance," into which we now had to fit the state of Israel, and then the call to the young people to build a future in "the spirit of *tikkun olam*, the repairing of the world." All of this was thrown together as giving Israel a "special place in the history of mankind," except that Pelosi wanted to add the vertical register as well. Not content with history, she had the Israeli astronaut take the Torah to the stars.[2] On top of both registers, she invoked the basic mythical distinction between darkness and light, twice: first with the darkness of the twentieth century to one of its brightest stars, Israel, and then with the darkness of the Shoah to the light, again, of Israel.

On top of these categories—of history, the heavens, and the opposition of darkness and light—the flood of terminology that evokes the master myth of Genesis–Joshua is hardly a surprise, especially the terminology of Exodus and Exile. So we find references to walking the "long thorny path," a path that included Nazism, communism, authoritarianism, and the Shoah. There were the heroes who prevailed against overwhelming odds, and since then "all those who have defended Israel through decades of struggle and sacrifice." Or, as George W. Bush (2004b) once said, repeating the classic formulation, "We're both founded by immigrants escaping religious persecution in other lands."

Here Condoleezza Rice, the one-time globe-trotting mythmaker for the United States, came in to flesh out the Exodus dimensions of Pelosi's effort:

> In 1776, cynics and skeptics could not see an independent America, so they doubted that it could be so. They saw only 13 colonies that could never hang together and would surely hang separately. But there were others who had a vision, a vision of the United States as a free and great nation, a democracy, and one day, a complete multiethnic society. With perseverance, the American people made that vision a reality. In 1948, cynics and skeptics could not see *the promise of Israel*, so they doubted it, said it could never be fulfilled. They saw only a *wounded and wandering people* beset on all sides by hostile armies.
>
> But there were those who had another vision, a vision of a Jewish state that would *shelter its children*, defend its *sacred homeland*, turn its desert *soil* green and reaffirm the principles of freedom and democracy. With courage, the Israeli people made that vision a reality. (Applause.) (Rice 2005, emphasis added)

This was by no means the first time such a story of American self-understanding has been rolled out. But the terms Rice used were deeply biblical: "the promise of Israel" is none other than an echo of the dual promise to Abraham and then Jacob of a great people and a land (Genesis 12:1–3; 15:1–5; 17; 18:18; 22:15–18; 28:13–16; 32:12; 35:11–12; 46:3–4); the "wounded and wandering people" are the Israelites in the wilderness; and then of course the image of the Promised Land that is both a shelter and a sacred homeland. Indeed, Rice's little myth echoed very strongly the crucial "creedal statements" that sum up every now and then the political myth of Genesis–Joshua.[3] Although the terms of that myth were applied to Israel in this piece of spin by Rice, they stuck to the United States like flypaper by the sheer parallels of the two stories. Except that for Rice, at least in her time, the United States set the agenda and Israel followed. If only it had been so in the Bible.

The second paragraph I quoted from Rice is far more ominous. In her "vision" she lined up progeny and soil with that weary code for American values, freedom, and democracy. But what has happened here is that sheltering the children, defending a sacred homeland and turning its soil for food have begun to sound a little too close to the invocation of blood and soil that was (and is again with the supposed "threat" of Islam) so favored by myths on the Right, most notably that of National Socialism.

Rice, who at times trots out her own family's background in slavery in the southern United States as yet another narrative of the Exodus from slavery and oppression to freedom, managed to tie all of these threads neatly together by playing off cynicism against vision:

> With our support, the people of the region are demonstrating that all great human achievement begins with free individuals who do not accept that the reality of today must also be the reality of tomorrow. Of course, there will always be cynics and skeptics who hold the misguided belief that if they can not see their goal, then it cannot be possible. They will try to elevate their cynicism by calling it realism and they will criticize all who echo the stirring words of Theodore Hertzel, "If you will it, it is no dream." (Applause.) (Rice 2005)

Theodor Herzl, a Viennese journalist and writer in the late nineteenth century, was one of the founders of political Jewish Zionism, a movement in the which the dreams of revolutionary Labor Zionism faded in the face of a liberal capitalist agenda.[4] Herzl produced a coherent and rational argument for a Jewish state, arguing that this was the only way to short-circuit the inevitable persecution Jewish minorities face in other states. But he also argued that the Jews should follow the European example of colonialism. In his 1898 missive, "Who Fears a State?," he wrote, "As a consequence of overpopulation, and of the resultant ever more acute social question, many nations are endeavoring to found overseas colonies in order to channel the flow of emigration there" (quoted in Smith 2001: 55–56).

All of this is, to say the least, a rather potent mythical remix: the biblical political myth of Genesis–Joshua, a reach into the full length and breadth of history and the heavens, Zionism, and echoes of the Nazis. But now there is a crucial twist, for the United States becomes central to that myth. It was as though the United States had stepped into the biblical political myth to draw it down into the present. Pelosi's triple blessing at the close of her speech sounds like nothing other than a benediction or perhaps a hymn:

"America stands with Israel now. America will stand with Israel forever. We will never abandon Israel. We will never abandon Israel."

Culture

Such a stride into the center of the political myth of Genesis–Joshua could hardly take place in a vacuum. Indeed, the geopiety I mentioned is as much a feature of popular culture as it is of political positioning. The one can hardly take place without the other. I will restrict myself to brief comments on three signal moments: Leon Uris's *Exodus*, the rise of Holy Land theme parks and tours, and the *Left Behind* series of novels.

The novel and then especially the film *Exodus* are, as Edward Said (2004: 101; see also Weissbrod 1999) pointed out, the most influential sources for popular opinion concerning Israel and Zionism in the United States. Both Uris's (1958) novel, which has gone into more than eighty printings in the United States, and Otto Preminger's film in 1960 were inspired by the journalist Ruth Gruber's (1947, 1999) dispatches, collected in *Destination Palestine: The Story of the Haganah Ship* Exodus, *1947*. Gruber's book concerns a particular ship, originally called the *President Warfield* but renamed *Exodus* when it left France carrying "illegal" refugees, many of them Holocaust survivors, for Palestine (still under British mandate), only to be turned away and towed by the British to Germany. Needless to say, Gruber's reporting created much sympathy around the world for the Zionist cause. The evocative name of the boat, the emerging consciousness of the gas chambers just at the war's end, Gruber's newspaper reports, and the high-handed behavior of the British, who saw their empire collapsing around them, all made for a highly charged and passionate atmosphere.

Following Gruber's book, Uris's novel *Exodus* may be seen as a thoroughly deliberate piece of mythmaking, or rather remaking. A Jew of Polish and Russian background, he knew his audience in the United States and Europe would largely be Christian, so the link with the biblical narrative of Exodus and the Promised Land was a crucial move to gain sympathy and support, not just for Jews as such but specifically for the state of Israel. The book is still sold at airports and in the travel sections of bookstores as an introduction to Israel and its history. I can recall the power that the connection had for me as a teenager. *Exodus*—of course, it's just like the Exodus in the Bible. More than one Zionist was created by this book, Jewish or otherwise. The book is a historical novel whose period is the recent past. It tells its story by focusing on everyday characters with unimaginative names like Kitty, Barak, and Dov and an everyday story centered on an Adamic farmer, Ari ben Canaan, who would rather plough and reap than take up arms. Rough and poorly written (with words like "plip-plopped"), it has no pretensions to classic status. Yet its claim to mythic status is directly proportional to its ordinariness.

One other feature of the novel was crucial to its success in the United States: Kitty is an American nurse. The Preminger movie would make this far more explicit, with Paul Newman taking the lead role of Ari ben Canaan. Newman's "I'm a Jew, and this land is mine" becomes in this film another part of the United States stepping into the reclaimed political myth. It really is a direct expression of American geopiety. In the same way that Newman is an American Jew, so the United States claims Israel as its own.

Indeed, the second cultural moment of the fantasy of Israel does claim "This land is mine." These are the Holy Land theme parks that began dotting the United States in the nineteenth century along with the touring audiovisual displays and models that sought to bring the Holy Land to the people. As Burke Long (2003) shows, for those who could not afford the time or expense to tour the actual sites of Palestine and Israel, these theme parks set out to re-create in careful and scaled detail the geography of that countryside, but now within the United States. From Palestine Park in Chautauqua in Upstate New York to New Holy Land in Eureka Springs, Arkansas, these sites were part of a larger process of imagining and claiming the "holy land" for the United States, a process that included some of the most prominent Christian and Jewish biblical scholars, such as W. F. Albright and Max Margolis. In various ways one could and can follow in the footsteps of major moments in the Bible, for geographical knowledge was, after all, essential for salvation. If you can't actually get there, then it is here anyway. In fact, that is the implicit claim: that the Holy Land is in fact here and not there, or that there is a small extension of it here. It is a little like going to Disneyland or Disney World instead of, or even better than, going to Europe or Asia or Africa, or perhaps to Quebec for a cheaper European holiday.

The third moment is the *Left Behind* book series phenomenon. As the sales of the initial seven books keep mounting—now beyond the 100 million mark—and the spinoffs also cash in, such as the teenage *Left Behind* series, the spoofs, the film, and even the DVD you can buy to give to your loved ones should the Lord whisk you and not them away to heaven, the *Left Behind* series marks a new wave of conservative Christian Zionism. The books are based on a fundamentalist preconstruction of the last days before Christ's return that begins with the "rapture," the moment when all "Bible-believing" Christians will suddenly be drawn up to heaven. Then come the Antichrist, world domination, and eventually the return of Christ at the final battle of Armageddon. The novels follow the story of a small group who come to a fundamentalist version of the Christian faith too late for the rapture but just in time for the Second Coming of Christ, although they suffer a great deal before he finally decides to turn up. One key in the novels is the crucial role of Israel: the Jews must be converted, or at least 144,000 of them, as a precondition of the last days. Arabs, Muslims, liberal Christians, the United Nations, abortionists, and sundry other sinners will not be saved, but converted Jews will, and the land of Israel will be the scene for the final showdown, at none other than the ancient battlefield of Armageddon. Although fundamentalist Christians might debate the details of the reconstruction, the power of such novels is astonishing. As David Shepherd, senior vice president of the fundamentalist publisher Broadman and Holman points out, pro-Israel evangelical Christian books that interpret the situation in the Middle East through the lens of messianic eschatology have increased in popularity following the success of the *Left Behind* series ("Religion Update" 2004).

The *Left Behind* books bring into relief an anomaly with the fantasy of Israel in the United States: in the end Christian Zionism has no place for Jews or indeed for the state of Israel. For Christian Zionists, the Palestinians must be expelled, the Jews must be converted, and the land must become distinctly Christian—albeit a Christianity with a fundamentalist flavor to it (see Mezvinsky 2005). The tightening of fundamentalist support for Israel is based on the belief that it is a precursor for the Second Coming, if only the Jews would acknowledge the First Coming and join the saved. For Israel, which banned such evangelizing many years ago, the immediate benefits of such support seem to be worth the trade-off. So much so that the oldest English-language newspaper in Israel, the *Jerusalem Post*, has moved to the schizophrenic option of publishing Jewish and Christian editions for two different Zionist audiences (McGreal 2005).

Ideology: Beacons of Liberty and Justice
Not only are the United States and Israel part of the same biblical myth, and not only is the Holy Land to be found as much in the United States as in Palestine, but the two States share the same ideologies, patched neatly onto the fantasy. Here we find that the Christian fantasy of Israel becomes markedly capitalist, a Christian capitalist fantasy, if you will. Let me return to the delightfully hyperbolic Nancy Pelosi (2003), who shows us

that Democrats can outdo Republicans on this issue any day: "The United States stands with Israel because of our common history—two beacons founded on the ideals of liberty and justice." George W. Bush (2004b) was a little more pedestrian: "Our nation, and the nation of Israel, have much in common. . . . We have both built vibrant democracies, built on the rule of law and market economies."

Indeed, nothing is peddled as incessantly and nothing is greeted with quite as much weary cynicism as the claim by the United States of America to uphold the ideals of freedom, democracy, the rule of law, and market economics, and that somehow they all fit seamlessly together. It is astonishing how often one comes across the claim, especially on the world stage, by the likes of one secretary of state or president after another. It is equally astonishing how few outside the United States, and indeed within the United States, actually believe it. The two seem to feed off each other: the more cynicism there is, the more stridently it is proclaimed, and then the deeper the cynicism becomes. The long line of pro-U.S. despots and dictators propped up by the United States in Latin America and in the Arab world is well known. Less well known perhaps is that Israel, claimed to be the "only democracy in the Middle East," plays the same game. Given that the propaganda of democracy and freedom is coupled with the concrete walls and electric fences in the Occupied Territories of East Jerusalem and the West Bank, with the apartheid system of ethnic separation, and with the continued occupation of Syrian land in the Golan Heights and the Sheba farms region of Lebanon (both with U.S. approval and based on the need for water), one suspects that it is less of a contradiction, or indeed hypocrisy, than that this type of democracy—parliamentary democracy—goes hand in hand with such activities, that they are two sides of the same coin.[5] Alain Badiou (2003a) is correct, it seems to me, in pointing to the sheer bankruptcy of such a notion of democracy.

It seems as though little will change in the near future, given the positions (as I write) of two leading women in U.S. politics, Condoleezza Rice and Hillary Clinton, one a Republican, the other a Democrat. Let me quote the Democrat first, who in a speech from 2005 was keen to spell out the pedigree of freedom and democracy:

> I want to start by focusing on our deep and lasting bond between the United States and Israel. . . . These are bonds forged in a common struggle for human rights, for democracy, for freedom. These are bonds

that predate the creation of the state of Israel, that *really predate the creation of the United States* because they are rooted in fundamental beliefs and values about the dignity and rights of men and women to live in freedom, free from fear, free from oppression. And there is no doubt that these incredibly strong bonds and values will remain as *the lodestar* of our relationship with our democratic friend and ally, Israel. (Clinton 2005, emphasis added)

I am tempted to refer to the "bonds of democracy" after Clinton's speech, especially as a mark of the paradox I noticed earlier, and I can't help but notice the way stars and indeed beacons keep turning up, especially in light of their presence on both flags. But above all it is the claim to an age-old tradition, which Clinton pushed back in her speech to before the creation of the United States. Hillary Clinton is not stupid, and yet it is astonishing how much she has bought into the fantasy. But just in case we—or rather, everyone else in the Middle East—is not sure what "democracy" might mean, Clinton comes to our aid:

Now, Israel is not only, however, a friend and ally for us, it is a *beacon* of what democracy can and should mean. It is, after all, a *pluralistic democracy*. It is, as many of us know from personal experiences, a very *dynamic democracy* with many points of view, and those are expressed with great frequency and vigor. So if people in the Middle East are not sure what democracy means, let them look to Israel, which has been and remains *a true, faithful democracy*. (Clinton 2005, emphasis added)

This is far more sinister. A true and faithful democracy is pluralistic, dynamic, and vigorous. Clinton has neglected the fact that the government in Israel typically relies on one or more parties of the Religious Right, who tend to get their way with domestic policy, above all with regard to restrictive policies on immigration, continued occupation of Palestinian land, and Orthodox religious control over family law. This is curious: in Israel the influence of the Religious Right is a sign of a vigorous democracy; in other Arab countries it is a sign of the absence of democracy. Here Clinton's speech becomes menacing: in other countries of the Middle East there is not merely an absence of democracy, but an absence of "true" and "faithful" democracy. That is, they do not have parliamentary democracies that operate according to the dialectic of hypocrisy. If they want an example of that type of democracy, they should look to the United States or Israel.

In the same year the Republican Rice made a rather similar point, but then got herself in a further tangle:

> Some in the Arab media have even asked why the only *real democracies* in the Middle East are found in the "occupied lands" of Iraq and the Palestinian territories. What an incredible thought. Today, citizens in the region are demanding that their governments respond to this simple, audacious question.
>
> In Lebanon, hundreds of thousands of citizens have demanded an end to the foreign suffocation of their country. (Applause.) (Rice 2005, emphasis added)

"Real democracies"—not just any old democracy—were spreading, it seemed, first to Iraq and the Palestinian territories, and then to Lebanon. But then Rice managed to get herself in trouble: on the one hand, democracy has appeared in occupied countries; on the other, the sign of democracy is the call for the end of occupation. Does she admit the paradox of totalitarianism and democracy, namely, that the two go hand in hand? Or are the Palestinian demands that Israel get out of their land and the Iraqi wish for the last foreign soldier to leave signs of democracy? If so, then the election of Hamas to a majority in the Palestinian Parliament in the 2005 elections was an example of precisely this type of democracy. Or did she unwittingly speak the truth about the United States and Israel: that they constitute "foreign suffocation"? All of the above, it seems to me.

At a deeper level, however, Islam finally enters this complex fantasy of Israel, for the "Middle East" becomes a zone of the absence of freedom, democracy, the rule of law, and the market. Once these spread, so will "peace" in the Middle East: "The United States looks to a future and has a vision of a day when Israel is no longer the sole democracy in the Middle East. (Applause.) This aspiration shapes the very heart of our approach to the Israeli-Palestinian conflict as well" (Rice 2005). The first foothold is Israel, and from there the rest of the Muslim Middle East awaits the arrival of such beacons of light—conveniently neglecting the fact that they have been part of global capitalism for a good while now.

Let me sum up the argument thus far. The fantasy of Israel is in U.S. hands a Christian capitalist fantasy characterized by stepping into the biblical political myth, a cultural and political geopiety focused on Israel, and an ideological loading of that fantasy with the curious juxtaposition of freedom and the market.

Like the Australian version, the U.S. form of the fantasy of Israel has its anomalies. I have already hinted at a few, but the Left's common strategy is to present the facts as an answer to spin, to seek to undermine falsehood with the truth—an agenda it shares with journalists and historians at least. To my mind, this is a necessary and useful strategy that carries on the spirit of Marx's demystification, and that the Left must not relinquish. I will engage in precisely this strategy in a moment. But there is a catch, and it is a big one. Political myths such as this—the fantasy of Israel—are largely impervious to such a strategy. In the face of a potent mix that includes the biblical political myth of Genesis–Joshua, along with associated cosmological and historical claims, a few facts will not go very far. For this reason I pursue the deeper anomalies of the U.S. fantasy of Israel.

The Problem of Facts, or, Stalin and the Origins of Israel
Unearth new information and rewrite the history books: this process begins with historians such as Benny Morris and Zeev Sternhell. They are among the so-called new historians in Israel, a catchall phrase that embraces a variety of people who have begun to reexamine the founding of the state of Israel. Morris's (1987, 2004a) *Birth of the Palestinian Refugee Problem, 1947–1949* is the groundbreaking work here, since he was the first to make use of declassified official documents concerning the origin of the modern state of Israel. Given the fiery passions surrounding these problems, Morris writes as dispassionately as possible, in the process deflating both Zionist and Palestinian versions of events. He concludes that in the pressure and confusion of those early war years, the Israelis were able to clear sufficient land of its Palestinian population by a number of means, some of which involved deliberate programs of population removal and destruction of villages. His argument is that the Palestinian Exodus was born "of war, not design." Other historians, such as Norman Finkelstein (1991), have challenged Morris's work, especially the holes and inconsistencies in his use of documentation concerning policies of expulsion. A notable example of this work is Parsons's (2001) analysis of the role of the Druze minority in Palestine. She focuses on documents explicitly directing the nascent Israeli forces *not* to destroy Druze villages or remove the populations—even those that fought against the Israelis!—rather than those still largely classified documents that contained orders *to* expel or destroy. The underlying desire was that the Druze and other minorities, such as the

Maronites of Lebanon, would become allies, or at least form a significant buffer zone, since, according to Israeli opinion, they would be happy to be under Israeli control.

Zeev Sternhell (1997) is more interested in the ideological and political origins of Zionism, establishing that a "constructive socialism" lies at the basis of Zionism. This was Stalin's idea of "socialism in one state" rather than the global communism of Marx and Lenin, a policy with which many of the Eastern European Zionist leaders were well acquainted. In light of these ideological and political alignments of the early Zionists, the USSR and the other states of Eastern Europe supported their moves. Hence Stalin's position as "the grandfather of Israel"—although the shipments of arms the USSR and its allies sent during the 1948 conflict also helped with this image. The crucial assistance came during the final ceasefire, when, in contravention of a U.N.-brokered ceasefire, the USSR sent arms through Yugoslavia and enabled the final putsch that produced the troubled borders—the "green line"—that now exist in Palestine. But what happened to the socialist elements of Zionism? The proletariat in the "constructive socialism" of early Israel was to subordinate itself to the state and the bourgeoisie: all were to put class conflict aside and unite behind the program of the state of Israel. What there was of a socialist agenda was always mired in nationalism and disappeared from the political and social horizon until we have the situation today, where the United States is Israel's main supporter.

If the 1948 war was Stalin's moment, the 1967 war was the moment of the United States. After the so-called miraculous victory of this war—in which Arab forces armed with Soviet weapons were convinced by the USSR on the dawn of battle that Israel would not attack them if they did not attack first—the United States and arguably Australia saw in Israel both the possibility for an ally against Soviet expansion as well as a model for how the West and its colonies could deal with the growing threat of anticolonial uprising. As George W. Bush said in 2004, "The Israeli people have always had enemies at their borders and terrorists close at hand. Again and again, Israel has defended itself with skill and heroism. And as a result of the courage of the Israeli people, Israel has earned the respect of the American people" (Bush 2004b). Or, at the very least, proved their usefulness.

Further, contrary to the image of an equal partnership, one in which the United States shares in the narrative of origins, or indeed steps into the biblical political myth itself, the relationship that developed from this point is a chronically unequal one. So much so that Israel, argued

Henry Kissinger, became "dependent on the United States as no country is on a friendly power. . . . It takes a special kind of heroism to turn total dependence into defiance, to insist on support as a matter of right [rather] than as a favour" (quoted in La Guardia 2005: 32).

There is a distinct value in such recasting of the narrative, of beginning again and challenging the accepted historical narratives. This was of course Foucault's genius. But it is, as I mentioned earlier, a limited strategy unless the new narrative catches on and displaces the old. However, putting out the facts themselves and expecting them to be efficacious because they tell what "really happened" is not going to get us very far at all: the Right plays the same game. They have little effect in puncturing a fantasy like this one.

Once Again, the Dialectics of Peace and Violence

So let me move to a second level and pursue the tensions a little further into this U.S. fantasy of Israel. The tension that shows up rather quickly is very similar to the one I tracked in the Australian version, namely, between hoped-for peace and ongoing violence. I begin by returning to Benny Morris. The one who began the debates concerning the founding of Israel effectively ended them with the second edition of *Birth of the Palestinian Refugee Problem, 1947–1949* in 2004 (Morris 2004a). In an interview at the same time, Morris (2004b) pointed out that more documents had become available that showed "far more Israeli acts of massacre" than even he had previously thought, along with orders for the expulsion of Palestinians signed by Ben-Gurion and the darling of Western liberals, Yitzhak Rabin. In an essay first published in the leading Israeli broadsheet, *Haaretz*, on January 8, 2004, and later reprinted in *New Left Review*, Morris shocked readers with his brutal honesty. After detailing new revelations of massacre, rape, and a policy of transferring the Palestinian population, Morris (2004b: 44) makes the following point:

> I know this stuns the Arabs and the liberals and the politically correct types. But my feeling is that this place would be quieter and know less suffering if the matter had been resolved once and for all. If Ben-Gurion had carried out a large expulsion and cleansed the whole country—the whole Land of Israel, as far as the Jordan River. It may yet turn out that this was his fatal mistake. If he had carried out a full expulsion—rather than a partial one—it would have stabilized the State of Israel for generations.

In case the link with the United States was unclear, Morris points out, "Even the great American democracy could not have been without the annihilation of the Indians. There are cases in which the overall, final good justifies harsh and cruel acts that are committed in the course of history" (43).

This dialectic of peace and violence showed up as well in George W. Bush's comments concerning Israel. Without even blinking at the contradiction, he managed to slip from peace to violence within a few seconds: "Freedom is also at the heart of our approach to bringing *peace* between Israel and the Palestinian people. . . . Israel is a democracy and a friend, and has every right to defend itself from *terror* (Applause)" (Bush 2004b). Before we know it peace and violence are rubbing up against one another. Of course, the standard line here is that the hindrance to peace in Israel and the Middle East is the "terrorism" of Arab opposition to Israel. If only that hurdle could be overcome, then peace would sprout forth, or at least free trade. At a pinch, trade would come first: "Our vision is a Middle East where borders are crossed for purposes of trade and commerce, not crossed for the purposes of murder and war (Applause)" (Bush 2004b).

At this point there is an extraordinary parallel between the United States and Australia, not least because Australia depends on the United States for information to use as travel warnings. Compare the following travel warning with the one for Australia in the preceding chapter (this one from January 16, 2006, emphasis added):

Travel Warning
This information is current as of today, Mon Jan 16 12:22:53 2006.
ISRAEL, THE WEST BANK AND GAZA
This travel warning is being issued to update information on travel restrictions for U.S. government personnel in the West Bank and to reiterate threats to American citizens and interests in Israel, the West Bank and Gaza. It supersedes the Travel Warning issued April 7, 2005.

The Department of State urges U.S. citizens to carefully weigh the necessity of their travel to Israel in light of the risks noted below. The Department also urges U.S. citizens to defer unnecessary travel to the West Bank and avoid all travel to Gaza.

Terrorist *attacks* within Israel have declined in both frequency and associated casualties. However, the potential for further *violence* remains high. ***Resentment against efforts to promote peace,*** *and ongoing Israeli military operations in the Occupied Territories could incite further violence in Israel and* the Occupied Territories. *Israeli security services report that they are investigating between 40 and 60 planned terrorist attacks at any given time.* The February 25 suicide bombing of a Tel Aviv nightclub is a reminder of the precarious security environment, even when a cease-fire has been declared.

The anticipated evacuation of Israeli from Gaza could lead to violence in Israel by settler groups. *Settler organizations* have already organized a series of large-scale demonstrations and are reportedly planning acts of *civil disobedience* and other protests that at best will be severely disruptive and *at worst may result in physical confrontations leading to violence.*

The U.S. Government has received information indicating that *American interests within Israel could be the focus of terrorist attacks.* For that reason, American citizens are cautioned that a greater danger may exist in the vicinity of restaurants, businesses, and other places associated with U.S. interests and/or located near U.S. official buildings, such as the U.S. Embassy in Tel Aviv and the U.S. Consulate General in Jerusalem.

Throughout Jerusalem, the State Department urges American citizens to remain vigilant while traveling, especially within the commercial and downtown areas of West Jerusalem. Israeli security services report that they continue to receive information *of planned terrorist attacks* around Jerusalem. In addition, American citizens should stay away from demonstrations and generally *avoid crowded public places, such as restaurants and cafes, shopping and market areas and malls, pedestrian zones, public transportation of all kinds, including buses and trains and their respective stations/terminals, and the areas around them.* Spontaneous or planned protests within the Old City are possible, especially after Friday prayers. Some of these protests have led to violent clashes.

American employees of the U.S. Embassy in Tel Aviv and the U.S. Consulate General in Jerusalem are *prohibited from using all public transportation.* The Old City of Jerusalem is *off-limits to them after dark all week and between the hours of 11:00 A.M. and 2:00 P.M. on Fridays.* U.S. government employees are *also forbidden from patronizing discos and nightclubs.*

American citizens in Gaza should depart immediately, a recommendation the State Department has maintained since the deadly roadside bombing of a U.S. Embassy convoy in Gaza on October 15, 2003. U.S. government personnel are *prohibited from all travel in Gaza.* Overall conditions of *lawlessness* prevail, Israeli military operations continue, and *areas of violent conflict shift rapidly and unpredictable.* Militants have abducted Western citizens and held them for short periods, and the Hamas terrorist organization has threatened attacks against U.S. interests.

In September and October 2004 and February 2005, *citizens of Western nations, including Americans, involved in pro-Palestinian volunteer efforts were assaulted and injured in the Occupied Territories by* **Israeli settlers** *and harassed by the Israeli Defense Forces. Those taking part in* **demonstrations, non-violent resistance,** *and "direct action" are advised to cease such activity for their own safety.*

For official operational needs only, U.S. Government personnel are permitted to travel to and stop in cities and towns in the West Bank, depending on prevailing security conditions. For limited, personal travel, U.S. government personnel and family members are permitted to transit the West Bank on primary roads to reach the Allenby/King Hussein bridge and the Dead Sea coast, north of Ein Gedi and Masada, in the south. For safety and security reasons *all cities, towns and settlements in the West Bank, including Jericho and Bethlehem, remain strictly off-limits for personal travel by U.S. government personnel and family members.* U.S. government personnel and family members are expressly prohibited from using Route 443 between Modi'in and Jerusalem for personal travel.

All travelers who enter or travel in Gaza or the West Bank should exercise *particular care when approaching and traveling through checkpoints and should expect delays and difficulties.* Travelers should also be aware they might not be allowed passage through checkpoints.

Any American Citizen who intends to travel to Israel, the West Bank or Gaza in spite of this and prior warnings should carefully review the Consular Information Sheet for Israel, The West Bank and Gaza. That reference describes other potential dangers and difficulties and offers detailed security recommendations. ***Palestinian-Americans face many additional obstacles and regulations that are described in that document.***

. . . As a consequence of the current limitations on official travel to the West Bank, and the prohibition on travel by U.S. government employees to Gaza, *the ability of consular staff to offer timely assistance to U.S. citizens in these areas is considerably reduced.*

Although we find similar talk and hope for peace, the warnings of the dangers for U.S. citizens in Israel and Palestine are more urgent and explicit than in the Australian statement. Words such as "violence," "terrorist," "confrontation," and "attack" litter the text, and there are a series of explicit curfews and prohibitions for U.S. Embassy and consular staff. However, I would like to focus on a few items that are even more telling. First, note how the Gaza Strip is characterized as a zone of "lawlessness" where even the

Israeli occupying army has trouble. Further, Israelis living in Gaza are "settlers," not colonists. One wonders, of course, how the image of lawlessness sits with the idea of settlers, unless of course we are in the ideological construct of the Wild West of the United States. Second, an inconspicuous sentence says far more than at first appears: "Palestinian-Americans face many additional obstacles and regulations that are described in that document." An unfortunate group? From a U.S. perspective, they are a migraine headache. But the sentence points to another element forgotten in the clean ethnic and religious lines that are drawn in these various texts: What of the Palestinian Americans, whether Muslim, Jewish, Christian, or anything else? And what of the Arab Jews (Sephardic Jews) or even Ethiopian Jews?

Finally, the violence from Palestinian groups is the result of "resentment against efforts to promote peace," an extraordinary example of doublespeak if ever there was one. Then we find that Americans and others involved in pro-Palestinian demonstrations and "non-violent resistance" have triggered violence from Israelis, especially the colonists. Everyone, it seems, is becoming violent in the face of peace. Or rather, the threat of peace generates violence from both Palestinians and Israelis. At this point the U.S. State Department's travel warning makes explicit the logic of the fantasy of Israel. In the previous chapter I suggested that the fantasmatic kernel, the unresolvable trauma in that fantasy, is not violence but peace itself. The real terror is peace, and any effort toward peace generates further violence. I repeat the point I made there: should peace inexplicably break out in the Middle East, then without the uniting force of a foreign foe Israel and Palestine would tear themselves apart through the internal political, religious, and class conflicts that have been kept at bay.

Nancy Pelosi in her speech of 2005 made a desperate attempt to put the usual spin on such a situation when she reflected on a congressional trip to Israel, Egypt, Lebanon, Jordan, and Iraq:

> One of the most powerful experiences was taking a helicopter toward Gaza, over the path of the security fence. We set down in a field that belonged to a local kibbutz. It was a cool but sunny day, and the field was starting to bloom with mustard. Mustard is a crop that grows in California, and it felt at that moment as if I were home.
>
> And then we were told that the reason we had to land in that field, as opposed to our actual destination, was because there had been an infiltration that morning, and they weren't sure how secure the area was. And that point alone brought us back to the daily reality of Israel:

even moments of peace and beauty are haunted by the specter of violence. (Pelosi 2005, emphasis added)

Not quite, for she should have said: even moments of violence and danger are haunted by the specter of peace.

A Christian Capitalist Fantasy, or, Bush and Islam

The third and by far most intriguing anomaly was George W. Bush, especially his public statements on Islam. Much to the dismay of his handlers and speech writers, he was known to depart from the text of his speeches and make ad lib comments. That this made him far more interesting goes without saying. But first let me return to my discussion of the fantasy of Israel in Australia. There I argued that the fantasy of Israel is a distinctly Christian fantasy that quietly removes Judaism from the "Judeo-Christian" pair. If in Australia it takes the path of a "relaxed and comfortable" Australia, in the United States it takes the form of Christian Zionism, a position that is loudly proclaimed and reasonably well known in the United States and Israel, so much so that it can be exploited for Israel's benefit.

However, it also takes the form of what I called a Christian capitalist fantasy, one that is loaded with that curious ideological mix of freedom and the market. In this case we find that Israel, just like the United States, embodies precisely these elements, and the hope is that they will spread throughout the Middle East. The problem is that there always seems to be some hindrance to the realization of that fantasy, and now that hindrance takes the shape of terrorists, or Palestinians, or Muslims, or Arabs, or Canaanites, which is really the same amorphous thing for such a fantasy. If only this hurdle can be overcome, if only peace could be achieved, if only the last terrorist were to be hunted down, then unfettered capitalism would sweep through the world. The current situation is in fact rather frustrating, since it looked as though capitalism had indeed broken through with the end of the cold war and the collapse of an effective alternative in communism. Exit the communists, enter the Muslims.

Here my argument concerning Australia is relevant. The Australian Christian fantasy embodies an unstable vision of Australia that identifies specific hindrances which need to be removed for the fantasy to be realized. The paradox for the fantasy is that, should such a dream be realized, it would collapse. If we turn to the United States, we need to ask: What is most feared in terms of the U.S. fantasy of Israel, or rather, this Christian capitalist fantasy? What, in other words, is the fantasmatic kernel of this fantasy? The terrorist bomb in an airplane or railway station? The breeding hordes of Arabs taking over the world? The hurricane that strikes a major U.S. port-city? No: what is feared is the full realization of the fantasy itself, namely, unfettered capitalism throughout the globe, especially in Arab countries and Muslim majority states. To put it bluntly, if communism and then the Arab world were not actual opponents to unfettered capitalism, then they would have to have been invented. Or rather, as monochrome blockages to capitalism they have been and are invented. For this is the function of the fantasy: to hold out the hope for such a world and then block it.

At this point George Walker Bush turned out to be very intriguing. He was in fact rather good on Christian-Muslim relations and in countering anti-Muslim violence in the United States following the September 11 attacks, often at the expense of his Evangelical allies. Bush visited a mosque six days after the September 11 attacks and declared, "Islam is peace. Muslims contribute much to the country; [they] are doctors, lawyers, law professors, members of the military, entrepreneurs, shopkeepers, moms and dads, and they need to be treated with respect." In response to anti-Muslim violence he commented, "I've been told that some [Muslim women] fear to leave [their homes], some don't want to go shopping for their families, some don't want to go about their ordinary daily routines because, by wearing cover [*hijab*], they're afraid they'll be intimidated. That should not and will not stand in America" (quoted in "Bush Visits Mosque" 2001: 12).

In response to comments by his Evangelical allies Pat Robertson, who said, "Adolf Hitler was bad, but what the Muslims want to do to the Jews is worse," and Jerry Falwell, who called the Prophet Muhammad "a terrorist," Bush replied on November 13, 2002, "Some of the comments that have been uttered about Islam do not reflect the sentiments of my government or the sentiments of most Americans" (quoted in "In the Capital" 2002: 3). The initial problem was to keep a lid on anti-Muslim violence in the United States, but was this necessary a year after the September 11 strikes? Bush seemed to be concerned about the extent of the dirty little relationship his administration had with the leading Evangelicals. On this occasion he went on to say, "Islam, as practiced by the vast majority of people, is a peaceful religion, a religion that respects others. Ours is a country based upon tolerance . . . and we respect the faith and we welcome people of all faiths in America."

Contrary to his usual practice, Bush remained consistent. In early 2004, he once again attracted the ire of Evangelical Christians when he declared, notably during a press briefing alongside British Prime Minister Tony Blair, that Christians "worship the same god" as Muslims. Responding to a question, Bush declared, "I do say that freedom is the Almighty's gift to every person. I also condition it by saying freedom is not America's gift to the world. It's much greater than that, of course. And I believe we worship the same God." A key Bush ally, Ken Lund of the Southern Baptist Convention, responded, "We should always remember that he is commander in chief, not theologian in chief. The Bible is clear on this: The one and true God is Jehovah, and his only begotten son is Jesus Christ" (both quoted in "In the Capital" 2004: 3).

What are we to make of this? Was Bush alienating a sizable portion of his voting base? At the time it seemed that this was not the only group that was in a hurry to put as much distance as possible between themselves and Bush. Liberals, social democrats, and the Left in all its varied colors always found Bush and his neoconservative power base obnoxious, but in the second year of his second term as president all shades of the Right began to abandon him as well. Internationally the disastrous invasion and occupation of Iraq was waiting to take its toll. On top of that, domestically the two major moments were the failure to respond decisively and rapidly to the aftermath of Hurricane Katrina in New Orleans in 2006 (why would you bother when those left are blacks, Latinos, and poor white trash?) and then the dismay and furor at his approval of the purchase of six U.S. ports by a company owned by the government of a key U.S. ally, the United Arab Emirates.

Either Bush had lost the plot, as his allies and supporters seemed to think, or, as I prefer, perhaps he was a little *too close to the plot*. On these matters, the Right is worth listening to, especially when it votes with its feet. The problem for the Right is that with these acts Bush gave us a glimpse of a realized fantasy, a fantasmatic kernel laid bare. What was implied with declarations of worshipping the same god, or Muslim peace and tolerance, or selling U.S. assets to Muslims is precisely what the fantasy I have been tracking in its various forms holds forth: unfettered capitalism throughout the globe. But whenever Bush gave, however unwittingly, those who hold most strongly to that fantasy a glimpse of its possibility, they dumped him and ran for the hills. For they knew, equally unwittingly, that the realization of that fantasy would be the end of what it promised. They want their myth, but they want its blockages too.

What, then, is to be done? If realizing the myth, if grasping the fantasmatic kernel should lead to the unraveling of capitalism, then that is what the Left should do. In other words, the Left should call capitalism's bluff.

CHAPTER SEVEN

Mythmaking for the Left

[The Left is] the locus where the question of politics, and above all of the limits of the political . . . can be formulated and dealt with.

—Julia Kristeva (1996: 174)

Now it is time to take the hazardous path of mythic construction. It is all too easy to criticize the abuse of myth, but quite another to engage in mythmaking itself. And that myth asks, What if? What if we pushed the political myth of the Right to its logical end? What if we reveal the con of such myths of the Right that I have explored in the previous chapters and revealed their grisly underside? What if we bring the fantasmatic kernel out from its corner? In this sense it is a negative myth for the Left, for it calls on us to embrace the myth which the Right has presented to us and tell the myth's full story with all its consequences.

Why would I want to take this path? It relies on what I have called Ernst Bloch's cunning of myth. This cunning has been part of the earlier discussions as an underlying, submerged concern. Here it becomes the main voice. To recap: the cunning of myth means that the subversive possibilities are not merely repressed by reactionary ones; rather, sedition arises from within the dynamics of reaction. Myths, especially of the political variety, have a sly knack of undermining the dominant ideology that so often seeks expression in such myths. This wily dimension of myths shows up in two major aspects of my discussion: calling the bluff on the unbearable truth of a realized capitalist utopia and invoking the Real of chaos from my discussion of the master myth of Genesis–Joshua, a myth that remains so important for contemporary political myths. Indeed, a reuse of this myth enables us to take the side of rebellion, of natural and political chaos that runs deep in the Hexateuch.

Four major steps structure this chapter. I begin by drawing together various threads from the preceding chapters, particularly the definition of political myth that I developed in the first chapter and then worked through in the subsequent chapters. Second, I touch on the work of one of the great mythmakers of capitalism, Milton Friedman, who constructs an Edenic myth of capitalist plenty. Its premise is that if capitalism can get past its various hindrances, whether government interference, greenies, socialists, or others, then it can come into its full glory. There is, however, another side to this utopian myth, and that is a dystopian myth of the destructive effects of unfettered capitalism. In order to build this alternative dimension, I move on to focus on the fundamental tension between capitalism's need to expand and environmental limits. This tension forms the basis of an alternative myth, one that is repressed by the one-sided account of Friedman and his ilk. I ask the same question Freidman does: If we remove the various hindrances and blockages to the full realization of capitalism, what might capitalism look like? In the conclusion I ask how we might respond to such a myth.

THREADS

Let me begin by returning to the definition of political myth that I developed in the first, theoretical, chapter. Political myths are characterized by six elements: the labyrinth of language, a dialectic of reaction and subversion, the psychoanalytic notion of fantasy, cunning, virtual power, and eschatology. Or, to put these terms in relation to one another, political myth is marked by a labyrinth of language, a labyrinth that creates worlds which play with the dialectical tension between subversion and reaction. The psychoanalytic description of fantasy outlines the workings of such a dialectic in precise detail. However, through cunning, myths work around this tension and open up political possibilities that may be characterized as eschatological "fictions of completed truths." Such myths are not merely reactions to, or imaginary resolutions of, political situations; they may also have a virtual power over such situations.

In light of this definition, the mythmaking of this chapter comes out of the preceding two chapters. In other words, by reworking the dialectic of reaction and subversion, I ask how positive, progressive possibilities might emerge from the largely reactionary myth that I called the fantasy of Israel in both its Australian and U.S. versions. This reworking seeks to uncover the political myth of the Right in all its destructive glory in order to uncover that myth's cunning.

Before diving into this delectable task, one point of clarification is needed. In this book I have traced a certain slippage in the content of the political myths that interest me. I began with the comprehensive political myth of the Hexateuch, of the stretch of text from Genesis through Joshua in the Hebrew Bible. Part of that exploration involved identifying a distinct fantasy of Israel within the biblical political myth, a State-in-waiting and a sacred economy that would never be realized in any way close to its depiction in the text. In the next step, my discussion of Australia, I began with the fantasy of Israel as a central feature of a certain Australian political myth. Although that fantasy manifested itself most obviously in Australian foreign policy it became apparent that these were not its only features: the other side of the fantasy is a distinctly Christian fantasy that projects a domestic myth of Australia. Thus far the development is from political myth to a specific content of the fantasy of Israel to a Christian fantasy. The final step came with my discussion of the United States, for here the fantasy of Israel is not merely a Christian fantasy, it is also very much a capitalist one, a Christian capitalist myth, if you will. Although the content of these myths moved from a Hebrew political myth to a Christian capitalist myth, the form remains remarkably similar. There is a distinct mythic logic that appears again and again through the midst of the changing content. It is that logic that I exploit once more in what follows.

CAPITALIST MYTHOLOGY

I begin with the one-sided utopian political myth of capitalism as it has been expounded and developed by one of its most accomplished mythmakers, Milton Friedman. Indeed, this myth is a final step on the path from the Hebrew political myth to the Christian capitalist fantasy. Friedman draws deeply on precisely the material that has been the subject matter of this book, namely, the mythic material of Genesis–Joshua. For Friedman capitalism is the nature not of fallen man, but of redeemed man. Were capitalism's dream to be realized, were we to overcome the final hindrances that block its way, we would find ourselves in a state that is both a prelapsarian Paradise and a postconquest Promised Land.

Nobel Prize winner, writer, and presenter with his wife, Rose Friedman, of a TV documentary series called *Free to Choose* in 1980, market evangelist, and untiring traveler, Friedman is an accomplished ideologue, mixing detailed analysis with sweeping statement. Thus, while we find his and his disciples' work studded with the paraphernalia of the hard sciences and mathematics—graphs and formulae such as the "quantity theory of money" (Friedman 1956) and the "expectations-augmented Phillips Curve"—we also find passionate arguments in favor of capitalism. Much of the literature presents Friedman as a monetarist and therefore an opponent of a Keynesian economics that he once espoused, but reading his *Capitalism and Freedom* (2002; see also Friedman 1984), originally published in 1962, one soon realizes that communism is the great enemy. To counter the appeal of the USSR, Friedman, as is well known, links "economic freedom" with "political freedom": in a command economy there is no economic freedom, hence no political freedom. This means that government interference with the economy in any form is bad; laissez faire is therefore good, and the Market should rule. The history of economics, according to Friedman, shows that depressions, as well as fluctuations in prices, output, and employment, are the result of government interference, especially through federal reserve banks, and not market forces (Friedman and Schwartz 1963). And so we get, linked in with Friedrich von Hayek's (1960) *The Constitution of Liberty*, what became so much a part of the political and economic propaganda during the Reagan and Thatcher years: small government, privatization, deregulation in all areas, and an attempted return to the old laissez faire. Friedman has pushed his agenda into any part of the world that will hear him, from the United States to Chile, arguing for the end of compulsory education and the introduction of school vouchers, the legalization of drugs, the privatization of social security, the end of the draft and of tariffs and protection, the deregulation of retirement benefits and old-age pensions, the removal of federal reserve banks, the removal of licensing in medicine and law, the futility of economic sanctions against other countries, and more.

Friedman is quite clearly an old-fashioned liberal, advocating the values of free choice and laissez faire. But with this background, I am interested in Friedman's ability as a mythmaker and defender of capitalism. A mythical figure himself,[1] often touted by his supporters as a rebel and a visionary, his personal narrative is tied up closely with the master myth: as a sole pioneer in the early sixties, set upon on every side by critics and unbelievers, he won through to widespread success.

Along with this personal narrative, Friedman smothers his writing in great dollops of myth. Let me give two examples. The first, from the 1982 preface to *Capitalism and Freedom*, is more tame, although the narrative sweep is impressive. It passes from an Egypt of big government, whether communist or capitalist welfare state, through the wilderness of disillusion to the victorious conquest of Ronald Reagan. All the while Friedman (2002: viii) casts himself as a Moses figure at the service of the Market:

> The change in the climate of opinion was produced by experience, not by theory or philosophy. Russia and China, once the great hopes of the intellectual classes, had clearly gone sour. Great Britain, whose Fabian socialism exercised a dominant influence on American intellectuals, was in deep trouble. Closer to home, the intellectuals, always devotees of huge government and by wide majorities supporters of the national Democratic party, had been disillusioned by the Vietnam War, particularly the role played by the Presidents Kennedy and Johnson. Many of the great reform programs—such guides of the past as welfare, public housing, support of trade unions, integration of schools, federal aid to education, affirmative action—were turning to ashes. As with the rest of the population, their pocketbooks were being hit with inflation and high taxes. These phenomena, not the persuasiveness of the ideas expressed in books dealing with principles, explain the transition from the overwhelming defeat of Barry Goldwater in 1964 to the overwhelming victory of Ronald Reagan in 1980—two men with essentially the same program and the same message.

The grab bag of evils and hindrances is impressive: communism, Fabian socialism, trade unions, public housing, aid to education, the Democrats, affirmative action, to name but a few. "Huge government" in whatever form is the problem, but note the rhetoric: one by one they have "gone sour," are "in deep trouble," are "disillusioned," and have "turn[ed] to ashes." There is also an undercurrent of an ethical-cum-theological loading in this narrative, for all of these things are evil and need to be overcome.

However, my favorite text in the collection is the following. Let me quote it first before commenting:

> The fecundity of freedom is demonstrated most dramatically and clearly in agriculture. When the Declaration of Independence was enacted, fewer than 3 million persons of European and African origin (i.e., omitting the native Indians) occupied a narrow fringe along the eastern coast.

Agriculture was the main economic activity. It took nineteen out of twenty workers to feed the country's inhabitants and provide a surplus for export in exchange for foreign goods. Today it takes fewer than one out of twenty workers to feed the 220 million inhabitants and provide a surplus that makes the United States the largest single exporter of food in the world.

What produced this miracle? Clearly not central direction by government. . . . Unquestionably, however, the main source of the agricultural revolution was private initiative operating in a free market open to all. (Friedman and Friedman 1980: 3)

An extraordinary text, is it not? I hardly need to point to the conjunction of the Garden of Eden and the Promised Land in this text, a land, to borrow a phrase, flowing with milk and honey (minus the indigenous peoples!). Or, in Friedman's terms, we have the "fecundity of freedom," a "miracle," a "revolution" produced by "private initiative operating in a free market open to all." This, I hate to say, is not my experience of the United States, where I found myself time and again witnessing the stark contrast between a vast sea of poverty surrounding islands of privilege.

But Friedman needs to be careful, for one might be mistaken in believing that the Promised Land of this myth has been achieved in the United States. So he must play off the specific example with the myth still to be realized. Agriculture is but a glimpse of what lies before us, for a far greater world of fecundity and freedom awaits us if only we can get past the hurdles presented by the interference of government. But what does that myth look like? Apart from bowing to the will of the Market, the key lies with the status of general equilibrium: in the ideal state, in which the market is complete, consumers are rational, and there are no external disruptions, all factors of a capitalist economy will achieve equilibrium. Thus supply meets with demand, wages come together with prices, no one is wealthy and no one is poor; in short, the price and quantity of goods stabilize so that all prices are exactly what they should be and the quantity of all goods and services is exactly sufficient to meet all wants. This is the moment of optimal equilibrium (or what is known as pareto optimality). But it can happen only when the market is given free rein, fulfills its mission, and is not hindered in any way by the external forces. An Edenic, utopian picture, is it not, in which the market realizes its great mission?

We are in fact in the realm of Adam Smith's manifesto of capitalism, *The Wealth of Nations*, which, for all its economic arguments that Marx would pull to pieces and then use to build his theory, ultimately relies on a mythical construction. As Susan Feiner (2002: 13) points out, the title of Smith's book comes from Isaiah 60:4–5:

> Lift up your eyes round about, and see;
> They all gather together, they come to you;
> Your sons shall come from far,
> And your daughters shall be carried in the arms.
> Then you shall see and be radiant,
> Your heart shall thrill and be enlarged;
> Because the abundance of the sea shall be turned to you,
> *The wealth of nations shall come to you.*

UNLIMITED CAPITAL ON A LIMITED PLANET

Surely this myth is hopelessly one-sided, telling only part of the story. Let us see what that underside looks like. I begin with exactly the same premise as Freidman and others like him: if we can remove the various blockages, whether government interference, welfare, regulation, and now greenies, anticapitalist protestors, feminists, and so forth, only then will capitalism finally come to fruition. The trap is that such a full-blown capitalism looks somewhat grimmer than Freidman et al. would have us believe.

One line in developing this underside to the myth of capitalist plenty is to point to the volatility of capitalist market economics, with its waves of boom and bust, with its economists still guessing how it does indeed work and what to do about it to keep some semblance of stability. Such a line has been taken by many before me (see, e.g., Mandel 1975), so I take another path. The underside to this myth of unrestricted plenty generated by capitalist markets lies, I suggest, in two fears that send the pulse of the West racing more than any others in the early twenty-first century: the fear of Islamic "terror" and the fear of environmental destruction and collapse. My premise is that both fears are codes for another, deeper fear, namely, the end of capitalism. I have already written of the first in my dissections of the Australian and U.S. versions of the fantasy of Israel, so here my focus is on the second. In doing so, I invoke directly the chaos of the Real that came through in my reading of Genesis–Joshua, particularly in the form of political rebellion and natural chaos.

The reason for focusing on the tension between capitalism and the natural environment (variously recast as resources, raw materials, or "natural" capital) is that we have at this time a distinct convergence between socialism and various green movements. It is part of a resurgence of the Left in all manner of new forms that include the return of socialism in South America, vast numbers of radicalized youth after anticapitalist protests from Seattle to Melbourne and Genoa, the renewed appeal of anarchism for teenagers, and the spiritual and religious Left. As for the Greens, they have more than once been described by the Right as watermelons: green on the outside and red on the inside. Absolutely correct, it seems to me. The convergence is premised on the fact that the Greens, along with the socialists, are by definition opposed to capitalism. This is, of course, a bold statement to make, for there are any number of mild green groups for whom a slightly more concerned capitalism is needed: one with solar and nuclear power, with "ethical" investments, and so forth. However, such positions are really severe compromises, for at its heart the green movement is anticapitalist.[2] My basis for this definition, a common one among the Greens, is that the unlimited growth of capitalism stands in profound tension with a limited planet. Thus, if the Greens want to preserve the latter, then they must be against the former. I will explore this tension more in moment, but it will suffice for now to point out another contradiction: capitalism relies on such limits to function in the first place, and yet those limits inhibit the full realization of capitalism.

Of course, there are multiple variations of the green movement, from radical groups like Sea Shepherd, Earth First!, and the Animal Liberation Front, through the New Age Left (what I like to call lovingly the Loopy Left) and the media-savvy Greenpeace to genteel middle-class bird watching groups like the Audubon Society and even the pro-capitalist Planet Ark. With green political parties we find a coalition of many such groups developing and pushing a common agenda. The radical groups have provided a great service to the green movement as a whole, for in recoiling from programs that include direct action and ecoterrorism, the agendas of more moderate groups have been widely accepted. Thus, with support from an increasing number of scientific studies, from climatologists to the U.S. Geological Survey and the Intergovernment Panel on Climate Change, along with on-the-ground experiences of ever hotter summers and melting glaciers, one belief is very widely held: global warming is a reality and human beings are responsible for it. There might be more difference of opinion over whether killing whales and dolphins and baby seals is bad, or whether genetically modified food harms your health, or whether kangaroos are a pest or not, but global warming is different. Those who deny it are like those who deny that smoking is bad for you or who argue that the earth is flat.

Global warming has become the basis for the fear of widespread environmental destruction. For this reason, global warming has become the focus of intense political debate. Thus we find the covert silencing of scientists and the suppression of scientific studies that verify global warming by the governments of John Howard in Australia (Murphy 2006) and George W. Bush in the United States. And when such a position becomes no longer tenable, various other positions come forward, such as changing the terminology from global warming to "climate change" or even "climate shift." But this act is far less interesting than the reason for such resistance: that any environmental restrictions on industry are bad for business ("Stark Warning over Climate Change" 2006).

Even more intriguing is the way scientists become political figures. Thus Professor Sir David King, the government's chief scientist in the United Kingdom, pointed out in an interview on April 14, 2006, that even an average 3 degree (Celsius) rise would be catastrophic ("Stark Warning over Climate Change" 2006; Alok 2006). King based his comments on a report from the Hadley Centre, the U.K. government's center for research into climate change (Jenkins et al. 2006), and the outcomes of a conference in early 2006 (Schellnhuber et al. 2006). He outlined a picture of the loss of crops threatening 400 million people, the destruction of major rain forests, the loss of half the world's wildlife reserves, the possibility of up to 3 billion people losing safe water supplies as the result of flooding, and the destruction of major coastal cities such as Edinburgh, Dundee, and Inverness and large parts of London. The key lies with the level of the greenhouse gas carbon dioxide (CO_2): once it gets to 550 parts per million (ppm) it would be about twice the level as at the beginning of the Industrial Revolution. To put this in perspective, typical periods of cooling in the past have generated 220 ppm of CO_2, while during periods of warming the level has been around 270 ppm. Until 1800 the level of CO_2 had not been above 280 ppm; by 2005 it was 380 ppm, and it continues to rise. Despite the EU's agreed level of 2 degrees Celsius, the 3 degree rise is the minimum level that the U.K. government feels achievable given the refusal of the United States (and Australia) to make any effort to reduce such greenhouse gases, along with the rapid economic growth of India and China. Despite some encouraging words, King doubted the will to make changes to achieve even this level.

The information changes rapidly, and yet the basic picture is now rather well known. While the Hadley Centre report and the book *Avoiding Danger-*

ous Climate Change (Schellnhuber et al. 2006), or even the widely discussed *Fourth Assessment Report* of the Intergovernment Panel on Climate Change (2007), provide often conservative pictures of the possible effects of global warming, events seem to outstrip the reports. All the same, their assessments are strikingly apocalyptic: a change of 3 degrees Celsius will begin the process of melting the Greenland ice sheet; melting the Arctic sea ice (7.5 percent since 1970) to the point where there will be no sea ice in summer by about 2030 at the latest; releasing methane from the warming of cold ocean floors; and slowing and possibly switching off the warm Gulf Stream. There will be effects on major "carbon sinks" such as the Amazon forests, where drying and warming will lead to the extensive dying off of the rain forest; the rise in precipitation in other areas; and the production of weather and temperature extremes, such as flooding and the wider range of hurricanes as tropical weather moves farther north and south.

What immediately strikes anyone who considers the problem is how radically insufficient the various solutions seem to be. It is a little like treating cancer with aspirin. Thus, in the face of the widespread agreement on global warming and various scenarios of its long-term effects, we find campaigns to encourage us to use energy-efficient light bulbs, to turn off the tap while brushing our teeth, and to restrict our showers to three minutes. One day a year the community is urged to gather up the rubbish in waterways and parks and put it in plastic bags to take to the garbage dump. We should recycle glass, plastic, and paper and compost our fruit and vegetable waste. We should write a letter to our local politician or perhaps even a senator or government minister about the oil crisis, forgetting in the process that nearly all such politicians are pro-capitalist. Or we might consider catching a bus one day a week rather than drive our car. Or we may wish to invest our money in "ethical investments" (is that not an oxymoron?), particularly green investments. Or when we connect to the electricity network, we can opt for green power, or better still install solar power and gain credits for putting power into the grid.

As for David King, his message has been a mixed one. While he talks about the urgent need of setting measures in place now to deal with climate change, he also argues that such change, at least at 3 degrees, is inevitable. The fact that environmental groups such as Friends of the Earth find him too pessimistic, arguing that such a gloomy future is not inevitable, says much about the status of such groups in the debate ("Stark Warning over Climate Change" 2006). However, what I find most intriguing are King's comments concerning the built environment (Climate Group 2004). Even with recent hot summers such as the one of 2003–4, there were billions of dollars in damage, thousands of lives lost, and a steep rise in insurance claims. Sixteen of the world's nineteen large cities sit on the coast and are vulnerable to rising sea levels and would suffer significant destruction through storms and rising sea levels. With further temperature rises the effects on such infrastructure will rise. I hardly need to point out that what King is actually talking about is capitalism. In other words, the real fear is not that we will have a dead planet, not even that human beings will cease to exist as a species on the globe (which, in my more pessimistic moments, I think may well be a good thing), but that capitalism would come under severe stress.[3]

Here the politics of science comes into full play. Rather than some hippy on the high seas, David King is a professor of physical chemistry and head of the University of Cambridge's Chemistry Department. Yet even he is small fry compared to the international scientific weight of the Intergovernmental Panel on Climate Change, a U.N. body that draws upon the work of more than two thousand scientists from around the world. Let me take two responses to this material, both by Australians. One is sympathetic yet offers a message of hope; the other is vociferously unimpressed. Both are, of course, eminently qualified. Tim Flannery (2005b) is a professor in Macquarie University's Division of Environmental and Life Sciences, and he has been at the forefront of global warming commentary since his book *The Weather Makers* appeared. Flannery has been sounding warnings about the effects of climate change, especially in Australia, where much farming is already marginal and the majority of the continent is arid or semiarid (Flannery 2005a; Jones 2005). For instance, the cities of Melbourne, Sydney, and Adelaide, all in the southeastern corner of the continent, are now in a zone of long-term drying due to three effects: the hole in the ozone layer (remember that?), which has drawn rain-bearing weather systems southward into the Southern Ocean; the El Niño effect in the Pacific Ocean, which now brings back-to-back dry spells to the southeastern section of Australia; and global warming itself. The total effect is to put all three cities on a path of severe water shortages within a decade, cities in which well over half of the total population of Australia lives. Although Flannery agrees with King, he offers a more hopeful view, arguing that there are still ten to twenty years to turn things around and make long-term changes. An offer of hope and warning against an eschatological scenario, is it not? The question, however, is: Why offer such hope? Apart from quibbles over interpreting scientific data, the underlying desire is to motivate people to bring about sufficient change in order to preserve our current way of life—that is, again, to preserve capitalism.

The third figure is Ian Plimer, one of a group of climate change skeptics (Fyfe 2004) and a professor of geology at the University of Melbourne. Though he has challenged the evidence and arguments for global warming as dogma and not fact, he now accepts that global warming is happening, but argues that it is due to natural causes and is part of a longer cycle of global warming and cooling (Plimer 2001). The responses to the Intergovernment Panel on Climate Change and other reports he describes as hysteria and superstition. His economic reading is what interests me. We should welcome such warming, he says, since global warming is good for business: "Thriving of life and economic strength occurs during warm times" (Plimer 2006: 12). A few meters of sea level and a few degrees of climate change are no great problem, argues Plimer, in the overall evolution of the earth. However, he goes one step further, suggesting that any policies of curtailing global warming will have disastrous economic effects. In other words, let capitalism get on with its unfettered production and consumption. There are two points I want to make about this debate: global warming is accepted by all parties, and the debate is now purely over its causes and its effects. The latter is either good news for capitalism, or bad.

Into this scene comes the question of oil. Only a few years ago the mention of oil shortages in most social gatherings would at best generate the polite smiles and bored looks reserved for fanatics. With a few jolts in world oil prices, speculation on oil stocks, heated up trading on oil futures, hoarding all the way from Lufthansa to Chinese industry, the automobile industry's futile efforts to come up with mass-produced vehicles that run on alternative fuels, and the eventual admission that the invasions of Afghanistan and Iraq were for the sake of securing precious oil sources, oil is now a topic of newspaper headlines. One does not need to look at Internet newsletters of dubious origin to find information on current oil reserves.[4] Sources from inside the oil and energy industry as well as major government bodies such as the U.S. Geological Survey paint the following picture. The available reserves of oil have been known, whether "discovered" or "undiscovered," since the 1970s. Further, if it has not already happened, the famed "Hubbert's peak" is due to happen sometime before the end of the first decade of the twenty-first century. The name derives from Marion King Hubbert (1956, 1965), who argued already in the 1970s, to the chagrin of his employer, Royal Dutch Shell, that the crucial point with oil would not be when the last oil barons have dripped dry, but when petroleum output begins to decline and demand exceeds supply. Hubbert calculated 2000 as the year, and oil industry insider geologists such as Kenneth Deffeyes (2003, 2005) largely agree, give or take a year or two. Indeed, according to the Energy Watch Group (2007), an organization of independent German-based scientists, that moment arrived in 2006, after which we can expect a 7 percent drop in oil production per year, precisely at a time of ever-increasing demand. Needless to say, the price in oil will generally continue to move skyward.

However, unlike the widespread belief in global warming and its deleterious effects, the response to oil shortages is more curious: here we find an equally widespread belief that "they" will find an alternative fuel. Some suggest nuclear power, but this is much more costly to produce, both in building the facilities (three times the cost of a conventional power station) and to operate (Frew 2006). Others point to hydrogen cell units with zero pollution, neglecting the point that it takes more energy to produce such units than the energy that comes out of them. Others point to solar power, yet others to coal-rich countries such as Australia. It seems as though there is an inverse ratio: the closer the peak, the greater the denial. Or rather, the closer the crisis, the greater the blind belief in a solution. Thus the oil crisis is real, but "they" will come up with another fuel. Or, as the code runs, capitalism will survive without too much disturbance to my way of life.

The catch with all of this is that the oil crisis seems a far more solvable problem than other environmental conundrums. It is, after all, just a fuel, a source of energy, however vital, not quite as huge a problem as global warming. Are there not other sources of fuel and energy? The answer is yes, but at far greater cost, for each of the alternatives is far more expensive to produce. Like coal, oil is an extraordinarily cheap energy source. For instance, while the ratio of energy input to output for oil is 1:20, for fuel from cereal crops it is 1:2, and for the hydrogen cell it is 1:0.8, a net loss. Nor will such changes in energy come without those positioned—the old owners of capital, the new holders of finance capital—to take advantage of a new situation. It is not a matter of putting a little device in your car and running it on, say, methane collected from sewage plants and one's individual fart power. Given the crucial role of oil in transport by sea, land, and air, in industries that rely on such transport from delivery all the way from raw materials through production to distribution and consumption, in the production of plastics (20 percent of world oil production), steel, aluminum, glass, cement, and machines, and in agricultural production, the effect will be profound. Even cultural habits will be affected: gone will be the satisfaction for an angry hormone-filled teenager to hit the accelerator and squeal the tires of her or his old car. Humming off in a small solar-powered vehicle or clanking the pedals on one's bicycle does not produce quite the same effect.

My point in bringing together global warming and the oil crisis is that the two are directly related. For it is the fossil fuels, coal and oil and natural gas, that produce the greenhouse effect with carbon emissions. The worst possible scenario is if some massive unknown oil reserve or two is found, flooding the globe and its spreading industries with yet more cheap oil. This would merely accelerate the process of global warming and its associated problems.

With this broad picture in place, none of which is particularly earth-shattering news, let me draw it all together with some key theoretical points concerning capitalism and its limits. The first comes from Fredric Jameson (2005), who points out that a fully fledged capitalism is only just beginning to be glimpsed with globalization. The battles over globalization—producing either widespread celebration or deep angst—suggest a transition within capitalism, but it is a step toward a fuller realization of the logic of capitalism. Thus, with the increasing commodification of nature, of the genome, of plant species, of air and water, we begin to see what a fully commodified world might look like. Jameson, who first championed what is now the widely held position that postmodernism is not merely a style one may adopt or shake off at will, but the cultural logic of late capitalism (Jameson 1991), now argues that globalization is the flip side of that postmodernism. It would seem that globalization is a better term for the nature of capitalism now, rather than Mandel's (1975) troubled notion of "late capitalism." And in a move that remains unpalatable for the Left, Jameson points out that the intelligent conservatives—always worth listening to—are right: globalization is a fact of our existence under capitalism.

The second theoretical point comes from Slavoj Žižek, who argues that one of Marx's great discoveries was the constitutive exception. In his search for the secret of the commodity form, Marx took the anomalies of capitalism, the perceived blockages and distortions of the system, as the secret of the system itself: in short, the constitutive exception. Thus, the cycles of boom and bust, economic crises, and wars are not deviations that stand in the way of the full realization of capitalism, but symptoms of the system, revealing the fundamentally antagonistic and unstable nature of capitalism. In other words, as Žižek points out time and again, drawing from Marx's third volume of *Capital*, the limit of capitalism is capital itself, the capitalist mode of production: the limit to the system is that which provides the very possibility of that system. Hence, in light of the constant tension between the forces and relations of production, the constant need to revolutionize itself to survive, the "normal" state of instability and imbalance, "it is this very immanent limit, this 'internal contradiction,' which drives capitalism into permanent development" (Žižek 1989: 52). For instance, the dream of open competition sees the great hurdle not merely in terms of tariffs imposed by the governments of various nation-states, but in monopolies. Yet the desire to outstrip one's competitors has as its final goal precisely such a market monopoly, which then becomes the condition of possibility, the constitutive limit, of the "free market."

One of Žižek's most astute observations is the way he turns Marx's discovery of the constitutive exception, or the symptom, back upon him. The characteristic Žižekian move is to identify what is excluded or, even more profoundly, the methodological assumption that cannot be identified—variously the Real, the surplus object, objet petit a, the fetish, or woman—as the secret to the structural logic of the system, of thought, society, economics, or whatever. As far as socialism itself is concerned, the fundamental problem is that socialism is not possible if we stick with Marx's logic. Thus, in light of the argument that the very possibility of a particular system may be found in its limits, socialism must therefore operate with similar blockages, anomalies that both forestall the full realization of socialism and thereby enable its very existence. In terms of the tension between the relations and forces of production, Marx was right when he saw this tension as the very logic of capitalism itself, the instability and constant revolutionizing that are the result of this tension or limit. But Marx was wrong when he argued that a socialist revolution arises when the forces of production outstrip their relations, and that socialism would rearrange the relations of production in order to release the forces of production. In other words, actually existing socialism could not help but replicate capitalism: "Is it not already a commonplace to assert that 'real socialism' has rendered possible rapid industrialization, but that as soon as the productive forces have reached a certain level of development (usually designated by the vague term 'post-industrial society'), 'real socialist' social relations began to constrict their further growth?" (Žižek 1989: 53). In other words, the dream and promise of socialism, as it was conceived, was unfettered production without the limits of capitalism. But is this not at the heart of the myth of capitalism? If only we can get past these last hurdles, if only we can get rid of the nuisance of the union movement, if only we can arrange the workforce so that it does as it's told, then capitalism will walk into its Promised Land. The inevitable conclusion is that the reason socialism, as it was conceived and practiced, is so unbearable for capitalism is that it provides a glimpse into the realization of the myth of capitalism.

Above all, however, I want to draw from Žižek the point that the full realization of the myth of unfettered production and consumption, of complete commodification without restrictions, would mean the end of capitalism, for then it would be in the impossible state of operating without limits. So far I have drawn upon Jameson and Žižek, but finally I turn to one of David Harvey's (1998) most important but nearly neglected essays. Harvey takes Marx's dictum concerning history—that history may shape men, but men shape history—and extends it to the natural environment. Although human beings may be formed by nature, they also form nature itself. In other words, the natural environment may shape a particular social formation, but that social formation fundamentally shapes the natural environment that shapes the formation. Thus the availability of raw materials, the types of animals and plants available in an area, the climate, rainfall, and fertility of the soil obviously shape the type of social formation that may arise. It is not for nothing that a hunter-gatherer existence characterized life in Greenland for centuries, while the naturally occurring sheep, goat, cow, and pig in Mesopotamia profoundly influenced the development of a sacred economy there. But mode of production also shapes nature. For instance—adding to Harvey's examples a few of my own—the imposition of capitalism on Greenland from the time of Danish colonization in the eighteenth century not only shifted the economy to a fish-based export one, but also produced the global warming that now affects nature directly and rapidly, from the melting Greenland icecap to changing fish types with warmer waters. In Australia, the introduction of a host of plant species since British colonization in the late eighteenth century, along with animals such as the cat, dog, goat, deer, camel, water buffalo, and rabbit—all of which have gone feral—means that nature in Australia means something far different under capitalism than it did under an earlier mixture of hunter-gatherer economy and settled agriculture economy. Add to this the fact that much of the arable land is shaped by a mix of fertilizers and pesticides, and any notion of an Australian "nature" is impossible to separate from capitalism.

All of this may seem like common sense, but too often one comes across the assumption that nature has ultimate precedence, that it is the most basic of all materialisms, setting the agenda for language, culture, textual production, and society. Harvey's argument puts paid to that assertion.

But his argument also puts a new spin on Barry Commoner's first law of ecology: "Everything is connected to everything else." Commoner's law of interconnectedness overcomes the opposition between human beings and nature, asserting that human beings are part of a much larger nature; Harvey shows that, more extensively than other species, human beings are part of nature by profoundly shaping it. There is nothing more or less natural, for example, about a freeway overpass than a field full of grass and trees.

However, Harvey also has his eye on political change. His final two points are the most telling. First, what we know as nature is held together and sustained by capitalism—all the way from agribusiness, with its pesticides, herbicides, patented hybrids, and genetic modification, to forest management and national parks. Second, if capitalism were to break down, so would nature as we know it. For this reason he advocates gentle political change, a long program of winning control of government and wielding political power according to a socialist agenda. For otherwise, he argues, in the ensuing social chaos fascism is far more likely to arise.

For Harvey then, capitalism constructs a certain form of nature which would undergo severe stress and readjustment if capitalism were to be removed. But this is where the contradiction I have been tracing comes to a head, for if we turn everything around and make Harvey's conclusion our starting point, then *capitalism constructs its own limit*, that is, nature. We have, then, a further contradiction: capitalism constructs the nature on which it relies, but that nature in all its many facets is ultimately a limited resource.

Let me draw together the three contributions from Jameson, Žižek, and Harvey. While capitalism is inspired by a myth of the unfettered growth of production and consumption, by the perpetual increase of the "wealth of nations," it can operate only with the limits it simultaneously produces and yet so desperately wishes to overcome. Perhaps the ultimate self-produced limit is that of nature: if nature as we know it is created and sustained by capitalism, nature is crucial for capitalism to continue. Remove one, the other collapses.

IT'S THE END OF THE WORLD AS WE KNOW IT (AND I FEEL FINE)

The picture I have been constructing in the preceding section—the dialectical tension between an unfettered capitalism and a limited environment of its own making—is the first step to telling the other side of the myth of capitalist plenty. That myth is predicated on the need to remove all the limits and hurdles to the full realization of capitalism. In telling the second part of the story, I ask exactly the same question: What if we dispense with those hindrances, such as various oppositional groups or even government interference? So I would like to speculate a little, conjure a myth of what a fully realized capitalism of endless production and expansion might look like.

This is a myth in which the forces of chaos break through. Rather than the program of control and order that constantly struggles to keep chaos at bay, chaos breaks the dams and surges forth. At the point where demand exceeds supply and production begins to fall, the cost of oil begins to climb steadily. At first it has a mild inflationary effect, from air travel to private vehicles to the transport of goods. Since it has been at historically low prices, oil reaches a more realistic price. However, the massive oil-hungry economic growth of India and China heightens the crisis, and small-minded commentators blame these two for the oil crisis. Stockpiling, the frantic scramble to secure dwindling oil reserves, invasions of one oil-producing country after another, exploration and expensive extraction in the Arctic and Antarctica all add to the price spikes. Soon cheap air travel comes to an end and major airlines go bankrupt. Small cars replace large cars and there is a rush for alternative fuels, including steam, solar, hydrogen cell, and nuclear, but they have only limited success as their production and prior-to-sale transport require far more energy than it takes to actually power the vehicles. Before long small cars for private use disappear as available fuels, from dwindling oil to limited alternatives, are reserved for military, police, medical, and government services. Those countries with coal, such as Australia, may do a little better, since their existing power generation mostly relies on coal. However, with oil now a scarce resource, coal becomes highly desirable. Australia makes a short-term fortune on selling coal to the world, but that runs down the coal supply all the more quickly and accelerates global warming. The languishing nuclear power industry becomes an apparent savior as massive resources are pumped into building nuclear power stations. But their high cost of production and short lifespan add to the cost of energy. They turn out to be no less polluting than oil, mainly due to the huge amount of energy required to build the facilities. A handful of meltdowns later, the occasional bomb, and before we know it the pollution from nuclear power turns out to be far more potent than oil pollution ever was. The transport of goods shifts decisively from trucks back to steam trains while coal is available. As the oil crisis deepens, cities that were built relying on the motor vehicle for transport start to break up. Suburbs become small towns, linked to others by rail. The freeways and motorways and highways stand empty, great monuments to the false confidence of the past as people begin to use some as cycle ways, breaking others up to use for landfill, building materials, paving, and whatnot. In the United States, Eisenhower's great freeway network—originally planned as an alternative to rail should there be a nuclear strike from the USSR—is now commandeered by the military to maintain control against rising civil unrest.

A single crisis like that of oil will not bring about the end of capitalism. Indeed, those strategically positioned make huge profits from the skyrocketing oil prices, from coal reserves, and from the frantic research into other fuels. But coal produces even more, and nuclear power produces almost as many greenhouse gases as oil does. The days of oil begin to look like an Edenic period of environmental care. Global warming accelerates; the Arctic pack ice begins to break up, disappearing entirely in September each year; the process of melting the Greenland ice sheet begins in earnest; and more ice shelves off Antarctica break off and melt away. In each area—the Arctic, Antarctic, and Greenland—the once prohibitively expensive extraction of small oil reserves adds to the process of breakup and melting. With the rising sea levels and temperatures the Gulf Stream—paradoxically—wanes and the areas it has warmed start to cool, areas such as Norway and the rest of Scandinavia. Methane begins to be released from the ocean floor as the oceans warm, acidic levels rise in the oceans, and the carbon sinks of the great tropical rain forests fade away as they dry out and the trees die off. The extinction of species, already under way in the age of oil, now becomes massive. In the Caribbean and the Gulf of Mexico huge hurricanes become the norm. Tropical zones begin to spread farther north and south, and hurricanes ravage the coasts from southern Australia to northern China. In Australia old cycles of rain and drought cease, replaced with continuous drought. The already marginal agriculture in much of the country ceases as the arid zones spread, as also in Africa. The cities of Sydney, Melbourne, and Adelaide depopulate as people move to areas with water. Above all, the sea begins to creep over Bangladesh and over low-lying islands in the Pacific and the Indian Oceans such as the Maldives. The dikes in the Netherlands hold, but only because the Dutch engage in the age-old practice of letting a little water in rather than keeping it all out. But given the new conditions, they trade off by flooding a good part of the country to keep the rest. Most of the major coastal cities, ports, and industrial centers around the world begin to feel the pressure. From Rotterdam to London to Lisbon to New York to Copenhagen to Los Angeles to Vancouver, the nodes of trade and finance inexorably shrink and disappear under the waves. And with them goes much of the infrastructure of large population centers. In some places, mostly in the overdeveloped centers of capital, people relocate and rebuild at great cost, but in many Third World countries they simply abandon the sites altogether. Already weakened by the oil crisis, the global economy shakes and shifts and desperately tries to adapt.

The human cost of such relatively rapid change is of course immense. Environmental refugees soon outnumber political refugees, and governments become increasingly intolerant of refugee claimants. Following the examples of Australia and Sweden, they throw them in concentration camps, chase them away, or sink their boats. The remnants of the welfare state, itself the West's effort to counter the appeal of communism, are discarded. The belief in the Market above everything else soon sours as masses of poor surround smaller and smaller islands of privilege. The increasing underclass challenges the small and powerful owners of capital, whom the armed forces encircle in protective cordons. Civil unrest and spontaneous outbursts of violence are dealt with brutally by the armed forces. With the breakdown of agriculture, especially the production and distribution of fertilizers, pesticides, genetically modified seeds and animals, as well as the loss of formerly arable land to arid zones and floods, crop production and animal husbandry fall away rapidly. Apart from the obvious effect of widespread starvation, the greater effect is large-scale environmental breakdown. Barren, saline, dry, or wild, much of what used to be regarded as picturesque now looks more like an industrial wasteland or a Tarkovsky movie set. Crops, if they are planted, are no longer able to survive, overcome by crop-eating pests and weeds hardened by decades of adapting to herbicides and pesticides, and the flocks of domesticated animals die from disease without their chemical mix of inoculations, or they are seized and slaughtered by hungry human beings or go feral.

Fundamentalisms of every stripe—Christian, Jewish, Muslim, Buddhist, Hindu—gain sway in many areas. Christian fundamentalism becomes the state-enforced ideology of the United States, although it fails elsewhere. Before long it comes into conflict with the remnants of capitalism. Despite a close allegiance of the Religious Right and market economics, the economic models developed from the Bible turn out to be incompatible with the extractive economics of capitalism. Politically, people seize on a whole range of options, from anarchism to fascism and every possibility in between. Splintered and decimated, what is left of the Left faces the paradoxical situation of both having lost credibility as an alternative political force with any cohesion and providing a massive resource for the explosion of new social and economic options.

With the great age of mass global transport over, or indeed driving some distance in one's car, with the loss of transport networks and the splintering of cities, with starvation and environmental collapse, new social formations develop for the sake of food, shelter, survival, and protection from others. In Australia, if one is lucky enough to have been able to move to a place that has adequate rainfall without being too hot, it is not that uncommon to find wombat stew on the menu. Technology, which was severely restricted under capitalism—most of what was made was useless, and what was useful was clumsy and didn't last long—may gain a new burst of life, but in entirely different directions. Perhaps the Thule people, who lived in northern Greenland for eight centuries or so since 1000 CE, provide a limited example: in the extremely harsh conditions of living close to the polar cap, they produced some of the most astonishing technological developments, from whalebone houses to waterproof wetsuits, with the most limited resources. The global population will be smaller, for whatever mode of production follows capitalism it will not be able to support the mass numbers that were fed under capitalism. Food supplies will be much more local, transport more limited to walking, bicycle, and perhaps beast of burden. Who knows what the social, economic, and political formations will be? Released from the possibilities and strictures of capitalism, hitherto unimagined social and economic forms may well emerge.

This little myth of unfettered capitalism fills out the missing half of the myth of plenty that I traced a little earlier. The reader will be reminded of any number of apocalyptic dystopias, ranging from films such as *Mad Max* to *An Inconvenient Truth* (2006) and *Crude Awakening* (2007). It is customary to dismiss them as millenarian or apocalyptic speculation, refer to the fateful history of earlier forms of such stories, and then move on. Yet what I have cast as a myth with its own embellishments is regarded by many as highly likely, and is used both as prophetic prediction and warning to act now to save our world as we know it. I suggest that the Left needs to take a different tack, namely, to say that we do indeed want the end of the capitalist world as we know it. The last thing we want to do is save it.

Conclusion

How might we respond to this myth of unfettered capitalism in all its tarnished glory? There are two possibilities, it seems to me, and they both draw upon themes that run throughout this book. In my discussion of the permutations of the political myth of Genesis–Joshua I identified two linked features of the chaos of the Real, one natural and the other political. The first shows up in stories such as the Flood and Korah's rebellion; the other comes to the fore with the murmuring stories in the wilderness and what I called the demimonde, the rebellious undercurrent of the text. The possible responses to this myth of unrestrained capitalism may well follow similar paths.

As for the first response, which pertains to the natural world, it really involves calling on capitalism to realize its myth as soon as it can, for then it will bring about its own end through this internal contradiction between unlimited capital and a limited environment. Here it is a case of eschewing visions of better societies, or offering concrete models and plans of what to do and how to go about doing it. Instead, this option foregrounds the chaos engendered and repressed by capitalism as a way out of capitalism. It brings what is nothing less than a doomsday scenario to bear on capitalism and espouses it as a strategic move. Only by taking such a hard line will the ultimate contradiction arise. It is, to borrow a saying from Paul Keating, a former Labor prime minister of Australia, like skiing down a slope on one ski without poles.

It is the age-old response that we find in the myth of the Flood in Genesis 6–9: in the face of unending evil, God destroys all life on earth except for Noah's Ark. The problem is that there is no guarantee that social and economic life after the deluge will be qualitatively different. Capitalism is, after all, immensely adaptable and elastic. Capitalist relations and means of production may well return in a new form.

The second response picks up the other, more political element of the chaos that the political myth of Genesis–Joshua perpetually attempts to close down. We saw it in the story of the woman's rebellion in the narrative of the Fall, in the various insurrections cast as sin against the deity, indeed in the whole people themselves who become rebels when they take on Moses and Aaron. As for how this political element of chaos might work as a possible response to the full myth of capitalism, I suggest that the source of that rebellious opposition comes from precisely those elements that are cast as hindrances or hurdles to the complete realization of capitalism. Earlier I took as my premise for both halves of that myth the need to remove those blockages. Now I would like to bring those various hindrances back into the picture.

They embody the cunning of myth of which I am so fond—the way myths of repression have an uncanny knack of undermining themselves and showing how they might come unstuck. They are the various annoyances that John Howard would have liked to dispense with in his quiet walk in the evening of his middle-class suburb, or the terrible blight on the United States in the eyes of its neoconservatives: the greenies, hippies, ferals, feminists, indigenous activists, anticapitalist protestors, religious Lefties and critics, trade unionists and socialists, even with the odd social democrat thrown in. If we are to believe the different versions of the political myth of capitalist plenty, then this riffraff is not merely a hindrance to the full flowering of capitalism, they are in fact a real threat to its very possibility. They embody all the chaotic elements that capitalism could well do without. This is where the political myth of the Right is absolutely correct: should these forces of chaos have their way, capitalism would putter to a standstill.

What would the globe look like if these greenies, anarchists, socialists, religious Lefties, and whatnot had their way? What kind of political myth might emerge if they were to set the agenda? Here I come face to face not with a famine of the imagination, but a great wealth of political myths. Full of utopian dreams, visions, plans, and political agendas, they spill out in all directions. But then the Utopians too are used to dealing with the realms of political myth. In light of all of these myths, the myth of capitalist plenty begins to look sparse indeed.

They are a mixture of old and new. Communism has its own myth, captured by the slogan "From each according to his abilities, to each according to his need!" (Marx and Engels 1975–2004, vol. 24: 87). Anarchists too have their myth, of the absence of the state and the self-organization by collectives, all of which is captured in Bakunin's (1980: 77) principle of "absolute rejection of every authority including that which sacrifices freedom for the convenience of the state." Pacifism too has a long heritage, predicated as it is on a social and economic system in which peaceful cooperation is the rule rather than conflict and warfare. At its deepest level, pacifism argues that all forms of human society have been built around conflict, so what is needed is an entirely different social formation that is cooperative rather than conflictual.

Or there is the old tradition of Christian communism that has inspired one movement after another, including various religious collectives, Winstanley's Diggers of the seventeenth century, Étienne Cabet's (1788–1856) Icarian communities, the "Old Believers" in nineteenth-century Russia, and the International League of Christian Socialists today. The source of their ideal is the mythic image from Acts 2:44–45: "And all who believed were together and had all things in common; and they sold their possessions and goods and distributed them to all, as any had need."

These are more or less well known, with rather long histories, but they do constitute the basis of differing political myths. However, I am also interested in the wide variety of newer political myths. I might call upon the variety of feminist myths, not so much those that provide an image of an egalitarian capitalist society in which women can acquire as much capital as men, but rather a postcapitalist and postpatriarchal society. What that might look like is the subject of much debate, but it is premised on the point that all forms of human society have featured the complex dominations of one sex over another. Does the end of such patriarchies lead to equality, separate economic and social systems, or the celebration of difference?

Like the feminists, the Greens have all manner of political myths, although they all turn on an economy and society that does not destroy the natural environment of which we are a part—whether in terms of global warming, the extinction of species, monoculture, or pesticides and herbicides. Among the Greens there is an immense amount of discussion, planning, and debate concerning the shape of society, new forms of global government, uses of technology and science, the role of religion, and, of course, the structure of the economy. All of it is very much part of the process of constructing political myths of alternatives to capitalism.

The possibilities may keep multiplying, and I am sure the reader will be able to come up with a few more. Some are wilder, some more practical. Some would resist the characterization of political myth, claiming that they embody concrete programs rather than mythical stories. I would point out that we still need a myth or two to underlie such programs. Many of them overlap with each other, sharing similar concerns, critiques, and images, embodying the concerns of one or more of the others within their own myths, such as ecofeminism, ecosocialism, or primitivist anarchism.

Given the range of such myths, how would they interact with each other should they be given the chance to do so? The imposition of one master myth over the others is a fatally flawed procedure, since it all too quickly runs into the problem of being undermined by reaction, by the emergence of the fantasmatic kernel. A plurality of such myths rather than one master myth would avoid such a self-destructive pattern. Or indeed, if one goes to ground and turns in on itself, then it would be a lesson learned, not to be repeated. Do they fight it out by force of arms? Perhaps the pacifists need to have a word here and take over the ministries of defense. Above all, it seems to me that all these political myths and more should be on the table, that the process would be one of constant debate, argument, negotiation, experiment, failure, and beginning again. A distinct element of chaos in this vast procedure would not be a bad thing.

Let me return, finally, to Georges Sorel. There is one point that stays with me, apart from his examples of the general strike, Marx's catastrophic revolution, the French Revolution, Mazzini's efforts at Italian unification, the failed hopes of the first Christians based on the myth of the immanent return of Christ, and the revolution driven by the pessimistic myth of Calvinism, which changed everything from top to bottom (Sorel 1961: 42, 125–26). And that is his point that one of the features of political myths is that despite repeated setbacks and failures, these myths provide the source of the continued determination of the political movements in question.

Appendix

■ *Speech*

ALEXANDER DOWNER
Melbourne, August 15, 2003
At the International Conference on Islam and the West
Introduction

Distinguished guests, ladies and gentlemen.

I'm very pleased to be here today to open this international conference "Islam and the West: The Impact of September 11."

It hardly needs saying that the subject matter is topical. But the conference itself is also timely.

It is almost exactly ten years since Samuel Huntington, writing in *Foreign Affairs*, put forward his hypothesis about the so-called "clash of civilisations."

This phrase has sparked intense debate and become part of the popular lexicon—both in the West, but also, significantly, in many Islamic countries.

Ten years is not a long time in international politics.

But it is probably enough to get a feel for how much of Huntington's hypothesis has been borne out by developments.

And certainly the events of September 11 and subsequent terrorist spectaculars, including the Bali bombings, make such an assessment even more apposite.

Proponents of Huntington's thesis point to these attacks as symptomatic of the war of cultures that he predicted.

Even for opponents of Huntington, September 11 has, in many cases, provoked serious head-scratching about whether he might, in the end, be right.

I for one do not believe that September 11 is the realisation [of] Huntington's clash of civilisations. And I would like to use my address today to put forward three important reasons why.

I would like to explore how Islamist-inspired terrorism largely sits at odds with Australia's own experience of Islam in our region . . .

. . . to explain why I believe that terrorism threatens moderate Islam and moderate Muslims as much as it does the West . . .

. . . and to look at how terrorism, rather than promoting conflict between Islam and the West, is in some instances actually encouraging cooperation.

Religion as a Source of Conflict

Central to Huntington's argument was his view that religion was increasingly becoming, quote, "a basis for identity and commitment that transcends national boundaries and unites civilizations."

Huntington argued that religion was contributing to the division of the world into distinct "civilisations." And that this in turn was drawing new lines of conflict in international politics—in particular between the Islamic world and the West.

Recent decades have indeed seen a growing Islamic identity or affiliation in South East Asia.

Most often it is manifest as a greater observance of Muslim practices and dress codes, particularly among young Muslims.

But Islamic organisations have also become increasingly prominent and active on university campuses and in politics more generally.

Some of these groups have played significant roles in the process of political reform, notably in Indonesia.

Much of this is evolutionary rather than revolutionary.

Islam is not new to the region. Islamic influences in South East Asia date back to the 14th century, much of it the result of trade between the region and the Middle East.

Indeed Islam has played an integral role in the development of the modern day nation states of the South East Asia archipelago through the 19th and 20th centuries.

But does this necessarily mean that, as Huntington would have it, Australia is destined for conflict with its Muslim neighbours? I think not.

Certainly we are not sanguine about the future directions of political Islam in the region.

Many countries in the region face significant social, political and economic challenges.

There remains a strong body of popular anti-western sentiment on which extremists can feed.

And we have also seen the pernicious role that external groups, such as Al-Qaeda, are playing in the promotion of radicalism and violence.

But equally we should not be overly alarmist and maintain some perspective.

We should certainly not confuse the growing incidence of Islamic observance in the region with the emergence of Islamist-inspired terror of the likes of Jema'ah Islamiyya and Abu Sayyaf.

It is a simple point, but one that often needs re-stating.

The Bali bomber Amrozi no more represents the majority of Muslims in South East Asia than Osama Bin Laden represents the majority of Muslims in the Arab world.

Amrozi is a part of a minority—possibly a sizable minority—that should not be allowed to inform our perception of Islam, even political Islam, in the region.

Indeed the reality of Islam in South East Asia stands in pretty stark contrast to the hateful rhetoric of Amrozi and his colleagues.

By and large the Islam practiced by the majority of Muslims in South East Asia is generally moderate, pluralist in character, and largely tolerant in outlook.

For example, in Indonesia, the world's largest predominantly Muslim country, greater Islamic observance among the population has not translated into a greater desire by people to be ruled under an Islamic system of Government.

In the 1955 election Islamist parties gained 43 per cent of the vote. In the 1999 election that support dropped to 38 per cent.

And Islamic parties that supported a constitutional amendment obliging Muslims to uphold Sharia law won just four per cent of the vote.

Mainstream organised Islam has played a positive role in Indonesian politics.

In particular, Indonesia's two largest Islamic organisations were central to the successful transition to democracy—which if you believe the extremists or Huntington for that matter, is an alien, western value, incompatible with Islam.

It is also worth remembering that for many of these countries Islam may be an important characteristic, but it is not necessarily the defining one.

Indonesia, the Philippines, Thailand and Malaysia are also modern, increasingly open economies, with a record of moderate secularism and increasingly vibrant democratic traditions and institutions.

The Targets of Islamist Terror

The distinction between radical and mainstream Islam in South East Asia was illustrated at a joint press conference held last week in Jakarta by Indonesia's two largest Muslim organisations.

At that press conference NU Chairman Hasyim Muzadi said that all Indonesians, and not only the individual victims, had been injured by the recent terrorist bombing at the Marriott hotel in Jakarta.

Together with the Head of the Muhamadiyah he called on the Indonesian security services to act decisively to bring the culprits of this outrage to justice.

Muzadi's comments and the condemnations of the bombing by other Muslim figures in Indonesia underline what I believe is perhaps the strongest reason for rejecting the Huntington thesis.

That is, that Islamist inspired terror strikes as much at moderate Islam and moderate Muslim countries as it does at the West.

Certainly much of the rhetoric used by the extremists echoes Huntington's theme of irreconcilable cultural differences between Islam and [the] West.

And there is no denying that a strong current of anti-western sentiment lies at the core [of] Islamist extremism.

But increasingly a great many Muslims also understand that they and their moderate vision of Islam, is also under threat.

Whether it be from the terrorist's vision of building Taleban-style theocracies in moderate Muslim countries . . .

. . . or from the extremists' misappropriation of their faith . . .

. . . or indeed, as we saw last week in Jakarta, from acts of violence and terror.

That perception is not limited to Islam in South East Asia.

Bin Laden rails against the West but his chief target has always been the government of Saudi Arabia.

In Egypt, in the not so distant past, we saw how Islamist terrorists neatly combined their antipathy toward the West with their goals of overthrowing the Mubarak government by attacking foreign tourists.

And many of Al-Qaeda's operatives were first blooded in violence directed against their own Government in the Middle East.

Nor is the threat or its method unique to Islam. The style and psychology of the extremists finds [*sic*] parallels in the history of the West.

It echoes the violent "propaganda by deed" philosophy of some late 19th century European anarchists.

Or like Baader Meinhof or the Italian Red Brigade, Al-Qaeda and Jemaah Islamiy[y]ah, don't care that their violence is unlikely to produce immediate results in terms of their political program; it is the act of violence which is important.

All of this serves to underline the fact that what we face today is not some new clash between civilisations.

Rather, it is the age-old clash between moderates and extremists; between tolerance and intolerance; between those who uphold the integrity of their faith and those prepared to kill innocents in its name.

Cooperation Rather than Conflict

In assessing the impact of September 11 on relations between Islam and the West it is all too easy to focus on the negative.

Often lost in the discussion are tangible examples of how, since September 11 cooperation between Muslim and non-Muslim states has in fact increased in some areas; in practical, tangible, but still meaningful ways.

The obvious case is the fight against terror.

As governments and people in Muslim countries come to understand that they are the common victims of the extremists, their willingness to cooperate across Huntington's cultural divide has also increased.

Today we see greater cooperation between Muslim and non-Muslim states in combating terrorism than perhaps we have ever seen.

Quiet and but [*sic*] very effective collaboration between the United States and Saudi Arabia has, for example, replaced the more cautious and fitful cooperation of some years ago.

Muslim countries that once supported the Taleban, helped to remove it and Al-Qaida from Afghanistan.

Muslim and non-Muslim countries have worked to freeze over $137 million in terrorist assets since September 11.

Around 65 per cent of senior Al-Qaeda members have been captured or killed—an outcome which would have been impossible without the cooperation of Muslim countries.

In our own region a network of bilateral counter-terrorism MOUs [Memorandum of Understanding] have facilitated practical, operational-level cooperation between our security, intelligence and law enforcement agencies.

Australia has signed six counter-terrorism MOUs with regional countries: Indonesia, Malaysia, Thailand, the Philippines, Cambodia and Fiji.

We co-hosted with Indonesia, a regional conference on money laundering and terrorist financing and are exploring options for further such summits.

And of course, Australian and Indonesian police forces cooperated closely and effectively in the joint Bali investigation, and more recently in Indonesia's investigation of the Marriott hotel bombing.

Clearly there has been a strong focus on pragmatic and effective cooperation with regional countries against the terrorist threat.

What is also clear is that Muslim and non-Muslim countries have generally shown a willingness to work together to address a common threat.

Think how difficult—and ineffective—the fight against terror would have been without this cooperation.

But not only is this cooperation effective, it also builds confidence and helps dispel misapprehension between Islamic countries and the West.

Of course our effort to bridge between our cultures cannot stop here.

We have to look at other mechanisms—including things like this conference—to both help promote greater understanding, and to address the root cause of extremism.

In Australia's case, in parallel with our enhanced security cooperation with Indonesia we have established a Muslim exchange program, under the auspices of the Australia-Indonesia institute.

It is our hope that it will help promote linkages both between our respective Muslim communities, but also between Muslims and non-Muslims in each country.

Similarly we are working with regional governments to strengthen democratic institutions and promote good governance; to alleviate poverty and to help local communities be participants in the global economy rather than bystanders.

I do not believe that poverty is the cause of terrorism—as we have seen with Al-Qaeda, terrorists come from all backgrounds, rich and poor.

But it is important to ensure that for ordinary people there are alternatives to the politics of despair, peddled by extremists.

The Muslim world also has a role to play. In particular it cannot cede the agenda to the extremists. It must speak up—as it has since September 11—to condemn terrorism unequivocally.

It must help us to highlight an Islam that we know is practised by the majority of the world's Muslims, including those in Australia; strong in its faith, proud in its traditions, but willing to engage with people of other religions and cultures on the basis of mutual respect.

Conclusion

Ladies and gentlemen

September 11 and subsequent terror attacks are not necessarily symptomatic of Huntington's clash of civilisations. But that does not mean that such a clash will not occur.

Ultimately it is up to us to determine what our relations will be; whether they will be marked by a clash or by cooperation.

We must strive to understand that diversity and nuance characterise the Islamic world as much as it does the West.

We must recognise that while our prayers might be different our hopes and our fears are more often than not very similar; that values of openness, tolerance, and democratic principles are not things that divide us but things we share.

I am confident that today's conference will do much to promote increased understanding of the complex relationship between Islam and the West.

I wish you well in your deliberations.

■ *Speech*

ALEXANDER DOWNER
August 27, 2003
At the Sir Thomas Playford Annual Lecture

It's a privilege to be invited to deliver the Sir Thomas Playford Lecture.

Much has been written and said about the success, the authority and the honesty of Sir Thomas's political career.

But it was also a career that was profoundly influenced by his Baptist upbringing and lifelong commitment to Christian principles.

It's from them and the sometimes turbulent relations between Church and State that I take my theme today.

Let me begin with a personal anecdote.

Listening to the ABC's [Australian Broadcasting Commission's] AM on Saturday morning 19th October I was dumbfounded to hear the announcer Hamish Robertson say "well, the head of the nation's Anglican Church says the Bali Bomb attack was an inevitable consequence of Australia's close alliance with the United States . . . Dr. Peter Carnley says terrorists were responding to Australia's outspoken support for the United States and particularly its preparedness to take unilateral action against Iraq."

Here was the head of my own church, reported by the ABC as rushing to judgment and blaming the Australian Government for bombing incidents in which so many of our people were killed or terribly injured.

Whether this report was fair or not, it struck me hard.

There was no concentration on comforting the victims and their families, no binding up of the broken-hearted while a shocked nation mourned.

Yet surely that first and foremost is what was needed and what we were entitled to expect.

It was a stark reminder of the tendency of some church leaders to ignore their primary pastoral obligations in favour of hogging the limelight on complex political issues—and in this case a national tragedy—in ways which would have been inconceivable in the Playford era.

This is something that has troubled me for some time.

I will always defend the right of the Churches to enter the political debates of our time.

But they have special responsibilities—to the facts, to their congregations and to their faiths.

Too often, it seems to me, the Churches seek popular political causes or cheap headlines.

And this tends to cut across the central role they have in providing spiritual comfort and moral guidance to the community.

It may surprise some of you to know that an unusually high proportion of federal politicians on all sides are practising Christians who have a sense of faith and listen to what the churches tell us and the rest of the community.

Imperfect as we all too obviously are, we're sincere about the faith that nurtured Western Civilisation.

It's because of our beliefs that we tend to see public life as a vocation—a calling, not just a job.

Beyond the theatre of question time, some of the most impressive and heartfelt speeches in Parliament arise over questions of conscience where shared values make unexpected allies and cross-party acquaintances develop into lasting friends.

Despite deep differences, Don Dunstan the young Labor turk and one-time Anglican synodsman developed a friendship like that with Playford over the years when the premier very often gave him a lift home in his car, on those nights the house was sitting late.

Playford was a religious Non-Conformist. My own denomination is, as I've said, Anglican.

These days that means that, like my denomination, I'm very often torn between hope in "the church militant here on earth" and near-despair at her divisions.

I remember where once there was a confident global communion, with room for civilized doctrinal disagreement under a canopy of shared belief.

Those days are long gone.

In their place, uncertainty or disbelief in the fundamental tenets of Christianity are commonplace among senior clergy.

Not since the Enlightenment swept through France has clerical scepticism been so much on the ascendant.

I'm reminded of the dilemma faced by Louis XVI and his advisers, when the see of Paris fell vacant.

In the Gallican church the king had almost as much of a say in senior appointments as in England.

The problem was one of finding someone both suitable and orthodox.

When, in 1785 the Archbishop of Toulouse was recommended, Louis replied "Ah, no; the Archbishop of Paris must at least believe in God."

The last forty years of the church has seen even core issues of faith such as the resurrection become the subject of vigorous dispute.

Of course it is possible to believe in God in some sense, or other, without believing in the resurrection, as many good Jewish and Muslim Australians do.

But the Christian church has always taught that belief in the resurrection was the central tenet of Christianity.

As a politician, I offer no judgement on this issue: just the observation that some church leaders have moved away from their core beliefs.

Not surprisingly then, it's often said that we are entering a post-Christian age.

Whether there is a terminal decline in Australia remains an open question.

It depends in part on whether you place more reliance on what people say they believe or in their actual church attendance.

43 per cent of Australians believe the resurrection was an actual historical event, yet 20 per cent attend church frequently according to the ACS [Australian Church Life Survey] 1998 survey.

It may be that the gap can best be explained by what contemporary congregations experience in the pews.

Confidence in the church has fallen in recent years—from 56 per cent in a comparable survey in 1983 to 39 per cent.

Still, the growing role of televised services for an ageing population and the unexpected strength of new Pentecostal, Evangelical and Catholic youth movements may not have been captured in the survey.

However, a post-Christian age poses a relentless question to politicians and everyone concerned with the character of our society.

Family life, the education system and the moral instruction provided by other faiths all play an important part.

But without consistent moral teaching and example from bodies like the churches, how can most Australians be expected to behave selflessly or consider the common good and abide by any kind of social contract?

Nature can be relied on to some extent through sturdy instincts like parental love.

But the ties of kith and kin are less binding; the weaving of the social fabric is less confidently and competently undertaken than in Playford's era.

Most of the givens and imperatives in his world view are now optional—relative rather than absolute.

When "everything is relative" is the best that many clergy have to offer on major moral questions, morality starts to become a matter of convenience, being seen to do the decent thing, what feels good at the time or what you can get away with.

This is a kind of ecclesiastical post-modernism.

Those categories may coincide with the good of society as a whole from time to time, but the erosion of a shared sense of the obligations enforced by conscience is disturbing.

I should stress immediately that Christian politicians prize their faith primarily because they believe in it, rather than as an instrumentalist might see it as a useful management tool to encourage civic virtue.

The lament is not for "the good old days" in any simple sense, but for foreshortening of a larger notion of what it means to be fully human.

Those clergy and theologians who have lost sight of the fundamentals have filled the vacuum with all manner of diversions.

For some, social work has become the be all and end all.

Environmental causes, feminist and gay agendas and indigenous rights provide constant grandstanding opportunities.

Most intoxicating of all, and most divisive for their congregations, is overtly partisan politicking.

Apart from disdain for traditional pastoral duties and pontificating self-regard, how best to explain the clerics who issue press releases at the drop of a hat on issues where the mind of the church itself is unresolved or not yet engaged?

The then Bishop of London, Graham Leonard, put it this way: "The Church today, having lost her nerve, shows at times an almost pathetic desire to be loved by the world."

Ingratiating oneself with current popular opinion is a doomed strategy.

Dean Inge summed it up, saying "He who marries the spirit of the age will soon become a widower."

Perhaps that is partly why 29 per cent of Australians feel negative and another 39 per cent neutral or unsure about the church.

As Graham Leonard was wont to remark—bishops and theologians in their public utterance are remarkably vague and uncertain about matters which their faith should teach them with certitude but remarkably certain and dogmatic on matters of considerable complexity and ambiguity about which they have no particular expertise.

Hence political and social judgements are delivered with magisterial certainty while utterances on fundamental Christian doctrines are characterised by scepticism and doubt.

I think it's a polite way of saying that if you can't rely on what they say about what they're supposed to understand, why take all that seriously their opinions on anything else?

It's of a piece with the ADF's [Australian Defence Force's] Anglican bishop, Tom Frame, recently counselling caution about presuming to know the divine mind on strategic questions.

I am not always in agreement with Bishop George Browning of Canberra and Goulburn, but I do agree with his remark that the Church had become involved in the social agenda of Western governments with "indecent speed."

A temperate approach to political engagement would be as welcome now as the end of Labor's attitude to the Catholic Church as a wholly-owned subsidiary.

As Gerard Henderson remarked, the 30 per cent of Catholics on the Howard Government's front bench "is about the same as the percentage of Catholics in the Australian community."

The old legacy of sectarian bitterness which meant that, Judith Brett noted, "Catholics did not join the Liberal Party up until recent times because they felt unwanted" has disintegrated.

Unfortunately, the integration of the Catholic Church into the broader body politic as represented in Parliament has not prevented some of its bishops from making intemperate denunciations of Australia's participation in the Coalition of the Willing in Iraq.

The churches, and in particular the Catholic Church, had called for the application of humanitarian intervention in Rwanda, the Balkans and East Timor.

They were right to do so—but this contrasts dramatically with the approach of many church leaders to the brutal dictatorship of Saddam Hussein.

Few church leaders appeared concerned about the grotesque human rights abuses within Iraq of the Saddam Hussein regime—already the remains of at least 300,000 people have been found in mass graves since the end of the war.

Few church leaders expressed concern that Saddam Hussein had used chemical weapons not only against other countries but against his own people.

Few church leaders seemed concerned that Saddam Hussein had invaded neighbouring countries at the cost of over one million human lives.

Surely that is enough evil to enrage even the most placid church leader.

Instead vocal church leaders seemed more engaged in an esoteric debate about whether the Coalition of the Willing was adhering to international law—when in fact it was Saddam Hussein who was in breach of that law.

To debate international law is fair enough, but these commentators provided a one-sided moral message on war that offered no insight into the moral price the world would pay if it failed to address the vile immorality of the Saddam Hussein regime.

These commentators neither confronted that difficult moral dilemma, nor gave clear guidance.

In some cases they apparently failed to understand that for god-fearing people there was a moral dilemma that needed to be confronted.

Symptomatic of these types of problems was the retiring address by the President of the Uniting Church, Professor James Haire.

He said "We live in a time of profound turning away from God in much of our social and national life."

He went on to say that he believed "egged on by both political groupings in the country, we as a nation had reached new depths of political depravity, especially with the duplicity and harshness of the *Tampa* incident, and the total inability of the Federal Opposition to act as an opposition in the nation, thus depriving this nation of any genuine democratic debate leading up to the election."

I find the accusation of political depravity—not just misguidedness in particular policies, mind you, but depravity—profoundly personally offensive as well as foolish.

That he was attacking both the major parties is no comfort.

As I said at the beginning of this speech Archbishop Carnley, the Anglican Primate, was almost as outspoken and ill-advised on the issue of the Bali Bombings.

Not content with his radio performance, he went so far as to issue a press release, compounding the offence.

He expressed his "concern that by targeting two Bali nightclubs in which large numbers of young Australians were known to gather, terrorists were responding to Australia's outspoken support for the United States."

I felt obliged to respond to this premature and, as later events demonstrated, erroneous posturing and made it clear that we did not know precisely who was responsible for the bombing and the Archbishop needed to be careful before drawing any firm conclusions.

Dr Carnley was obliged to "do a little back tracking" as they say, especially when the bombers began to speak for themselves about their motives.

We have heard from them mostly that Australians were not deliberately targeted.

Rather the idea was to kill Americans and Westerners generally.

One alleged bomber, Imron, declaring "Australians, Americans, whatever—they are all white people."

But where one of these terrorists did mention targeting Australia, the motive was a world away from Iraq.

Imam Samudra said Australians were deliberately targeted because "Australia has taken part in efforts to separate East Timor from Indonesia which was an international conspiracy by followers of the Cross."

There were other reasons offered but the ending of the carnage in East Timor and its liberation, one of Australia's most significant foreign affairs achievements and one of which its people are generally and rightly proud, was uppermost in the conspirator's mind.

So Dr Carnley was wrong.

And sadly, he was wrong in a way that came dangerously close to suggesting that our foreign policy should somehow be dictated by the actions of terrorists.

I firmly believe that when we have to choose between doing the right thing and doing the wrong thing, we should not allow terrorists to influence our judgement.

As Foreign Minister, of course, I'm committed to using diplomatic means as all but the last resort in achieving outcomes in the national interest.

Diplomacy, once almost the special preserve of the clergy, requires patience, good manners and steadfastness in ascertaining the facts in any particular case—attributes which, among many modern clerics, are in short supply.

There are some signs of hope.

In particular, there's the resurgence of youth movements in some of the churches and the thousands of undergraduates who turned out formally to greet Archbishop George Pell when he first visited Sydney University as their new archbishop.

The link between the growing, well-documented social conservatism of many young people and religious observance is part of a pattern.

Demographically it fleshes out the increasingly plausible hypothesis that the baby boomers' children have tended to skip a generation and prefer the values of their grandparents rather than their parents.

Sir Thomas will be viewing that development with the same optimism that many contemporary politicians feel.

The Christian churches, as with other great religions, such as Judaism, Islam, Hinduism and Buddhism, have a central role to play in providing a moral compass to an increasing materialistic world.

While many people, although still too few, have material comfort, as they have achieved that state, they have lost much-needed spiritual sustenance.

The greatest challenge today for leaders of all religions is to forego the opportunity to be amateur commentators on all manner of secular issues on which they inevitably lack expertise, and instead to find the spark of inspiration to give our lives greater moral and spiritual meaning.

I know Tom Playford would have wanted them to rise to that challenge.

■ *Address to National Day
of Thanksgiving Commemoration,
Scots Church*

THE HON. PETER COSTELLO, MP
Treasurer
Melbourne
7.10 pm
Saturday, May 29, 2004

When Jesus told his disciples that they would be witnesses in Jerusalem, Judea, Samaria and the uttermost part of the earth, the known world consisted of the Roman Empire—the Mediterranean and surrounds.

No one in the Roman world, no one in the Jewish world, knew of Australia. From the then known world of the Mediterranean, Australia was beyond even the uttermost parts of the earth.

And yet the teaching of Jesus came to Australia. It took nearly 18 centuries. And we can pinpoint quite accurately the first time a Christian service was held on Australian soil. The sermon was preached by the Rev. Richard Johnson, Chaplain of the First Fleet. It was preached on Sunday 3 February 1788 under a large tree in Sydney. His text was from Psalm 116 Verse 12: "What shall I render unto the Lord for all his benefits toward me?"

The first Australian Christian service was a thanksgiving service. It was thanksgiving for a safe passage in dangerous sailing ships, on a dangerous mission half way around the world.

Two hundred and twenty six years later we meet tonight to mark a "National Day of Thanksgiving" for all the benefits rendered to us, in the modern Australia.

Of course, the members of the First Fleet were not the first people to come to Australia. The Aboriginal people were here long before that. And I am so proud that we have descendants of those first Australians who are here tonight and who we have just honoured.

But it was the First Fleet that brought the first chaplain and first knowledge of the Christian faith to Australia. This was the critical and decisive event that shaped our country.

If the Arab traders that brought Islam to Indonesia had brought Islam to Australia and settled, or spread their faith, amongst the indigenous population our country today would be vastly different. Our laws, our institutions, our economy would all be vastly different.

But that did not happen. Our society was founded by British colonists. And the single most decisive feature that determined the way it developed was the Judeo-Christian-Western tradition.

As a society, we are who we are, because of that heritage.

I am not sure this is well understood in Australia today. It may be that a majority of Australians no longer believes the orthodox Christian faith. But whether they believe it or not, the society they share is one founded on that faith and one that draws on the Judeo-Christian tradition.

The foundation of that tradition is, of course, The Ten Commandments. How many Australians today could recite them? Perhaps very few. But they are the foundation of our law and our society, whether we know them or not.

The first Commandments: Thou shalt have no other God before me; Thou shalt not make any graven image; Thou shalt not take the name of the Lord in vain; Remember the Sabbath and keep it holy; are the foundation of monotheism.

The Commandments: Honour thy father and mother; Thou shalt not commit adultery; are the foundation of marriage and the family.

The Commandment: Thou shalt not to kill; is the basis for respect for life.

The Commandment: Thou shalt not steal; is the basis for property rights.

The Commandment: Thou shalt not bear false witness against thy neighbour; and Thou shalt not covet thy neighbour's property; is the basis of respect for others and their individual rights.

These are the great principles of our society. On them hang all of the laws and institutions that make our society what it is.

When Moses gave the Ten Commandments he initiated the rule of law. From the moment that he laid down these rules it followed that human conduct was to be governed according to rules—rules which were objectively stated, capable of being understood and, if necessary, enforced by the Hebrew judges. Prior to that the people of the ancient world were governed by Rulers rather than rules. The ruler was much more subject to whim and capricious behaviour. Rulers were not subject to independent review or interpretation. The rule of law is the basis for our constitution and justice system.

And so we have the Rule of Law, respect for life, private property rights, respect of others—values that spring from the Judeo-Christian tradition.

Tolerance under the law is a great part of this tradition.

Tolerance does not mean that all views are the same. It does not mean that differing views are equally right. What it means is that where there are differences, no matter how strongly held, different people will respect the right of others to hold them.

I mention this because "The Age" newspaper reported (10 May 2004) that my appearance here tonight has been criticized by the Islamic Council of Victoria. According to the President of that Council by speaking here tonight I could be giving legitimacy to parties that the Islamic Council is suing under Victoria's Racial and Religious Tolerance Act 2001 (the Act).

It is not my intention to influence those proceedings. But nor will I be deterred from attending a service of Christian Thanksgiving. Since the issue has been raised I will state my view. I do not think that we should resolve differences about religious views in our community with lawsuits between the different religions. Nor do I think that the object of religious harmony will be promoted by organizing witnesses to go along to the meetings of other religions to collect evidence for the purpose of later litigation.

I think religious leaders should be free to express their doctrines and their comparative view of other doctrines. It is different if a religious leader wants to advocate violence or terrorism. That should be an offence—the offence of inciting violence, or an offence under our terrorism laws. That should be investigated by the law enforcement authorities who are trained to collect evidence and bring proceedings.

But differing views on religion should not be resolved through civil law suits.

My view on this is not new or recent. In 1994 I opposed a proposed Commonwealth Bill on Racial Vilification on the following grounds:

"The legislation is going to make certain subjects very difficult to discuss in an open way. It is going to vest a large supervisory role in Government appointees over exactly what can or cannot be said."

At the time I was worried that "vilification" legislation would inhibit free discussion of important political issues. Since then the Victorian

Parliament has passed the Act dealing with racial and religious "vilification." No one likes vilification.

We are an open and tolerant society. But if rival camps start sending informants to rival meetings so they can take legal proceedings against each other in publicly funded tribunals we shall not enhance our openness or tolerance.

The proceedings which have been taken, the time, the cost, the extent of the proceedings, the remedies that are available all illustrate, in my view, that this is a bad law.

We would be better to forget the litigation and work to reinforce the values drawn from the tradition that underlies our society—respect for individuals, tolerance within a framework of law, and mutual respect.

This is the legacy of our Judeo-Christian tradition.

Unfortunately today we see that legacy fraying all around us. It is almost as if the capital deposit has been drawn down for such regular maintenance that the capital is running out. The maintenance demands are unending. But we are not building up the capital required to service it.

We do not have to look far to see evidence of moral decay around us. We can see it and hear it in entertainment like rap music, in songs which glorify violence or suicide or exploitation of others.

As we speak drug barons compete for the distribution rights to sell drugs to our children in Melbourne. These rights are so lucrative that they are prepared to kill to protect their profits with 24 or 25 unsolved gangland murders in Victoria since 1998.

These barons sell young people into addiction. Drugs break up families and marriages. Many addicts end up in prostitution or burglary. These outcomes are the very antitheses of all those values set out in the Ten Commandments about how to order society.

People well known to the police apparently live in luxury with no visible means of support or explanation as to how they maintain their lifestyles.

And it seems to me that as a society we have become complacent about this issue, in some cases, the media has glamourised it.

A few weeks ago I called for a sense of outrage about what is happening in our midst. And I pledge that if Federal Tax authorities can assist in tracking and taxing the flow of money that sustains the lifestyles of these drug barons then everything that can be done will be done. We stand ready, anxious, to assist.

We have such a rich heritage. But in so many ways it is being run down. The values which it has given us—respect for life, respect for others, for property, respect for family—seem to be undermined in many ways.

What should we do?

At this point it is usual for some leading churchman from some well known denomination to appear in the media to call on the Government to fix things.

I do not want to suggest that there are no initiatives the Government should take. And what Government can do, it should do. But I do want to suggest something much more radical and far reaching. I want to suggest that a recovery of faith would go a long way to answering this challenge. A Government should never get into religious endeavors. But if our church leaders could so engage people as to lead them to genuine faith we should be much richer and stronger for it.

The Bible tells the story of the Prophet Elijah who got despondent about the state of decay all around him. He was running for his life. He fled out to the wilderness. He sat under a juniper tree and asked to die. He felt alone and let down. He had no supporters. He thought he was the only person left that was true.

But the still small voice of God came to him and lifted him and told him that there were still thousands that had not lowered the knee to the spiritual and moral decay all around him. (1 Kings, Ch 19)

And this is the point I would like to make to those who have gathered here tonight. There are many that have not, in their hearts, acquiesced to the kind of decay which is apparent around us. They do not believe it is right. They earnestly pray for the expansion of faith and yearn for higher standards.

They will get up tomorrow and go to their places of worship in suburbs and towns across the country, affirm the historic Christian faith, and go to work on Monday as law-abiding citizens who want their marriages to stay together, their children to grow up to be healthy and useful members of society, and their homes to be happy. They care deeply about our society and where it is going.

These people will not get their names in the media. They will not be elected to anything. They will not be noisy lobbyists. But they are the steadying influence, the ballast, to our society when it shakes with moral turbulence. They give strength and stability and they embody the character and the traditions of our valuable heritage. It is their inner faith which gives them strength. Our society won't work without them.

All citizens share in the heritage and the blessings that heritage brought to our country, something for which we can all give thanks. We should not take these blessings for granted. We should not become complacent. We should genuinely give thanks because we have been genuinely blessed. And each, to our own ability, should nurture the values which were so important in bringing us to where we are today and which we need so badly to take us on.

Notes

1 Alongside my analyses of political myth in Australia and the United States, one might wish to consult Lincoln's (2000) discussion of the mix of romanticism, nationalism, and Aryan triumphalism in the recuperation of myth by fascism.

2 I have done this elsewhere (Boer 2005–6), arguing that to the traditional categories of myth—cosmogonic, anthroponic, and theogonic—we need to add a fourth, the "poli-gonic."

3 For a Marxist reading of *Enuma Elish*, see Boer (2006).

CHAPTER ONE. TOWARD A THEORY OF POLITICAL MYTH

1 If we want such a definition, we can't do much better than Northrop Frye (1982: 35): "Myth is a form of imaginative and creative thinking." Or, in fuller form, myth tells a society "the important things for that society to know about their gods, their traditional history, the origins of their custom and class structure" (Frye 1990b: 30). As Flood (2002: 6–7) points out, most definitions seek a combination of narrative, subject matter, cultural status (myths as true for a distinct community), and social functions (ideology). Lincoln's (2000) concise definition—"ideology in narrative form"—captures most of these. To be avoided is the baleful affect of Mircea Eliade (1954, 1964) and the Chicago school of history of religions.

2 I am not interested here in detecting a repressed religious condition (à la Žižek), or indeed the odor of a theological corpse in his closet (for that is a game older than prostitution), but rather in exploring the way the category of the necessary fable emerges from within his thought.

3 Alain Badiou did in fact respond in this vein to a presentation of mine that made this point. It was at the "Singularity and Multiplicity" conference at Duke University, March 26, 2005, organized by the Institute for Critical Theory.

4 For Badiou, this is one of the three forms of disaster. The other two are ecstasy and terror. The phenomenologists against whom Badiou warns us are, especially, Paul Ricoeur in relation to psychoanalysis and hermeneutics (Badiou 2004: 129), Jean-Louis Chrétien, Louis Henry, and Jean-Luc Marion (see Janicaud et al. 2000).

5 In this respect, my reading heeds Bruno Bosteels's (2004) call to move beyond the stabilizing task of exegesis to rethinking specific situations in light of Badiou's work, although I suspect my reading of Badiou against himself is not quite what he meant.

6 Here is Badiou (2004: 109): "We have the undecidable as subtraction from the norms of evaluation, or subtraction from the Law; the indiscernible as subtraction from the marking of difference, or subtraction from sex; the generic as infinite and in excessive subtraction from the concept, as pure multiple or subtraction from the One; and, finally, the unnameable as subtraction from the proper name, or as a singularity subtracted from singularisation." You will immediately notice that Badiou has four operations here—undecidable, indiscernible, generic, and unnameable—but I have removed the fourth. Why? Badiou (2003a: 133) has said more recently that the problematic idea of the unnameable may become irrelevant in light of his theory of appearance, which he understands as the move from inexistence to existence. See the detailed discussion of subtraction in *Theoretical Writings* (Badiou 2004: 103–18) and *Infinite Thought* (Badiou 2003b: 61–68).

7 Badiou (2004: 127–28; see also Badiou 2006: 410–30; Hallward 2003: 135–39):

> The crucial point, which Paul Cohen settled in the realm of ontology, i.e. of mathematics, is the following: you certainly cannot straightforwardly name the elements of a generic subset, since the latter is at once incomplete in its infinite composition and subtracted from every predicate which would directly identify it in the language. But you can maintain that *if* such and such an element *will have been* in the supposedly complete generic subset, *then* such and such a statement, rationally connectable to the element in question, is, or rather will have been, correct. Cohen describes this method—a method constraining the correctness of statements *according to an anticipatory condition bearing on the composition of an infinite generic subset*—as that of *forcing.*

8 Feminist responses to Benjamin's work fall roughly into two groups, one criticizing his various representations of women and their uses in the structures of his thought (Chow 1989; Stoljar 1996; Wolff 1989), and the other arguing that Benjamin's work constitutes an insightful and political criticism of the uses of women within capitalism, art, philosophy, and so on, thereby providing a stimulus to contemporary feminism and politics (Leslie 2000: 106–14; Weigel

1996: 85–98; Rauch 1988). For efforts to move beyond the dichotomy of dismissal and appropriation, see Geyer-Ryan (1988) and especially the excellent essay by Eva Geulen (1996).

9   Or, in a very similar vein but on a very different topic, that of wine in French culture, Roland Barthes (1993: 61) comments, "There are thus very engaging myths which are however not innocent."

10 I have argued elsewhere (Boer 2007a) that Bloch is in many respects a fore-runner, neglected and forgotten, of a favored mode of reading by postcolonial critics: locating the underhand subversion found in many colonial texts.

11 Indeed, history is for Adorno somewhat polygamous in its dialectical partners: apart from enlightenment and myth, we find nature, metaphysics, and theology in *Negative Dialectics* (Adorno 1973: 354–60).

12 The original is: "As if real history were not stored in the core of each possible object of cognition; as if every cognition that seriously resists reification did not bring the petrified things in flux and precisely thus make us aware of our history" (Adorno 1973: 130).

13 For an excellent introduction to the key ideas and history of psychoanalysis for the uninitiated, see Patrick Vandermeersch's (2001) "Psychoanalytic Interpretations of Religious Texts: Some Basics."

14 Csapo (2005: 93) points out that the manifest-latent distinction underlies all theories of myth since Freud.

15 Numerous examples may be found in Freud, such as the "primal scene" (witnessing the sex act while still in the womb or that led to one's birth), seduction as a child by an adult, and for boys, the threat of being castrated (2001, vol. 16: 369–70); or the fantasy of a patient that concealed a wish that he, the analyst, would act in a "sexually provocative" manner to her, a revolutionary fantasy, the "frightful or perverse imaginary events" of hysterics, and so on (vol. 4: 150, 185, 211, 217).

16 This example is drawn from Slavoj Žižek's (1997: 3–44) essay, "The Seven Veils of Fantasy."

CHAPTER TWO. WOMEN FIRST?

1   The attempt to locate the most accurate portrait of the place of women in the socioeconomic order of ancient Israelite society relies on the same sources and in a way parallels, but is of course rather different from, the earlier attempts to locate the place of women in the *religious* sphere of ancient Israel (see Bird 1997).

2   In light of the debate concerning the minimalist or revisionist position in current Hebrew Bible scholarship, the reader will need to exercise a certain *epoché*, or suspension of judgment. But then, critics such as Yee and Simkins by and large ignore this whole debate in their discussions, for the minimalist position

seems to be restricted to historical and archaeological circles rather than social scientific studies. I will engage with this whole debate in chapter 4.

3 Or, as Carol Meyers (1997: 2) puts it, "The study of early Israel is nearly equivalent to the study of the family."

4 Wittfogel developed certain passing points from Marx's work in order to argue that the role of the oriental despot in controlling and organizing irrigation was the key to the AMP. What made his book palatable for Western scholarship was a conspiracy theory: Stalin supposedly pressured scholars of the ancient Near East to dispense with the AMP precisely because Stalinist communism was the epitome of "oriental despotism." Due to his wayward influence on biblical studies, we need to deposit Wittfogel quietly in a roadside recycling bin. See further the criticisms by Krader (1975: 290–91), Hindess and Hirst (1975: 208–20), and Butzer (1996).

5 Bachofen himself does not appear, but the key signal "Mutterecht" does (Jobling 1991: 241).

6 Later Meyers (1999) tones down such arguments, but only slightly. Thus, in her discussion of Ruth she writes of "informal female networks" that arose from their central role in agricultural labor outside the domestic zone.

7 For the fascinating argument that the emotional matriarchy of early childhood—where the mother is the prime caregiver and authority—provides the reason for the continued appeal of the myth of a prior historical matriarchy, see Jongsma-Tieleman's (2001) reading of Genesis 2.

8 The assumption is extremely widespread, and its incessant repetition does not make it true. Lemche (1998b: 93), for instance, takes the idea up without examining it.

9 A quirkiness that manifests itself in the grand evolutionary schema from savagery through various levels of barbarism to civilization, as well as the following quaint examples of nineteenth-century scholarship: "Having neither tables nor chairs for dinner service they had not learned to eat their single daily meal in the manner of civilized nations" (Morgan 1877: 192); "and, finally, to the railway train in motion, which may be called the triumph of civilization" (562).

10 Bachofen makes use of the myths concerning Lycia, Crete, Athens, Lemnos, Egypt, and India, all of them from Greek and Roman sources.

11 For all their historical concerns, Bachofen's works also involve a speculative, even mystical philosophy that has influenced the work of Freud, Nietzsche, and Deleuze, among others.

12 Both law and narrative texts contribute to the mythic structure. I am not after some actual social practice (should that be possible) that requires a distinction between an ideal legal system and narratives that might give us a glimpse of that actual practice (Brenner 1985: 10).

13 My reading here is not redemptive, motivated perhaps by some commitment to church or synagogue or even some larger moral and social agenda that seeks to detoxify the text. A shift from the huge wave of such redemptive and de-

toxifying readings is marked by some of the essays collected in the volume on Exodus to Deuteronomy in the second series of the *Feminist Companion to the Bible* (Brenner 2000), but especially in the sophisticated work of Judith McKinlay (2004). Cheryl Exum's *Fragmented Women* (1993) is an earlier notable effort, although she tends to slip back into a secular form of redemptive reading. At least Exum develops a much more complex perception of the patterns of ideological oppression.

14 Note that childbearing appears for the first time in this story in the curse of v. 16. Paradise would seem to be a state without reproduction, for childbearing is the result of the curse.

15 The key lies with Numbers 12:6: "If your prophets are active, I Yahweh will make myself known to them in a vision, in a dream I will speak with them" (my translation). Miriam is of course a "prophet" (see Exodus 15:20). So Yahweh's comment in Numbers 12:6 is directed at her: as she is a prophet, Yahweh *may* appear to her in a dream. But beyond her the sequence goes thus: Aaron, who may intercede with Moses, who then may approach Yahweh directly (see Numbers 12:7–8, 11–13).

16 In these laws, Phyllis Bird (1997: 21) argues, the concern is of course solely with male honor. Thus the form of address is not the generic *'adam* but the masculine *'ish*. The two cites separated by "/" in the Deuteronomy citation above and in biblical references throughout refer to chapter and verses in the Hebrew text (first) and the English translation (second). They are not always identical.

17 Bird (1997: 21–22) notes that men were the only ones considered by the law to be responsible beings, and as such they were equally responsible for their dependents, be they wives, children, or animals.

18 The last item is on the same level as a man having sex with his father's wife: the ban on menstrual sex appears three times (Leviticus 15:24; 18:19; 20:18), as though it were an unresolved trauma that is doomed to be repeated incessantly.

19 But see Rashkow (1998) for a psychoanalytic reading.

20 On these tensions between the stories and the legislation, see Brenner (1994b).

21 See Boer (2003: 14–41).

22 This law from Deuteronomy 25:11–12 is related to the penalty for an accidental miscarriage that results from two men fighting (Exodus 21:22–25). What is extraordinary about this text is that a miscarriage of a fetus does not count as harm, but injury to the woman does. In the first case a fine applies, in the second the lex talionis in a brutal moment of equality before the law.

23 However, for an intriguing psychoanalytic reading of Exodus 4:24–26 as a textual "Freudian slip," see Kessler (2001).

24 On the class implications of *na'ar* and *na'arah*, young man and young woman, see Boer (2003: 65–86).

25 See Cheryl Exum's (1994a, 1994b) trenchant self-critique on Exodus 1:8–2:10, where she castigates herself for once allowing herself to entertain the possibility of a liberating, redemptive text for women in the early verses of Exodus.

26 One of the dangers of Cheryl Exum's (1993) *Fragmented Women*.

27 See Brenner (2005: 82–98).

CHAPTER THREE. THE FANTASY OF MYTH

1 Or, as Rashkow (1998: 85–86) puts it with a therapeutic bent, "In mythology a whole *people* retains its psychic health, freeing itself from primal drives."

2 See, for instance, Rosemary Jackson (1981) and Aichele and Pippin (1992, 1998). The key texts that form a background to my discussion of fantasy are Freud's (2001, vols. 4–5) *Interpretation of Dreams*; the sections "God's and W̶o̶m̶a̶n̶'s Jouissance," "A Love Letter," and "Knowledge and Truth" in Lacan's (1998: 61–103) Seminar XX; and Žižek's (1997: 3–44) "Seven Veils of Fantasy." See also Freud (2001, vol. 16: 358–77; vol. 17: 175–204), Lacan's Seminar III (1993) and the section "Tuché and Automaton" in Seminar XI (1994: 53–64), Koehler (1996), J. Rose (1982), and the Bible and Culture Collective (1995: 187–211).

3 Here I gloss Žižek glossing Freud's famous example of the strawberry cake: "Fantasy does not mean that when I desire a strawberry cake and cannot get it in reality, I fantasize about eating it; the problem is, rather: how do I know that I desire a strawberry cake in the first place? *This* is what fantasy tells me" (Žižek 1997: 7). For Freud (2001, vol. 16: 372), nature reserves are a perfect analogy for fantasy, since fantasy enables the continuation of pleasures otherwise renounced.

4 The interpretation that follows is somewhat distinct from the scattered psychoanalytic readings of Genesis 1–3. Although I do draw on them at points—Bal's (1987) and Rashkow's (2000) are the most insightful—they tend to fall into some of the traps of psychoanalysis: a focus on the (nineteenth-century bourgeois) nuclear family, however metaphorical, and a reading of the text in terms of the development of the "child." Thus, for Kim Ian Parker (1999) and Deborah Sawyer (2002: 24–26), who follows him, Adam becomes the child who must pass through the Lacanian mirror stage in relation with his mother (a role filled by Eve) into maturity. For Ilona Rashkow (2000: 43–73) the story of Adam and Eve and the deity in these chapters is the "first" account of the dysfunctional family, with its benevolent yet tyrannical father and rebellious children. The problem is that the mother is missing—Eve and the deity function as a father-daughter pair—or rather is banished in the necessary process of maturation. Although Ilana Pardes (2000) begins her interpretation at Exodus 1, she reads the narrative of Israel in terms of the development of the child, from birth through to adulthood. See also Ellen van Wolde's (1989) detailed semiotic reading that often resembles more a mathematics text than textual interpre-

tation. In her detailed use of Greimas and Pierce she argues for the narrative necessity of eating from the tree and plays hard on the schemas of *'adam* and *'adamah*, *'ish* and *'ishah*. There are, however, even more redemptive and therapeutic feminist readings of Genesis 1–3 than there are redemptive psychological or psychoanalytical readings. See, for instance, Ellens (2004), Schotroff (1993), Schüngel-Straumann (1993), Meyers (1993), and Bledstein (1993). But see also Milne's (1993) unrelenting criticism of such redemptive readings. Indeed, such redemptive readings, especially for feminist criticism, were so dominant in the 1970s and 1980s that they may now be seen as a distinct mark of that historical period of feminist criticism.

5   For all his opposition to psychoanalysis, Northrop Frye (1990a: 136) glimpsed the fantasmatic kernel with his observation that "myth is the imitation of actions near or at the conceivable limits of desire."

6   For Lacan (1998: 95), "Everything we are allowed to approach by way of reality remains rooted in fantasy." It is "never anything more than the screen that conceals something quite primary" (Lacan 1994: 60).

7   This is Mieke Bal's (1987: 104–30) point. Indeed, she argues that Genesis 2–3 is one of the first stories of female subjectivity. Bal is responding to Phyllis Trible's (1978: 80–140) famous but troubled argument that up until Genesis 2:21–25 we have an undifferentiated human figure, Adam; only with the making and naming of the woman do we get differentiation.

8   We might add that a similar pattern shows up with the distinction between *'adam* and *'adamah*, especially if we follow Ron Simkins's (1998) argument that this forms a pair with *'ish* and *'ishah*: the construction of gender here characterizes the woman as the fertile earth into which the man puts his seed.

9   For those with Foucauldian ears, this example is close to Foucault's (1988: 121–22) take on the constitutive exception: "If politics has existed since the 19th century, it is because the revolution took place. The current one is not a variant or a sector of that one. Politics always takes a stand on the revolution."

10   I will not discuss here either the Oedipus complex, the gate through which the Symbolic is attained, nor the Imaginary, the zone of identity, sexual attraction, aggression, and the mediator between Symbolic and Real.

11   For this Lacan (1991a: 29) provides a hint: "The human order is characterized by the fact that the symbolic function intervenes at every moment and at every stage of its existence."

12   These texts are, of course, mired in the fascinating history of historical criticism, with its foundational distinction, running all the way back to Jean Astrúc, between the Yahwist and the Elohist.

13   Of course, only those animals that breathe air and live on land die. A rather large group are exempt from punishment: those that live in water.

14   I write "Reed Sea" since that is what the Hebrew actually says. It is through a popular and traditional mistranslation that it has become the "Red Sea."

1 Here is Althusser's (1971: 143) list of ISAs present in a capitalist nation-state: the religious ISA (the system of the different churches and other religious institutions); the educational ISA (the system of the different public and private schools and universities); the family ISA; the legal ISA; the political ISA (including the political parties); the trade union ISA; the communications ISA (press, radio, television, etc.); the cultural ISA (literature, the arts, sports, etc.). Obviously this list varies under different modes of production.

2 Elsewhere, in an essay on Freud's *Moses and Monotheism*, Assmann (2006) comes very close to this argument, for here he argues that Freud is right about trauma and guilt at the heart of religion: this remembering and forgetting is part of the necessary repression of other religions in the name of monotheism.

3 Although such a system has long been abhorrent in states operating with parliamentary structure, it's making a comeback in the United States, with the "war on terror" used as a means to return to trial by the executive branch, not the judicial.

4 Moses's death is rather strange if we take the narrative claim at face value that he wrote of his own death. In that case, would it not have been in his interest to make it as quick and as painless as possible?

5 For instance, in the collection edited by Mark Sneed (1999), *Concepts of Class in Ancient Israel*, one searches in vain for any reference to the Russian literature. Outside biblical scholarship even Pryor's (1990) paper on the economics of the Asiatic mode of production somehow misses the Russians and focuses on Western scholarship. Some limited interaction may be found in Schloen's (2001: 187–254) published dissertation.

6 And if there was any engagement in an intellectually impoverished West, it was with those who spent some time in Western institutions and wrote in English. I think here especially of D'iakonoff (see Schloen 2001: 197–99).

7 An early sustained attempt comes in *The German Ideology* (Marx and Engels 1976: 32–35), but the most complete discussions are from *Grundrisse* (Marx 1986: 399–439) and the preface to *A Critique of Political Economy* (Marx 1987: 261–65).

8 A number of such distillations exist, such as Bailey and Llobera (1981), Krader (1975, especially 286–96), Lichtheim (1990), and Shiozawa (1990). See also Pryor's (1990) survey of the Western literature up until 1980. The problem is that these summaries tend to lose sense of Marx's dialectical dynamic in dealing with precapitalist modes of production (see Boer forthcoming).

9 This section relies on Dunn's (1981) useful summary and the collections edited by D'iakonoff (1969a, 1991a). Dunn (1981) and Kohl (1991) both point out, against Wittfogel, that the often vigorous debates were not held with nervous glances over the shoulder to check on the censor.

10 Nothing shows up the tensions more than this sentence from D'iakonoff (1969b: 202): "In the ancient society the principal exploited class was not the commu-

nity members, but the slaves, even though a major part of public produce was still created by the labour of freemen, as a survival of conditions in the primitive community."

11 The published material from this stage of the debate is immense; see the references in Dunn (1981: 144–53).

12 For instance, too many of the essays in the collection edited by Powell (1987) are afflicted by empirical fixations, except for the essays by D'iakonoff (1987) and Dandamaev (1987).

13 In tracing out these nodes I have brought the basic categories from Soviet studies into contact with Western biblical scholars to indicate both their convergence and their divergence.

14 Indeed, Lemche's (1998b: 99–100) definition of a tribe applies as much to the village commune: "a collective, extensive and solid organization to which people look for their political and temporal requirements."

15 Weinberg's work has been sufficiently influential to warrant a detailed criticism by Charles Carter (1999: 294–307).

16 With his notion of a "palace-state" Lemche (1998b: 94) merely reiterates the old point concerning the Asiatic mode of production: that the state is the ruling class.

17 In terms of typologies, Lemche (1998b: 91) estimates 90 to 95 percent involved in agriculture, maybe 4 to 5 percent in cattle breeding (nomads), and the remaining 1 to 5 percent in government administration and trade. But then, astoundingly, he argues elsewhere that these figures mean there was no such thing as class (Lemche 1999), for such a small percentage of exploiters is hardly enough for a class.

18 For other samples, see the range of types of workers in Vinogradov's (1991: 163–68) discussion of Middle Kingdom Egypt and the variety among the Hittites (Giorgadze 1991: 282–83).

19 For this reason *allocation* is a better term than distribution, since the latter is based on the perspective of the object produced.

20 I outlined the theoretical background to the notion of regimes of allocation within regulation theory in an earlier work (Boer 2003).

21 For instance, Lemche (1998b: 93), who has the ability to juxtapose a good Marxist argument with one straight out of the myth of capitalist development, writes, "Humans try to maximize productivity and profitability when climatic conditions become erratic and water and food supplies dwindle." Even Carter (1999: 256–95), who is very careful, slips into capitalist terminology when speaking about trade in Yehud.

22 Unfortunately, Thompson calls this local barter "trade," distinguishing between internal and international trade. The terminology is misleading and drawn from contemporary capitalist models; Lemche's (1988: 24–25) distinction between barter and trade is much more useful. Thompson (1999: 124–27) also argues that international trade was important for Mesopotamia and Egypt, but that

Palestine by and large stayed out of it due to the absence of a state until very late. However, such long-distance trade would have been minimal, due to the huge costs involved (Thompson supplies no data on volumes).

23 I have much sympathy with Thomas Thompson's (1999: 31–33) idea of "survival literature"—the literature that arose from a group for which survival was a crucial issue—since he removes the intentionalist shackles of propaganda that bedevils so many arguments.

CHAPTER FIVE. THE AUSTRALIAN FANTASY OF ISRAEL

1 The trap of such analyses is that governments lose elections and that some characters lose their job. As I check the manuscript, it is some months since John Howard suffered a massive defeat in November 2007. The analysis that follows, however, remains pertinent for this element of the political Right in Australia, whether it is in power or not. It does not help matters that the Labor Party is also very conservative. The Labor and Liberal parties are really two factions of one pro-capitalist party.

2 Other statements might be added, but I restrict myself to one more. This is Downer departing from his scripted speech at the Israel-Australia Chamber of Commerce in 2004: "We admire your tenacity. We admire your courage. We admire your determination to build a society here in circumstances which are . . . somewhat embattled. And let me tell you, we will never turn our back on you. We will never turn our back on you, that is something you never need to worry about" (quoted in O'Loughlin 2004: 7).

3 In fact, in Australian universities at least, if not in all government organizations, we must now seek permission to travel anywhere in the world by providing the latest advice to our superiors from the Department of Foreign Affairs and Trade concerning the places where we want or need to travel.

4 But then he has a knack of hanging on, even through another eleven chapters in his dotage. Just when we think he is dead and buried (Joshua 14:29–32; Judges 1:1) he comes back to life only to die once more in Judges 2:6–9.

5 As a sample only, see Bal (1988), Polzin (1980), Auld (1984), Gray (1986), and Matthews (2004).

6 For a somewhat different use of psychoanalysis, especially the dialectic of love and violence, in the infamous white Australia policy, see Jennifer Rutherford (2000).

7 Ted Lapkin (2004) went one further: in *The Review: Australia/Israel and Jewish Affairs Council* he is overcome by a moment of Zionist paranoia and cannot help but accuse the U.N. of being hijacked by a pro-Palestinian agenda, hellbent on bashing and eliminating Israel, overwhelmed by a "dark morass of anti-Zionist demagoguery."

8 It has always struck me that anti-Semitism is as much a hatred of Arab and Muslim peoples—the conjunction of linguistic and religious terms is quite

conscious—as it is of Jews. This is, of course, a linguistic point as much as it is a social one, for Arabic is also very much a Semitic language. Closely related is the genetic point that Jews and Palestinians at least come from the same genetic Canaanite stock, closely related to Cretans, Egyptians, Iranians, Turks, and Armenians (see Ra'ad 2002).

9 The Victorian Islamic Council had brought a case before the Civil and Administrative Tribunal against two ministers of the Charismatic Catch the Fire Ministry for vilification against Islam. The case in question involved several Muslims who attended a sermon on Islam by ministers of the Catch the Fire Ministry in which Muslims were demonized. Those who attended later reported the incident to the Tribunal, which took action under the Racial and Religious Tolerance Act of 2001 (Victoria) that prohibits inciting hatred, contempt, or severe ridicule of a religious or ethnic racial group. The ministers were ordered by the Tribunal to acknowledge publicly that they had breached the law and to refrain from further breaches, which they have refused to do, appealing the decision and declaring that they would rather go to jail than apologize.

10 "Tolerance within a framework of law" is, ironically, precisely the basis of the Racial and Religious Tolerance Act of Victoria.

11 For an archive on the "children overboard affair," see the *Sydney Morning Herald* at http://smh.com.au.

12 Further, on the basis of some photographs of refugee children in the sea, Howard went on television just before the 2001 election saying that the children had been thrown overboard by their parents as a protest for not being allowed to enter Australia. Howard stated that "we" did not want these kinds of people in Australia, that is, people who would risk their children's lives to get into the country. Later, when it became clear that the children had not been thrown overboard but that they were escaping a sinking vessel, Howard claimed that he did not know at the time that the story was untrue. The affair had a substantial influence on the election that he won in 2001. With uncanny timing this infamous affair came back to haunt Howard in the 2004 election ("Aide Reveals Children Overboard Advice" 2004; Brown 2004): just when he seemed to have escaped blame for lying to the Australian public before the election in 2001, in August 2004 a senior defense official admitted that he had told Howard that the story was false before the 2001 election.

13 As is the way with writing about contemporary politics, things change. Since I first wrote this section the Howard government lost power in a catastrophic election that saw Kevin Rudd and the Labor Party sweep into government. Since November 2007 Rudd has made a formal apology to Aboriginal people for the former practice of removing children from their families, reinvigorated the reconciliation process, ratified the Kyoto Protocol, and has taken a leadership role on the issue of global warming. He has not, however, made any changes to the xenophobic refugee legislation. What these changes do, however, is set the policies of the Howard government of 1996–2007 in greater relief.

14 A constant refrain used by John Howard when he was in office—concerning the protests against the World Economic Forum in Melbourne in 2000; massive protests against the invasion of Iraq in 2002, to which Australia sent troops; when the leader of the Labor opposition in 2004 promised to bring Australian troops home by Christmas if he won the election; after the Greens senators Kerry Nettle and Bob Brown were removed from Parliament during a speech by George Bush; and so on—is that these and many other activities are "unAustralian" (Allard and Grattan 2004; Rule et al. 2000; Crabb 2003). In response, banners and T-shirts began appearing that proudly proclaimed their bearers to be engaged in "un-Australian" activities.

15 In his doomed election campaign of 2007 he argued that he could see no reason why Australia couldn't continue its economic surge indefinitely, that we needed to get past the mind-set that periods of bust follow boom. Not merely did he neglect to mention that Australia's resources-based boom was predicated on China's purchase of Australian resources, but the comments reinforced the increasing sense that he had lost touch with reality.

CHAPTER SIX. THE U.S. FANTASY OF ISRAEL

1 For a somewhat different analysis to which I am indebted, see Erin Runions's (2004b) discussion of the various papers and speeches of George W. Bush. Runions argues that the apocalyptic language of Bush's speeches, deeply enmeshed in the neoconservative agenda, postulated a personified History that called on him and the United States to defend and advance "freedom" in a way that conflated economic and religious desire. See also Runions's (2004a) earlier paper.

2 Not quite, since the shuttle didn't go out of Earth orbit. No mention, of course, of the Syrian cosmonaut who went up in a Soviet shuttle.

3 For instance, "When your son asks you in time to come, 'What are the testimonies and statutes and the ordinances which Yahweh your God has commanded you?' then you shall say to your son, 'We were Pharaoh's slaves in Egypt; and Yahweh brought us out of Egypt with a mighty hand; and Yahweh showed signs and wonders, great and evil, against Egypt and against Pharaoh and all his household, before your eyes; and he brought us out from there, that he might bring us in and give us the land which he swore to give to our fathers" (Deuteronomy 7:20–23).

4 Zionism as we now call it—the idea of a Jewish state in Palestine—existed centuries before Herzl, but as an apocalyptic Christian notion and political doctrine (Wagner 2002). It is useful to distinguish between humanistic Zionism, as it was developed by the Jewish writer Ahad Ha'am and then elaborated by Judah Magnes and Martin Buber; political Zionism, developed by the secular Herzl but which was to develop into versions of Left (Labor Zionism) and Right;

and religious Zionism, the move by Orthodox Jews for a theocratic state (see Mezvinsky 2005; Wheatcroft 1996).

5 For instance, in Australia voting is compulsory—an undemocratic law to ensure a full range of opinion in the demos.

CHAPTER SEVEN. MYTHMAKING FOR THE LEFT

1 In the words of Alan Greenspan, former chair of the Federal Reserve Bank, "There are many Nobel Prize winners in economics, but few have achieved the mythical status of Milton Friedman" (quoted in Formaini 2002).

2 My position comes closest to what has been called "ecosocialism" (Kovel 2002; Kovel and Löwy 2001; Fotopoulos 1997; O'Connor 1997; Benton 1996; Burkett 1999; Foster 2000). However, over against the view that this is but one strain among myriad green movements, I argue that it reveals the deeper logic of the green movement itself.

3 Indeed, much of the voluminous literature is devoted to precisely this issue: the economic effects of environmental collapse (as a small sample, see Association of British Insurers 2005; Congressional Budget Office 2003).

4 See, for instance, *Putting Energy in the Spotlight: BP Statistical Review of World Energy* (2005), which appears every June. Further information may be found at the BP website and the website of the U.S. Geological Survey, especially its "World Energy Assessment." Other articles from industry leaders may be found in *World Energy* (www.worldenergysource.com).

Bibliography

Aberbach, David. 2005. Nationalism and the Hebrew Bible. *Nations and Nationalism* 11 (2): 223–42.

Adorno, Theodor. 1973. *Negative Dialectics*. Translated by E. B. Ashton. London: Routledge and Kegan Paul.

———. 1989. *Kierkegaard: Construction of the Aesthetic*. Translated by R. Hullot-Kentor. Vol. 61 of *Theory and History of Literature*. Minneapolis: University of Minnesota Press.

———. 1994. *Briefe und Briefwechsel*. Frankfurt am Main: Suhrkamp.

———. 1999. *The Complete Correspondence 1928–1940*. Translated by N. Walker. Cambridge, Mass.: Harvard University Press.

Aichele, George, and Tina Pippin, eds. 1992. *Fantasy and the Bible*. Vol. 60 of *Semeia*. Atlanta: Scholar's Press.

Aichele, George, and Tina Pippin, eds. 1998. *Violence, Utopia and the Kingdom of God*. New York: Routledge.

Aide Reveals Children Overboard Advice. 2004. ABC News Online, August 16. Available at www.abc.net.au. Accessed August 20, 2004.

Allard, Tom, and Michele Grattan. 2004. Troops to Stay Well into Next Year: Howard. *The Age*, April 26, 6.

Alok, Jha. 2006. Death, Famine, Drought: Cost of 3C Global Rise in Temperature. *The Guardian*, April 15, 13.

Althusser, Louis. 1971. *Lenin and Philosophy and Other Essays*. Translated by B. Brewster. London: New Left Books.

———. 1994. *The Future Lasts a Long Time*. New York: Vintage.

Anderson, Perry. 1974. *Passages from Antiquity to Feudalism*. London: New Left Books.

Assmann, Jan. 1997. *Moses the Egyptian: The Memory of Egypt in Western Monotheism.* Cambridge, Mass.: Harvard University Press.

———. 2006. *Religion and Cultural Memory: Ten Studies.* Stanford: Stanford University Press.

Association of British Insurers. 2005. Financial Risks of Climate Change. Available at www.abi.org.uk. Accessed October 20, 2007.

Auld, A. Graeme. 1984. *Joshua, Judges, Ruth.* Philadelphia: Westminster.

Australian Department of Foreign Affairs and Trade. 2004. Travel Advice: Israel, the Gaza Strip and the West Bank. Available at www.smartraveller.gov.au. Accessed July 9, 2004.

Bachofen, J. J. 1967. *Myth, Religion, and Mother Right: Selected Writings of J. J. Bachofen.* Translated by R. Mannheim. London: Routledge and Kegan Paul.

Badiou, Alain. 1999. *Manifesto for Philosophy.* Translated by N. Madarasz. Albany: State University of New York Press.

———. 2000. *Deleuze: The Clamor of Being.* Translated by L. Burchill. Minneapolis: University of Minnesota Press.

———. 2002. *Ethics: An Essay on the Understanding of Evil.* Translated by P. Hallward. London: Verso.

———. 2003a. Beyond Formalism: An Interview. *Angelaki* 8 (2): 111–36.

———. 2003b. *Infinite Thought: Truth and the Return to Philosophy.* Translated by J. Clemens and O. Feltham. London: Continuum.

———. 2003c. *Saint Paul: The Foundation of Universalism.* Translated by R. Brassier. Stanford: Stanford University Press.

———. 2004. *Theoretical Writings.* Translated by R. Brassier and A. Toscano. London: Continuum.

———. 2005. *Handbook of Inaesthetics.* Translated by A. Toscano. Stanford: Stanford University Press.

———. 2006. *Being and Event.* Translated by Oliver Feltham. London: Continuum.

Bailey, Anne M., and Josep R. Llobera. 1981. The AMP: Sources of Information and the Concept. In *The Asiatic Mode of Production: Science and Politics,* edited by A. M. Bailey and J. R. Llobera. London: Routledge and Kegan Paul.

Bakunin, Mikhail. 1980. *Bakunin on Anarchism.* Montreal: Black Rose Books.

Bal, Mieke. 1987. *Lethal Love.* Bloomington: Indiana University Press.

———. 1988. *Death and Dissymmetry: The Politics of Coherence in the Book of Judges.* Chicago: University of Chicago Press.

Barthes, Roland. 1993. *Mythologies.* Translated by A. Lavers. New York: Vintage.

Benjamin, Walter. 1998. *The Origin of German Tragic Drama.* Translated by J. Osborne. London: Verso.

———. 1999. *The Arcades Project.* Translated by H. Eiland and K. McLaughlin. Cambridge, Mass.: Belknap Press of Harvard University Press.

Benton, Ted. 1996. *The Greening of Marxism.* London: Guildford.

Bible and Culture Collective. 1995. *The Postmodern Bible.* New Haven: Yale University Press.

Bird, Phyllis A. 1997. *Missing Persons and Mistaken Identities: Women and Gender in Ancient Israel*. Minneapolis: Fortress Press.

Bledstein, Adrien Janis. 1993. Are Women Cursed in Genesis 3.16? In *A Feminist Companion to Genesis*, edited by A. Brenner. Sheffield, England: Sheffield Academic Press.

Bloch, Ernst. 1972. *Atheism in Christianity: The Religion of the Exodus and the Kingdom*. Translated by J. T. Swann. New York: Herder and Herder.

———. 1985. *Ernst Bloch Werkausgabe*. 16 vols. Frankfurt on Main: Suhrkamp.

———. 1988. *The Utopian Function of Art and Literature: Selected Essays*. Translated by J. Zipes and F. Mecklenburg. Cambridge, Mass.: MIT Press.

———. 1995. *The Principle of Hope*. Translated by N. Plaice, S. Plaice, and P. Knight. 3 vols. Cambridge, Mass.: MIT Press.

———. 1998. *Literary Essays*. Translated by A. Joron et al. Stanford: Stanford University Press.

Boer, Roland. 2001. Yahweh as Top: A Lost Targum. In *Queer Commentary and the Hebrew Bible*, edited by K. Stone. Cleveland: Pilgrim Press.

———, ed. 2002. *Tracking "The Tribes of Yahweh": On the Trail of a Classic*. Sheffield, England: Sheffield Academic Press.

———. 2003. *Marxist Criticism of the Bible*. London: T. & T. Clark.

———. 2005–6. Phases of the Gonic: Re-reading Genesis to Joshua as Myth. *Literary Newspaper* (Bulgaria) 13: 18.

———. 2006. An Un-Original Tale. *Arena Journal* (double issue) 25–26: 136–52.

———. 2007a. *Criticism of Heaven: On Marxism and Theology*. Leiden: E. J. Brill.

———. 2007b. On Fables and Truths. *Angelaki* 11 (2): 107–16.

———. 2007c. *Rescuing the Bible: Blackwell Manifestos*. London: Blackwell.

———. 2008. *Last Stop before Antarctica: The Bible and Postcolonialism in Australia*. Revised edition. Atlanta: SBL Publications.

———. Forthcoming. A Titanic Phenomenon: Marxism, History and Biblical Societies. *Historical Materialism*.

———. In press. *Criticism of Religion: On Marxism and Theology II*. Leiden: Brill.

Bosteels, Bruno. 2004. On the Subject of the Dialectic. In *Think Again: Alain Badiou and the Future of Philosophy*, edited by P. Hallward. London: Continuum.

Boyer, Robert. 1990. *The Regulation School: A Critical Introduction*. Translated by C. Charney. New York: Columbia University Press.

———. 2000. Is a Finance-Led Growth Regime a Viable Alternative to Fordism? A Preliminary Analysis. *Economy and Society* 29 (1): 111–45.

Brenner, Athalya. 1985. *The Israelite Woman: Social Role and Literary Types in Biblical Narrative*. Sheffield, England: Journal for the Study of the Old Testament Press.

———. 1994a. Introduction to *A Feminist Companion to Exodus to Deuteronomy*, edited by A. Brenner. Sheffield, England: Sheffield Academic Press.

———. 1994b. On Incest. In *A Feminist Companion to Exodus to Deuteronomy*, edited by A. Brenner. Sheffield, England: Sheffield Academic Press.

————, ed. 2000. *Exodus to Deuteronomy, A Feminist Companion to the Bible* (Second Series). Sheffield, England: Sheffield Academic Press.

————. 2005. *I Am . . . Biblical Women Tell Their Own Stories*. Minneapolis: Fortress Press.

Brett, Mark. 2000. *Genesis: Procreation and the Politics of Identity*. London: Routledge.

Brown, Matt. 2004. Calls for New Senate Inquiry into Children Overboard Affair. Available at www.abc.net.au. Accessed August 21, 2004.

Brueggemann, Walter. 1982. *Genesis*. Atlanta: John Knox.

Bultmann, Rudolph. 1952–55. *Theology of the New Testament*. London: SCM.

————. 1958. *Jesus and the Word*. Translated by L. P. Smith and E. H. Lantero. New York: Charles Scribner's Sons.

————. 1966. *Faith and Understanding I*. Translated by L. P. Smith. London: SCM.

Burchill, Louise. 2000. Translator's Preface: Portraiture in Philosophy, or Shifting Perspectives. In *Deleuze: The Clamor of Being*. Minneapolis: University of Minnesota Press.

Burkett, Paul. 1999. *Marx and Nature: A Red and Green Perspective*. London: Palgrave Macmillan.

Bush, George W. 2004a. Remarks to the American Israel Public Affairs Committee (May 15). May 15, 2004. Available at www.state.gov. Accessed February 15, 2006.

————. 2004b. Remarks to the American Israel Public Affairs Committee (May 18). May 18, 2004. Available at www.state.gov. Accessed February 15, 2006.

Bush Visits Mosque, Warns against Violence. 2001. *Christian Century* 118 (26): 12.

Butler, Judith, Ernesto Laclau, and Slavoj Žižek. 2000. *Contingency, Hegemony, Universality: Contemporary Dialogues on the Left*. London: Verso.

Butzer, Karl W. 1996. Irrigation, Raised Fields and State Management. *Antiquity* 70 (267): 200–205.

Carter, Charles E. 1999. *The Emergence of Yehud in the Persian Period: A Social and Demographic Study*. Vol. 294 of *Journal for the Study of the Old Testament Supplement Series*. Sheffield, England: Sheffield Academic Press.

Cassirer, Ernst. 1947. *The Myth of the State*. New Haven: Yale University Press.

Chow, Rey. 1989. Walter Benjamin's Love Affair with Death. *New German Critique* 48: 63–86.

Climate Group. 2004. Interview: Professor Sir David King. The Climate Group, June 28. Available at www.theclimategroup.org. Accessed May 10, 2006.

Clinton, Hillary Rodham. 2005. Address to the 2005 American Israel Public Affairs Committee Policy Conference, May 24. Available at www.clinton.senate.gov. Accessed February 15, 2006.

Congressional Budget Office. 2003. The Economics of Climate Change. Available at www.cbo.gov. Accessed October 20, 2007.

Costello, Peter. 2004. Address to National Day of Thanksgiving Commemoration Scots Church, May 29. Available at www.treasurer.gov.au. Accessed August 21, 2004.

Crabb, Annabel. 2003. A Classic Aussie Bush Week as Greens Go Feral. *The Age*, October 28, 1.

A Crude Awakening: The Oil Shock. 2007. Directed by Basil Gelpke and Ray McCormack. Lava Production, Switzerland.

Crüsemann, Frank. 1996. Human Solidarity and Ethnic Identity: Israel's Self-Definition in the Genealogical System of Genesis. In *Ethnicity and the Bible*, edited by M. Brett. Leiden: E. J. Brill.

Csapo, Eric. 2005. *Theories of Mythology*. Oxford: Blackwell.

Damrosch, David. 1987. *The Narrative Covenant: Transformations of Genre in the Growth of Biblical Literature*. Ithaca, N.Y.: Cornell University Press.

Dandamaev, Muhammad. 1969. Achaemenid Babylonia. In *Ancient Mesopotamia: Socio-Economic History. A Collection of Studies by Soviet Scholars*, edited by I. M. D'iakonoff. Moscow: "Nauka" Publishing House.

———. 1984. *Slavery in Babylonia: From Nabopolassar to Alexander the Great (626–331 BC)*. DeKalb: North Illinois University Press.

———. 1987. Free Hired Labor in Babylonia during the Sixth through Fourth Centuries B.C. In *Labor in the Ancient Near East*, edited by M. A. Powell. New Haven: American Oriental Society.

Davies, Philip. 1998. *Scribes and Schools: The Canonization of the Hebrew Scriptures*. Louisville: Westminster John Knox.

Deffeyes, Kenneth S. 2003. *Hubbert's Peak: The Impending World Oil Shortage*. Princeton: Princeton University Press.

———. 2005. *Beyond Oil: The View from Hubbert's Peak*. New York: Hill and Wang.

Deleuze, Gilles, and Félix Guattari. 1987. *A Thousand Plateaus: Capitalism and Schizophrenia*. Translated by B. Massumi. Minneapolis: University of Minnesota Press.

Dever, William G. 2001. *What Did the Biblical Writers Know and When Did They Know It? What Archaeology Can Tell Us about the Reality of Ancient Israel*. Grand Rapids: Eerdmans.

D'iakonoff, Igor M., ed. 1969a. *Ancient Mesopotamia: Socio-Economic History. A Collection of Studies by Soviet Scholars*. Moscow: "Nauka" Publishing House.

———. 1969b. The Rise of the Despotic State in Ancient Mesopotamia. In *Ancient Mesopotamia: Socio-Economic History. A Collection of Studies by Soviet Scholars*, edited by I. M. D'iakonoff. Moscow: "Nauka" Publishing House.

———. 1974. The Commune in the Ancient East as Treated in the Works of Soviet Researchers. In *Introduction to Soviet Ethnography*, edited by S. P. Dunn and E. Dunn. Berkeley: Copy Centers of Berkeley.

———. 1987. Slave-Labour vs. Non-Slave Labour: The Problem of Definition. In *Labor in the Ancient Near East*, edited by M. A. Powell. New Haven: American Oriental Society.

———, ed. 1991a. *Early Antiquity*. Chicago: University of Chicago Press.

———. 1991b. Early Despotisms in Mesopotamia. In *Early Antiquity*, edited by I. M. Diakonoff and P. L. Kohl. Chicago: University of Chicago Press.

————. 1991c. General Outline of the First Period of the History of the Ancient World and the Problem of the Ways of Development. In *Early Antiquity*, edited by I. M. Diakonoff and P. L. Kohl. Chicago: University of Chicago Press.

Docker, John. 2001. *1492: The Poetics of Diaspora*. London: Continuum.

Downer, Alexander. 2002. National Press Club Address, Canberra, May 7. Available at www.dfat.gov.au. Accessed September 21, 2002.

————. 2003a. Speech at the International Conference on Islam and the West, August 15. Available at www.foreignminister.gov.au. Accessed August 28, 2003.

————. 2003b. Speech at the Sir Thomas Playford Annual Lecture, August 27. Available at www.foreignminister.gov.au. Accessed August 28, 2003.

————. 2004a. Speech to the Israel-Australia Chamber of Commerce, January 25. Available at www.foreignminister.gov.au. Accessed August 21, 2004.

————. 2004b. Visit to Israel, January 27. Available at www.foreignminister.gov.au. Accessed August 21, 2004.

Dunn, Stephen P. 1981. *The Fall and Rise of the Asiatic Mode of Production*. London: Routledge and Kegan Paul.

Eliade, Mircea. 1954. *The Myth of the Eternal Return*. Translated by W. R. Trask. New York: Pantheon.

————. 1964. *Myth and Reality*. London: Allen and Unwin.

Ellens, J. Harold. 2004. The Psychodynamics of the Fall Story: Genesis 2:25–3:24. In *From Genesis to Apocalyptic Vision*, edited by J. H. Ellens and W. G. Rollins. Westport, Conn.: Praeger.

Energy Watch Group. 2007. *Crude Oil: The Supply Outlook*. Ottobrun, Germany: Ludwig-Bölkow-Stiftung.

Engels, Friedrich. 1985. *The Origin of the Family, Private Property and the State*. Harmondsworth, England: Penguin. (Orig. pub. 1884.)

Evans, Gareth. 1995a. Australia, Israel and Peace in the Middle East, July 10. Available at www.dfat.gov.au. Accessed July 10, 2004.

————. 1995b. Peace In The Middle East: The Way Forward, September 10. Available at www.dfat.gov.au. Accessed July 10, 2004.

Exum, J. Cheryl. 1993. *Fragmented Women: Feminist (Sub)versions of Biblical Narratives*. Vol. 163 of *Journal for the Study of the Old Testament Supplement Series*. Sheffield, England: Sheffield Academic Press.

————. 1994a. Second Thoughts about Secondary Characters: Women in Exodus 1:8–2:10. In *A Feminist Companion to Exodus to Deuteronomy*, edited by A. Brenner. Sheffield, England: Sheffield Academic Press.

————. 1994b. "You Shall Let Every Daughter Live": A Study of Exodus 1.8–2.10. In *A Feminist Companion to Exodus to Deuteronomy*, edited by A. Brenner. Sheffield, England: Sheffield Academic Press.

Farouque, Farah. 2006. Howard Wants to See the Back of Burqa. *The Age*, February 28, 3.

Feiner, Susan. 2002. The Political Economy of the Divine. *Hawke Institute Working Paper Series* 18: 1–18.

Finkelstein, Israel. 1989. The Emergence of the Monarchy in Israel: The Environmental and Socio-Economic Aspects. *Journal for the Study of the Old Testament* 44: 43–74.

Finkelstein, Norman. 1991. Debate on the 1948 Exodus: Myths, Old and New. *Journal of Palestine Studies* 21 (1): 66–89.

Flannery, Tim. 2005a. Earth Needs a Climate of Change. *Sydney Morning Herald*, July 18, 16.

———. 2005b. *The Weather Makers: The History and Future Impact of Climate Change.* Melbourne: Text Publishing.

Flood, Christopher G. 2002. *Political Myth: A Theoretical Introduction.* New York: Routledge.

Formaini, Robert L. 2002. Milton Friedman: Economist as Public Intellectual. *Economic Insights* 7 (2). Available at www.dallasfed.org. Accessed April 13, 2008.

Foster, John Bellamy. 2000. *Marx's Ecology: Materialism and Nature.* New York: Monthly Review Press.

Fotopoulos, Takis. 1997. *Towards an Inclusive Democracy.* London: Cassell.

Foucault, Michel. 1988. *Michel Foucault: Politics, Philosophy, Culture.* Edited by L. D. Kritzman. New York: Routledge.

Freud, Sigmund. 2001. *The Standard Edition of the Complete Psychological Works of Sigmund Freud.* Edited by J. Strachey. 24 vols. New York: Vintage.

Frew, Wendy. 2006. Nuclear No Cure for Climate Change, Scientists Warn. *Sydney Morning Herald*, May 2, 8.

Friedman, Milton. 1956. *Studies in the Quantity Theory of Money.* Chicago: Chicago University Press.

———. 1984. *Market or Plan? An Exposition of the Case for the Market.* London: Centre for Research into Communist Economies.

———. 2002. *Capitalism and Freedom: Fortieth Anniversary Edition.* Chicago: University of Chicago Press.

Friedman, Milton, and Rose Friedman. 1980. *Free to Choose.* Chicago: University of Chicago Press.

Friedman, Milton, and Anna Schwartz. 1963. *A Monetary History of the United States.* Chicago: University of Chicago Press.

Frye, Northrop. 1982. *The Great Code: The Bible and Literature.* New York: Harcourt Brace Jovanovich.

———. 1990a. *Anatomy of Criticism: Four Essays.* Harmondsworth, England: Penguin. (Orig. pub. 1957.)

———. 1990b. *Words with Power, Being a Second Study of the Bible and Literature.* New York: Harcourt Brace Jovanovich.

Fyfe, Melissa. 2002. Economists Push PM to Ratify Kyoto Protocol. *The Age*, August 15, 3.

———. 2004. The Global Warming Sceptics. *The Age*, November 27, 8.

Garnaut, John. 2006. Costello to Violent Muslims: Get Out. *Sydney Morning Herald*, February 24, 1.

Geulen, Eva. 1996. Towards a Genealogy of Gender in Walter Benjamin's Writing. *German Quarterly* 69: 161–80.

Geyer-Ryan, Helga. 1988. Counterfactual Artefacts: Walter Benjamin's Philosophy of History. In *Visions and Blueprints: Avant-Garde Culture and Radical Politics in Early Twentieth-Century Europe*, edited by E. Timms and P. Collier. Manchester, England: Manchester University Press.

Giorgadze, G. G. 1991. The Hittite Kingdom. In *Early Antiquity*, edited by I. M. Diakonoff and P. L. Kohl. Chicago: University of Chicago Press.

Gottwald, Norman K. 1999. *The Tribes of Yahweh*. Sheffield, England: Sheffield Academic Press. (Orig. pub. 1979.)

———. 2001. *The Politics of Ancient Israel*. Edited by D. A. Knight. *Library of Ancient Israel*. Louisville: Westminster John Knox.

Gray, John. 1986. *Joshua, Judges, Ruth*. Grand Rapids: W. B. Eerdmans.

Gruber, Ruth. 1947. *Destination Palestine: The Story of the Haganah Ship* Exodus, *1947*. London: Wyn.

———. 1999. *Exodus 1947: The Ship That Launched a Nation*. London: Crown.

Hallward, Peter. 2003. *Badiou: A Subject to Truth*. Minneapolis: University of Minnesota Press.

Hamilton, Clive. 2004. Peter Costello Should Practice What He Preaches. *The Age*, June 9, 19.

Harvey, David. 1998. What's Green and Makes the Environment Go Round? In *Cultures of Globalization*, edited by F. Jameson and M. Miyoshi. Durham, N.C.: Duke University Press.

Hindess, Barry, and Paul Q. Hirst. 1975. *Precapitalist Modes of Production*. London: Routledge and Kegan Paul.

Homer. 1999. *The Odyssey*. Translated by R. Lattimore. New York: HarperCollins.

Horkheimer, Max, and Theodor Adorno. 1999. *Dialectic of Enlightenment*. Translated by J. Cumming. New York: Continuum. (Orig. pub. 1944.)

Howard, John. 1999. Address to the Australia-Israel Chamber of Commerce Melbourne, August 18. Available from www.pm.gov.au. Accessed August 21, 2004.

———. 2001a. Answer to Question without Notice from Mr Georgiou on the Israeli Election, February 7. Available from www.dfat.gov.au. Accessed July 10, 2004.

———. 2001b. Transcript of the Prime Minister, The Hon John Howard: Press Conference, Melbourne, October 8. Available from www.dfat.gov.au. Accessed July 9, 2004.

———. 2005. Prime Minister's Christmas Message. *The Age*, December 25, 1.

Hubbert, Marion King. 1956. Nuclear Energy and Fossil Fuels. (Presented before the Spring Meeting of the Southern District Division of Production, American Petroleum Institute. Plaza Hotel, San Antonio. March 7–9, 1956). Houston: Shell Development Company.

———. 1965. *History of Petroleum Geology and Its Bearing upon Present and Future Exploration*. Washington, D.C.: U.S. Geological Survey.

Huntington, Samuel. 1996. *The Clash of Civilisations and the Remaking of World Order*. New York: Simon and Schuster.

Ilan, Tar. 2000. The Daughters of Zelophehad and Women's Inheritance: The Biblical Injunction and Its Outcome. In *Exodus to Deuteronomy, A Feminist Companion to the Bible* (Second Series), edited by A. Brenner. Sheffield, England: Sheffield Academic Press.

An Inconvenient Truth. 2006. Directed by Davis Guggenheim. Paramount.

Intergovernment Panel on Climate Change. 2007. Fourth Assessment Report. Available at ipcc-wg1.ucar.edu. Accessed October 20, 2007.

In the Capital: Bush, Powell Condemn Rhetorical Attacks on Islam. 2002. *Church and State* 55 (11): 3.

In the Capital: Bush Isn't "Theologian in Chief," says Religious Right. 2004. *Church and State* 57 (1): 3.

Jackson, Rosemary. 1981. *Fantasy: The Literature of Subversion*. London: Routledge.

Jakobson, V. A. 1969. The Social Structure of the Neo-Assyrian Empire. In *Ancient Mesopotamia: Socio-Economic History. A Collection of Studies by Soviet Scholars*, edited by I. M. D'iakonoff. Moscow: "Nauka" Publishing House.

Jameson, Fredric. 1981. *The Political Unconscious: Narrative as a Socially Symbolic Act*. Ithaca, N.Y.: Cornell University Press.

———. 1991. *Postmodernism, or, The Cultural Logic of Late Capitalism*. Durham, N.C.: Duke University Press.

———. 2005. *Archaeologies of the Future*. London: Verso.

Janicaud, Dominique, Jean-François Courtine, Jean-Louis Chrétien, Michel Henry, Jean-Luc Marion, and Paul Ricoeur. 2000. *Phenomenology and the "Theological Turn": The French Debate*. New York: Fordham University Press.

Jankowska, Ninel B. 1969a. Extended Family Commune and Civil Self-Government in Arrapha in the Fifteenth–Fourteenth Century B.C. In *Ancient Mesopotamia: Socio-Economic History. A Collection of Studies by Soviet Scholars*, edited by I. M. D'iakonoff. Moscow: "Nauka" Publishing House.

———. 1969b. Some Problems of the Economy of the Assyrian Empire. In *Ancient Mesopotamia: Socio-Economic History. A Collection of Studies by Soviet Scholars*, edited by I. M. D'iakonoff. Moscow: "Nauka" Publishing House.

Janzen, J. Gerald. 1994. Song of Moses, Song of Miriam: Who Is Seconding Whom? In *A Feminist Companion to Exodus to Deuteronomy*, edited by A. Brenner. Sheffield, England: Sheffield Academic Press.

Jenkins, Geoff, Richard Betts, Mat Collins, Dave Griggs, Jason Lowe, and Richard Wood. 2006. *Stabilising Climate to Avoid Dangerous Climate Change: A Summary of Relevant Research at the Hadley Centre*. London: Met Office.

Jobling, David. 1991. Feminism and "Mode of Production" in Ancient Israel: Search for a Method. In *The Bible and the Politics of Exegesis: Essays in Honor of Norman K. Gottwald on His Sixty-Fifth Birthday*, edited by D. Jobling, P. L. Day, and G. T. Sheppard. Cleveland: Pilgrim Press.

———. 1998. *1 Samuel*. Collegeville, Minn.: Liturgical Press.

Jones, Tony. 2005. Hurricanes Can Be Tied to Climate Change. Australian Broadcasting Commission. Available from www.abc.net.au. Accessed May 10, 2006.

Jongsma-Tieleman, P. E. 2001. The Creation of Eve and the Ambivalence between the Sexes. In *God, Biblical Stories and Psychoanalytic Understanding*, edited by R. Kessler and P. Vandermeersch. Frankfurt-on-Main: Peter Lang.

Kautsky, Karl. 1953. *Foundations of Christianity*. Translated by H. F. Mins. London: Russell and Russell. (Orig. pub. 1908.)

Kellner, Douglas. 1997. Ernst Bloch, Utopia, and Ideology Critique. In *Not Yet: Reconsidering Ernst Bloch*, edited by J. O. Daniel and T. Moylan. London: Verso.

Kelso, Julie. 2003. Reading the Silence of Women in Genesis 34. In *Redirected Travel: Alternative Journeys and Places in Biblical Studies*, edited by R. Boer and E. Conrad. London: T. and T. Clark.

Kessler, Rainer. 2001. Psychoanalysis as a Hermeneutical Tool: The Example of Ex 4:24–26. In *God, Biblical Stories and Psychoanalytic Understanding*, edited by R. Kessler and P. Vandermeersch. Frankfurt am Main: Peter Lang.

Klengel, Horst. 1987. Non-Slave Labour in the Old Babylonian Period: The Basic Outline. In *Labor in the Ancient Near East*, edited by M. A. Powell. New Haven: American Oriental Society.

Koehler, F. 1996. Melanie Klein and Jacques Lacan. In *Reading Seminars I and II: Lacan's Return to Freud*, edited by R. Feldstein, B. Fink, and M. Jaanus. Albany: State University of New York Press.

Kohl, Philip L. 1991. Foreword. In *Early Antiquity*, edited by I. M. Diakonoff and P. L. Kohl. Chicago: University of Chicago Press.

Kovel, Joel. 2002. *The Enemy of Nature: The End of Capitalism or the End of the World?* London: Zed Books.

Kovel, Joel, and Michael Löwy. 2001. An Ecosocialist Manifesto. Ozleft: An Independent Forum of Strategy, Tactics and History in the Australian Left, Green and Labour Movements. Available at http://members.optushome.com.au. Accessed October 21, 2007.

Kozyreva, Nelly V. 1991. The Old Babylonian Period of Mesopotamian History. In *Early Antiquity*, edited by I. M. Diakonoff and P. L. Kohl. Chicago: University of Chicago Press.

Krader, Lawrence. 1975. *The Asiatic Mode of Production: Sources, Development and Critique in the Writings of Karl Marx*. Assen, Netherlands: Van Gorcum.

Kristeva, Julia. 1996. *Julia Kristeva Interviews*. Edited by R. M. Guberman. New York: Columbia University Press.

Lacan, Jacques. 1991a. *The Ego in Freud's Theory and in the Technique of Psychoanalysis 1954–1955*. Translated by S. Tomaselli. Edited by J.-A. Miller. Vol. 2 of *The Seminar of Jacques Lacan*. New York: Norton.

———. 1991b. *Freud's Papers on Technique 1953–1954*. Translated by J. Forrester. Edited by J.-A. Miller. Vol. 1 of *The Seminar of Jacques Lacan*. New York: Norton.

——— 1993. *The Psychoses 1955–56*. Translated by R. Grigg. Edited by J.-A. Miller. Vol. 3 of *The Seminar of Jacques Lacan*. London: Routledge.

————. 1994. *The Four Fundamental Concepts of Psycho-Analysis*. Translated by A. Sheridan. Edited by J.-A. Miller. Vol. II of *The Seminar of Jacques Lacan*. Harmondsworth, England: Penguin.

————. 1998. *Encore: On Feminine Sexuality: The Limits of Love and Knowledge 1972–1973*. Edited by J.-A. Miller. Vol. 20 of *The Seminar of Jacques Lacan*. New York: Norton.

La Guardia, Anton. 2005. It Wasn't Always Like This. *New Statesman*, October 31, 32–33.

Lapkin, Ted. 2004. Friends Indeed: Australia Comes Good at the UN. *The Review: Australia/Israel and Jewish Affairs Council* 29 (1). Available at www.aijac.org.au. Accessed June 20, 2005.

Larudee, Paul. 2005. The Blind Spot in Criticism of U.S. Policy toward Israel. *Washington Report on Middle East Affairs* 24 (27): 17–18.

Leemans, W. F. 1982. The Pattern of Settlement in the Babylonian Countryside. In *Societies and Languages of the Ancient Near East: Studies in Honour of I. M. Diakonoff*, edited by M. Dandamaev, I. Gershevitch, H. Klengel, G. Komoroczy, M. T. Larsen, and J. N. Postgate. Warminster, England: Aris and Phillips.

Lemche, Niels Peter. 1988. *Ancient Israel: A New History of Israelite Society*. Sheffield, England: Sheffield Academic Press.

————. 1998a. *The Israelites in History and Tradition*. London: SPCK.

————. 1998b. *Prelude to Israel's Past: Background and Beginnings of Israelite History and Identity*. Translated by E. F. Maniscalco. Peabody, Mass.: Hendrickson.

————. 1999. The Relevance of Working with the Concept of Class in the Study of Israelite Society in the Iron Age. In *Concepts of Class in Ancient Israel*, edited by M. Sneed. Atlanta: Scholars Press.

Leslie, Esther. 2000. *Walter Benjamin: Overcoming Conformity*. London: Pluto Press.

Levey, Geoffrey Brahm, and Philip Mendes, eds. 2005. *Jews and Australian Politics*. Brighton, England: Sussex Academic Press.

Lévi-Strauss, Claude. 1966. *The Savage Mind*. London: Weidenfeld and Nicolson.

————. 1968. *Structural Anthropology*. Harmondsworth, England: Penguin.

————. 1973. *Tristes Tropiques*. Translated by J. Weightman and D. Weightman. London: Cape.

————. 1994. *The Raw and the Cooked: Introduction to a Science of Mythology*. London: Random House.

Lichtheim, George. 1990. Marx and the "Asiatic Mode of Production." In *Marxian Economics*, Volume 1, edited by J. E. King. Aldershot, England: Elgar.

Lincoln, Bruce. 2000. *Theorizing Myth: Narrative, Ideology, and Scholarship*. Chicago: University of Chicago Press.

Liverani, Mario. 1982. Ville et campagne dans le royaume d'Ugarit : Essai d'analyse économique. In *Societies and Languages of the Ancient Near East: Studies in Honour of I. M. Diakonoff*, edited by M. Dandamaev, I. Gershevitch, H. Klengel, G. Komoroczy, M. T. Larsen, and J. N. Postgate. Warminster, England: Aris and Phillips.

———. 2005. *Israel's History and the History of Israel*. Translated by C. Peri and P. Davies. London: Equinox.

Long, Burke O. 2003. *Imagining the Holy Land: Maps, Models, and Fantasy Travels*. Bloomington: Indiana University Press.

Machiavelli. 1988. *The Prince*. Edited by Q. Skinner and R. Price. Cambridge: Cambridge University Press. (Orig. pub. 1532.)

Maddox, Marion. 2005. *God under Howard*. Crows Nest, New South Wales: Allen and Unwin.

Mandel, Ernest. 1975. *Late Capitalism*. London: New Left Books.

Marx, Karl. 1981. *Outlines of the Critique of Political Economy (Grundrisse)*. Vol. 28 of *Marx-Engels Collected Works*. Moscow: Progress Publishers (original German ed., 1939–41).

———. 1987. Preface. In *A Contribution to the Critique of Political Economy*. Vol. 29 of *Marx-Engels Collected Works*. Moscow: Progress Publishers (original German ed., 1859).

Marx, Karl, and Frederick Engels. 1975–2004. *Collected Works*. 50 vols. Moscow: Progress Publishers.

———. 1976. *The German Ideology*. Vol. 5 of *Marx-Engels Collected Works*. Moscow: Progress Publishers (original German ed., 1932).

Matthews, Victor Harold. 2004. *Judges and Ruth*. Cambridge: Cambridge University Press.

McGreal, Chris. 2005. Christian Leanings at the *Jerusalem Post. Sephardic Heritage Update*, November 16, 22–23.

McKinlay, Judith. 2004. *Reframing Her: Biblical Women in Postcolonial Focus*. Sheffield, England: Sheffield Phoenix Press.

McNutt, Paula M. 1999. *Reconstructing the Society of Ancient Israel*. London: SPCK.

Metherell, Mark. 2005. Finish Line Nowhere in View for Howard. *Sydney Morning Herald*, June 27, 1.

Meyers, Carol. 1988. *Discovering Eve: Ancient Israelite Women in Context*. New York: Oxford University Press.

———. 1993. Gender Roles and Genesis 3:16 Revisited. In *A Feminist Companion to Genesis*, edited by A. Brenner. Sheffield, England: Sheffield Academic Press.

———. 1994. Miriam the Magician. In *A Feminist Companion to Exodus to Deuteronomy*, edited by A. Brenner. Sheffield, England: Sheffield Academic Press.

———. 1997. The Family in Early Israel. In *Families in Ancient Israel*, edited by L. S. Purdue et al. Louisville: Westminster John Knox.

———. 1999. "Women of the Neighbourhood" (Ruth 4:17): Informal Female Networks in Ancient Israel. In *Ruth and Esther: A Feminist Companion to the Bible* (Second Series), edited by A. Brenner. Sheffield, England: Sheffield Academic Press.

Mezvinsky, Norton. 2005. The Impact of Christian Zionism on the Arab-Israeli Conflict, March. Available at www.nthposition.com. Accessed April 22, 2005.

Miller, Jacques-Alain. 2004. Religion, Psychoanalysis. *Lacanian Ink* 23: 6–39.

Milne, Pamela J. 1993. The Patriarchal Stamp of Scripture: The Implications of Structural Analyses for Feminist Hermeneutics. In *A Feminist Companion to Genesis*, edited by A. Brenner. Sheffield, England: Sheffield Academic Press.

Morgan, Lewis Henry. 1877. *Ancient Society, or, Researches in the Lines of Human Progress from Savagery through Barbarianism to Civilization*. Chicago: C. H. Kerr.

Morris, Benny. 1987. *The Birth of the Palestinian Refugee Problem, 1947–1949*. Cambridge: Cambridge University Press.

———. 2004a. *The Birth of the Palestinian Refugee Problem, 1947–1949*. 2nd ed. Cambridge: Cambridge University Press.

———. 2004b. On Ethnic Cleansing. *New Left Review* (2nd series) 26: 35–51.

Murphy, Damien. 2006. CSIRO Pressured to Shun Climate Scientists. *Sydney Morning Herald*, February 16, 3.

Nathan, Howard. 2000. Bonded by History: The ANZACS and Israel Share Many Chapters. *The Review: Australia/Israel and Jewish Affairs Council* 25 (June 6). Available at www.aijac.org.au. Accessed May 10, 2004.

O'Connor, James. 1997. *Natural Causes: Essays in Ecological Marxism*. London: Guildford.

O'Loughlin, Ed. 2004. Israel Dubs Sympathetic Downer an "Honorary Zionist." *The Age*, October 27, 7.

Overington, Caroline. 2004. Minority Votes with Backs to the Wall. *The Age*, July 22, 9.

Pardes, Ilana. 2000. *The Biography of Ancient Israel: National Narratives in the Bible*. Berkeley: University of California Press.

Parker, Kim Ian. 1999. Mirror, Mirror on the Wall, Must We Leave Eden, Once and For All? A Lacanian Pleasure Trip through the Garden. *Journal for the Study of the Old Testament* 83: 3–17.

Parsons, Leila. 2001. The Druze and the Birth of Israel. In *The War for Palestine: Rewriting the History of 1948*, edited by E. L. Rogan and A. Shlaim. Cambridge: Cambridge University Press.

Pelosi, Nancy. 2003. Address to the American Israel Public Affairs Committee, April 1. Available at www.democraticleader.house.gov. Accessed February 15, 2006.

———. 2005. Address to the American Israel Public Affairs Committee, May 23. Available at www.democraticleader.house.gov. Accessed February 15, 2006.

Plimer, Ian. 2001. *A Short History of Planet Earth*. Melbourne: ABC Books.

———. 2006. Global Warming a Damp Squib. *The Australian*, January 5, 12.

Polzin, Robert. 1980. *Moses and the Deuteronomist: Deuteronomy, Joshua, Judges*. New York: Seabury.

Powell, Colin. 2001. Remarks at the American Israel Public Affairs Committee, March 19. Available at www.state.gov. Accessed February 15, 2006.

Powell, Marvin A. 1981. *Labor in the Ancient Near East*. New Haven, Conn.: American Oriental Society.

Pryor, Frederic L. 1990. The Asian Mode of Production as an Economic System. In *Marxian Economics*, edited by J. E. King. Aldershot, England: Elgar.

Putting Energy in the Spotlight: BP *Statistical Review of World Energy.* 2005. London: British Petroleum.

Ra'ad, Basem L. 2002. The Cana'anite Factor: (Un)Defining Religious Identities in Palestine and Israel. *Palestine-Israel Journal of Politics, Economics, and Culture* 8 (4): 108–20.

Rashkow, Ilona. 1994. Daughters and Fathers in Genesis . . . or, What's Wrong with this Picture? In *A Feminist Companion to Exodus to Deuteronomy,* edited by A. Brenner. Sheffield, England: Sheffield Academic Press.

———. 1998. Daddy-Dearest and the "Invisible Spirit of Wine." In *Genesis, A Feminist Companion to the Bible* (Second Series), edited by A. Brenner. Sheffield, England: Sheffield Academic Press.

———. 2000. *Taboo or Not Taboo: Sexuality and Family in the Hebrew Bible.* Minneapolis: Augsburg Fortress Press.

Rauch, Angelika. 1988. The Trauerspiel of the Prostituted Body, or Woman as Allegory of Modernity. *Cultural Critique* 10: 77–88.

Reich, Chanan. 2002. *Australia and Israel: An Ambiguous Relationship.* Melbourne: Melbourne University Press.

Religion Update: Religion Is Politics. 2004. *Publishers Weekly* 251 (21): S4.

Rice, Condoleezza. 2005. Remarks at the American Israel Public Affairs Committee's Annual Policy Conference, May 23. Available at www.state.gov. Accessed February 15, 2006.

Roarty, Mike. 2002. The Kyoto Protocol: Issues and Developments through to Conference of the Parties (COP7). Available at www.aph.gov.au. Accessed August 21, 2004.

Rose, Deborah Bird. 1996. Rupture and the Ethics of Care in Colonised Space. In *Prehistory to Politics: John Mulvaney, the Humanities and the Public Intellectual,* edited by T. Bonyhady and T. Griffith. Melbourne: Melbourne University Press.

Rose, Jacqueline. 1982. Introduction II. In *Feminine Sexuality: Jacques Lacan and the École freudienne,* edited by J. Mitchell and J. Rose. London: Macmillan.

Rubenstein, Colin. 2000. Friend Honoured: John Howard in Israel. *The Review: Australia/Israel and Jewish Affairs Council* 25 (June 6). Available at www.aijac.org.au. Accessed May 10, 2004.

Rule, Andrew, et al. 2000. Battle of Melbourne. *The Age,* September 12, 1.

Runions, Erin. 2004a. Biblical Promise and Threat in U.S. Imperialist Rhetoric, before and after 9.11. *The Scholar and Feminist Online* 2 (2). Available at www.barnard.edu. Accessed May 10, 2004.

———. 2004b. Desiring War: Apocalypse, Commodity Fetish and the End of History. *The Bible and Critical Theory* 1 (1): 04.1–04.16. Available at www.epress.monash.edu. Accessed May 10, 2004.

Rutherford, Jennifer. 2000. *The Gauche Intruder: Freud, Lacan and the White Australian Fantasy.* Melbourne: Melbourne University Press.

Sahlins, Marshall. 1968. *Tribesmen.* Englewood Cliffs, N.J.: Prentice-Hall.

———. 1972. *Stone Age Economics.* New York: Aldine de Gruyter.

Said, Edward. 1988. Michael Walzer's *Exodus and Revolution:* A Canaanite Reading. In *Blaming the Victims*, edited by E. Said and C. Hitchens. London: Verso.

———. 2004. *From Oslo to Iraq and the Roadmap*. London: Bloomsbury.

Sarkisian, G. Kh. 1969. City Land in Seleucid Babylonia. In *Ancient Mesopotamia: Socio-Economic History. A Collection of Studies by Soviet Scholars*, edited by I. M. D'iakonoff. Moscow: "Nauka" Publishing House.

Sawyer, Deborah. 2002. *God, Gender and the Bible*. London: Routledge.

Schellnhuber, Hans Joachim, Wolfgang Cramer, Nebojsa Nakicenovic, and Tom Wigley, eds. 2006. *Avoiding Dangerous Climate Change*. Cambridge: Cambridge University Press.

Schloen, J. David. 2001. *The House of the Father as Fact and Symbol: Patrimonialism in Ugarit and the Ancient Near East*. Winona Lake, Ind.: Eisenbrauns.

Scholz, Susanne. 1998. Through Whose Eyes? A "Right" Reading of Genesis 34. In *Genesis, A Feminist Companion to the Bible* (Second Series), edited by A. Brenner. Sheffield, England: Sheffield Academic Press.

Schotroff, Luise. 1993. The Creation Narrative: Genesis 1.1–2.4a. In *A Feminist Companion to Genesis*, edited by A. Brenner. Sheffield, England: Sheffield Academic Press.

Schubert, Misha. 2006. Howard Accused of Inflaming Tensions. *The Age*, February 21, 5.

Schüngel-Straumann, Helen. 1993. On the Creation of Man and Woman in Genesis 1–3: The History and Reception of the Texts Reconsidered. In *A Feminist Companion to Genesis*, edited by A. Brenner. Sheffield, England: Sheffield Academic Press.

Shiozawa, Kimio. 1990. Marx's View of Asian Society and His "Asiatic Mode of Production." In *Marxian Economics*, edited by J. E. King. Aldershot, England: Elgar.

Silver, Morris. 1983. *Prophets and Markets: The Political Economy of Ancient Israel*. Boston: Kluwer Nijhoff.

Simkins, Ronald. 1998. Gender Construction in the Yahwist Creation Myth. In *Genesis, A Feminist Companion to the Bible* (Second Series), edited by A. Brenner. Sheffield, England: Sheffield Academic Press.

———. 1999. Patronage and the Political Economy of Ancient Israel. *Semeia* 87: 123–44.

Smith, Charles D. 2001. *Palestine and the Arab-Israeli Conflict: A History with Documents*. Boston: Bedford St. Martin's.

Sneed, Mark, ed. 1999. *Concepts of Class in Ancient Israel*. Atlanta: Scholars Press.

Sorel, Georges. 1961. *Reflections on Violence*. Translated by T. Hulme and J. Roth. New York: Collier.

Stark Warning over Climate Change. 2006. BBC News. British Broadcasting Commission, April 14. Available at news.bbc.co.uk. Accessed May 1, 2006.

Steinberg, Naomi. 1993. *Kinship and Marriage in Genesis: A Household Economics Perspective*. Minneapolis: Fortress Press.

Sternhall, Zeev. 1997. *The Founding Myths of Israel: Nationalism, Socialism, and the Making of the Jewish State*. Translated by D. Maisel. Princeton: Princeton University Press.

Stoljar, Margaret Mahony. 1996. Sirens of Gaslight and Odalisques of the Oil Lamp: The Language of Desire in the *Arcades Project*. In *"With the Sharpened Axe of Reason": Approaches to Walter Benjamin*, edited by G. Fischer. Oxford: Berg.

Struve, V. V. 1969a. The Problem of the Genesis, Development and Disintegration of the Slave Societies in the Ancient Orient. In *Ancient Mesopotamia: Socio-Economic History. A Collection of Studies by Soviet Scholars*, edited by I. M. D'iakonoff. Moscow: "Nauka" Publishing House.

———. 1969b. Some New Data on the Organization of Labour and on Social Structure in Sumer During the Reign of the IIIrd Dynasty of Ur. In *Ancient Mesopotamia: Socio-Economic History. A Collection of Studies by Soviet Scholars*, edited by I. M. D'iakonoff. Moscow: "Nauka" Publishing House.

Thompson, Thomas L. 1992. *Early History of the Israelite People: From the Written and Archaeological Sources*. Leiden: Brill.

———. 1999. *The Mythic Past: Biblical Archaeology and the Myth of Israel*. New York: Basic Books.

———. 2000. *Early History of the Israelite People from the Written and Archaeological Sources*. Leiden: Brill.

———. 2005. *The Messiah Myth: The Near Eastern Roots of Jesus and David*. New York: Basic Books.

Tommer, Yehonathan. 2004. Alexander's Odyssey. *The Review: Australia/Israel and Jewish Affairs Council* 29 (March 3). Available at www.aijac.org.au. Accessed May 10, 2004.

Trible, Phyllis. 1978. *God and the Rhetoric of Sexuality*. Philadelphia: Fortress Press.

———. 1994. Bringing Miriam Out of the Shadows. In *A Feminist Companion to Exodus to Deuteronomy*, edited by A. Brenner. Sheffield, England: Sheffield Academic Press.

Tyumenev, A. I. 1969a. The State Economy of Ancient Sumer. In *Ancient Mesopotamia: Socio-Economic History. A Collection of Studies by Soviet Scholars*, edited by I. M. D'iakonoff. Moscow: "Nauka" Publishing House.

———. 1969b. The Working Personnel on the Estate of the Temple of ᵈBa-Ú in Lagaš During the Period of Lugalanda and Urukagina (25th–24th cent. B.C.). In *Ancient Mesopotamia: Socio-Economic History. A Collection of Studies by Soviet Scholars*, edited by I. M. D'iakonoff. Moscow: "Nauka" Publishing House.

Uris, Leon. 1958. *Exodus: A Novel of Israel*. London: Kimber.

Vandermeersch, Patrick. 2001. Psychoanalytic Interpretations of Religious Texts: Some Basics. In *God, Biblical Stories and Psychoanalytic Understanding*, edited by R. Kessler and P. Vandermeersch. Frankfurt on Main: Peter Lang.

van Dijk-Hemmes, Fokkelien. 1994. Some Recent Views on the Presentation of the Song of Miriam. In *A Feminist Companion to Exodus to Deuteronomy*, edited by A. Brenner. Sheffield, England: Sheffield Academic Press.

Van Wolde, Ellen. 1989. *A Semiotic Analysis of Genesis 2–3*. Maastricht, Netherlands: Assen.

Vinogradov, I. V. 1991. The Middle Kingdom of Egypt and the Hyksos Invasion. In *Early Antiquity*, edited by I. M. Diakonoff and P. L. Kohl. Chicago: University of Chicago Press.

von Hayek, Friedrich. 1960. *The Constitution of Liberty*. Chicago: University of Chicago Press.

Wagner, Don. 2002. For Zion's Sake. *Middle East Report* 223: 52–57.

Wallerstein, Immanuel. 1983. *Historical Capitalism*. London: Verso.

Warburton, D. A. 2003. *Macroeconomics from the Beginning*. Winona Lake, Ind.: Eisenbrauns.

Weigel, Sigrid. 1996. *Body- and Image-Space: Re-Reading Walter Benjamin*. London: Routledge.

Weinberg, Joel. 1992. *The Citizen-Temple Community*. Translated by D. L. Smith-Christopher. Sheffield, England: Sheffield Academic Press.

Weissbrod, Rachel. 1999. Exodus as an Israeli Melodrama. *Israel Studies* 4 (1): 129–52.

Westermann, Claus. 1984. *Genesis 1–11: A Commentary*. Translated by J. J. Scullion. London: SPCK.

Wheatcroft, Geoffrey. 1996. *The Controversy of Zion*. Reading, Mass.: Addison-Wesley.

Wittfogel, Karl. 1963. *Oriental Despotism*. New Haven: Yale University Press.

Wohlfarth, Irving. 1997. Walter Benjamin and the "German-Jewish Parnassus." *New German Critique* 70: 3–86.

Wolff, Janet. 1989. The Invisible Flaneuse: Women and the Literature of Modernity. In *The Problems of Modernity: Adorno and Benjamin*, edited by A. Benjamin. London: Routledge.

Yassif, Eli. 1999. *The Hebrew Folktale: History, Genre, Meaning*. Translated by J. S. Teitelbaum. Bloomington: Indiana University Press.

Yee, Gale A. 2003. *Poor Banished Children of Eve: Woman as Evil in the Hebrew Bible*. Minneapolis: Fortress Press.

Zel'in, K. K. 1968. Principles of Morphological Classification of Forms of Dependence. *Soviet Anthropology and Archaeology* 6 (4): 3–24.

Zipes, Jack. 1979. *Breaking the Magic Spell: Radical Theories of Folk and Fairy Tales*. New York: Routledge.

———. 1983. *Fairy Tales and the Art of Subversion*. New York: Routledge.

Žižek, Slavoj. 1989. *The Sublime Object of Ideology*. London: Verso.

———. 1997. *The Plague of Fantasies*. London: Verso.

Indexes

Bush, George W. (*cont.*)
    Islam and, 4, 144, 166–67; Israel and,
    146–47, 150, 155, 159, 161
Butler, Judith, 33–34

Capitalism, ix, 154, 220; application of,
    to ancient Near East, 89, 101–2, 107,
    109–11, 222; Christianity and, 4–5, 154,
    165–67, 170–71; escape from, 7, 20–21,
    27, 33, 167, 174, 184, 186–92; fantas-
    matic kernel and, 140, 142, 165–67,
    181–83; freedom and, 5, 171–72; Greens
    and, 175–84; liberalism and, 136, 151;
    Marx and, 183; myth and, 4–6, 20–22,
    30, 142, 169–73, 182, 189–90, 221;
    nature and, 5, 174–81; secularism and,
    131; as unfettered, 6, 165–69, 184–89;
    as unstable, 171–72; Utopia and, 5, 168,
    170–73, 183. *See also* Nature
Chaos, 74–78, 192; appropriation of, by
    deity, 79–82; environmental destruc-
    tion and, 185–86; nature as, 3, 75–80,
    169, 174, 185, 189; politics and, 62–63,
    169, 189–90; punishment as, 82; Real
    as, 3, 62–63, 74, 79–83, 87, 168, 174,
    189–90; rebellion as, 3, 78, 168; sin
    as, 87, 190. *See also* Cosmos; Global
    warming; Myth
Children overboard affair, 223
Christianity: Australia and, 137–38,
    140–41, 207–8; communism and, 191;
    conservative, 132–33, 166–67, 187; de-
    mythologization and, 25, 30; fantasy
    and, 4–5, 136–38, 140, 154, 165, 170;
    Islam and, 4, 116, 127–28, 131, 133–35,
    154, 209–10; Israel and, 116, 127–29,
    133–36; *Left Behind* novels and, 163–64;
    liberal, 131–33, 201–3; messianic, 19;
    Reagan and, 146–47; revolution and, 5;
    secularism and, 132–33; settlement of
    Australia and, 134. *See also* Capitalism:
    Christianity and; Zionism: Christian
Clan. *See* Gens

Class, 3, 26, 29, 49, 56, 58, 81, 91, 99–106,
    109, 111–13, 124, 139, 159, 164, 172, 213,
    217, 220–21
Clientalistic mode of production, 3,
    37–38, 108–9, 112, 114
Clinton, Hillary, 4, 146, 155–56
Cold War, 3, 98, 142, 165
Colonialism, 145, 151, 159, 164, 183, 208,
    215
Communism: Christian, 191; Marxist,
    149–50, 159, 165–66, 171–72, 187, 191;
    primitive, 2, 5, 26, 36–40, 44–49, 61,
    94, 104–5. *See also* Mode of production
Communist Party (of Australia), 74
Constitutive exception, 2–3, 27, 32–34,
    62, 74, 142, 182, 219; capitalism and,
    165–67, 181–82; fantasy and, 2, 62, 74;
    Marx and, 181–82; rebellion and, 83,
    87–88
Cosmos, 3, 25, 75, 79–83, 87–88. *See also*
    Chaos; Myth
Costello, Peter, 4, 127–28, 134–39; text of
    speech of, 207–12
Cunning of myth, 1, 6, 16, 23–26, 31, 35,
    50, 56, 61, 73, 168–70, 190

Demimonde, 2, 57–61, 85–90, 95, 115, 189
Democracy, 4, 7, 130, 150–51, 161, 195;
    in Middle East, 156–57; paradox of,
    155–56; totalitarianism and, 157
Demythologization, 24–27, 30
Despotic state, 3, 100–106, 216
Dialectic, 14, 21, 33, 87, 101, 215, 220, 222;
    of capitalism and nature, 184–85; of
    enlightenment, 27–30; of history and
    myth, 31; of hypocrisy, 156; myth and,
    24–23; of peace and violence, 160–65;
    of reaction and subversion, 1, 24–27,
    34, 169
Dinah, 50, 52, 57, 59, 86, 94–95
Discernment of myth, 23–26
Division of labor, 26, 37, 39, 42–43, 47,
    98, 133

State, 105–6; of ancient Israel, 3–4, 29; as a class, 101; despotic, 100, 102, 106; formation of, 8, 29; 101, 104–5; in waiting, 3, 5, 90–97, 113, 115, 160
Stalin, Josef, 4, 144, 158–59, 216
Stolen children report (*Bringing Them Home*), 139
Symbolic, 3, 34, 62–63, 74–75, 78–83, 87–88, 142, 219. *See also* Psychoanalysis; Real; Rebellion

Tamar, 50, 54, 59, 94
sv *Tampa*, 132, 138, 205
Technology, 3, 43, 46, 108, 191
Temple-city, 3, 103–4
Ten Commandments, 92–93; use of, by Peter Costello, 135–36, 208–10
Terrorism, 70, 119, 127, 129–34, 159–66, 193–200, 205–6, 209
Theo-economics, 3, 102, 106–7, 111–15. *See also* Sacred economy
Totalitarianism, 33; democracy and, 157. *See also* Democracy
Trade, in sacred economy, 3, 89, 99, 102, 104, 107, 108–12, 221
Trauma, 32–33, 53, 62, 65, 73, 123–24, 142–43, 164, 217, 220
Tribute, in sacred economy, 3, 107–14

Unconscious, 74–75, 77, 113
United States, 4, 34, 125, 139, 186, 190; Bible and, 148–51, 187; fantasy and, 7–8, 116, 144–67; foreign policy of, 144–52; myth and, 170–73. *See also* Foreign policy
Uris, Leon, 4, 152–53
Utopia, 48–49, 190; capitalist, 5, 168–70, 173; dystopia and, 169; myth and, 23–25; liberal-conservative, 140–42; Paradox of, 67–68

Village commune, 3, 102–3, 106
Violence: dialectic of, 4, 160–65; peace and, 119–24, 140, 158–61; systemic, 140

Women (in the Bible): as alone, 57; egalitarian social structures and, 38–48; as exchange objects, 51–52; inheritance and, 42–48, 51, 54–55; law and, 51–56; punishment of, 51; rebellion of, 51, 56–59; subjugation of, 29, 39, 50; violence against, 51. *See also* Mode of production

Zelophehad, daughters of, 2, 46, 50, 54, 56, 86,
Zionism, 17, 124–25, 145, 151–52, 158, 222, 224–25; Christian, 153–54, 165; "honorary Zionist" (Alexander Downer) and, 125, 133; labor, 151, 159, 224; socialism and, 159. *See also* Anti-Zionism
Zipporah, 57, 86
Žižek, Slavoj, 1–2, 5, 32–34, 69, 142, 181–84, 213, 215, 218

INDEX OF BIBLICAL CITATIONS

Genesis		2–3	39, 50,	2:8	63–64
1	64, 72, 75		62–63, 68,	2:9	63–64
1:2	77		74, 80,	2:10–14	64
1–3	3, 218–19		86–88, 219	2:16	66
2	63–64, 72,	2:4	64	2:17	66–67
	75, 216	2:4–14	63	2:18	64

Roland Boer is research professor at the University
of Newcastle, Australia. He has written numerous
books and articles, the most recent of which are
Criticism of Heaven (2007), *Rescuing the Bible* (2007),
and *Symposia* (2007).

■

Library of Congress Cataloging-in-Publication Data
Boer, Roland
Political myth : on the use and abuse of Biblical
themes / Roland Boer.
     p. cm. — (New slant)
Includes bibliographical references and index.
ISBN 978-0-8223-4335-6 (cloth : alk. paper)
ISBN 978-0-8223-4369-1 (pbk. : alk. paper)
1. Mythology—Political aspects. 2. Myth in the
Bible. 3. Bible and politics. I. Title. II. Series.
BL313.B54 2009
220.6'8—dc22   2008040665